D0221146

Male and Female Violence
in Popular Media

Library of Gender and Popular Culture

From *Mad Men* to gaming culture, performance art to steampunk fashion, the presentation and representation of gender continues to saturate popular media. This series seeks to explore the intersection of gender and popular culture, engaging with a variety of texts – drawn primarily from Art, Fashion, TV, Cinema, Cultural Studies and Media Studies – as a way of considering various models for understanding the complementary relationship between 'gender identities' and 'popular culture'. By considering race, ethnicity, class, and sexual identities across a range of cultural forms, each book in the series adopts a critical stance towards issues surrounding the development of gender identities and popular and mass cultural 'products'.

For further information or enquiries, please contact the library series editors:
Claire Nally: claire.nally@northumbria.ac.uk
Angela Smith: angela.smith@sunderland.ac.uk

Advisory Board:
Dr Kate Ames, Central Queensland University, Australia
Dr Michael Higgins, University of Strathclyde, UK
Prof Åsa Kroon, Örebro University, Sweden
Dr Andrea McDonnell, Emmanuel College, USA
Dr Niall Richardson, University of Sussex, UK
Dr Jacki Willson, University of Leeds, UK

Library of Gender
& Popular Culture

Published and forthcoming titles:

The Aesthetics of Camp: Post-Queer Gender and Popular Culture
By Anna Malinowska

Ageing Femininity on Screen: The Older Woman in Contemporary Cinema
By Niall Richardson

All-American TV Crime Drama: Feminism and Identity Politics in Law and Order: Special Victims Unit
By Sujata Moorti and Lisa Cuklanz

Are You Not Entertained?: Mapping the Gladiator Across Visual Media
By Lindsay Steenberg

Bad Girls, Dirty Bodies: Sex, Performance and Safe Femininity
By Gemma Commane

Beyoncé: Celebrity Feminism in the Age of Social Media
By Kirsty Fairclough-Isaacs

Conflicting Masculinities: Men in Television Period Drama
By Katherine Byrne, Julie Anne Taddeo and James Leggott (Eds)

Fat on Film: Gender, Race and Body Size in Contemporary Hollywood Cinema
By Barbara Plotz

Fathers on Film: Paternity and Masculinity in 1990s Hollywood
By Katie Barnett

Film Bodies: Queer Feminist Encounters with Gender and Sexuality in Cinema
By Katharina Lindner

From the Margins to the Mainstream: Women On and Off Screen in Television and Film
By Marianne Kac-Vergne and Julie Assouly (Eds)

Gay Pornography: Representations of Sexuality and Masculinity
By John Mercer

Gender and Austerity in Popular
Culture: Femininity, Masculinity
and Recession in Film and Television
By Helen Davies and Claire
O'Callaghan (Eds)

Gender and Early Television:
Mapping Women's Role in
Emerging US and British Media,
1850–1950
By Sarah Arnold

The Gendered Motorcycle:
Representations in Society, Media
and Popular Culture
By Esperanza Miyake

Gendering History on Screen:
Women Filmmakers and
Historical Films
By Julia Erhart

Girls Like This, Boys Like That:
The Reproduction of Gender in
Contemporary Youth Cultures
By Victoria Cann

'Guilty Pleasures': European
Audiences and Contemporary
Hollywood Romantic Comedy
By Alice Guilluy

The Gypsy Woman: Representations
in Literature and Visual Culture
By Jodie Matthews

Love Wars: Television Romantic
Comedy
By Mary Irwin

Masculinity in Contemporary
Science Fiction Cinema: Cyborgs,
Troopers and Other Men of the
Future
By Marianne Kac-Vergne

Paradoxical Pleasures: Female
Submission in Popular and Erotic
Fiction
By Anna Watz

Positive Images: Gay Men and
HIV/AIDS in the Culture of
'Post-Crisis'
By Dion Kagan

Queer Horror Film and Television:
Sexuality and Masculinity at the
Margins
By Darren Elliott-Smith

Queer Sexualities in Early Film:
Cinema and Male-Male Intimacy
By Shane Brown

Male and Female Violence in Popular Media

Elisa Giomi and Sveva Magaraggia

BLOOMSBURY ACADEMIC

LONDON • NEW YORK • OXFORD • NEW DELHI • SYDNEY

BLOOMSBURY ACADEMIC
Bloomsbury Publishing Plc
50 Bedford Square, London, WC1B 3DP, UK
1385 Broadway, New York, NY 10018, USA
29 Earlsfort Terrace, Dublin 2, Ireland

BLOOMSBURY, BLOOMSBURY ACADEMIC and the Diana logo
are trademarks of Bloomsbury Publishing Plc

First published in Great Britain 2023

Copyright © Elisa Giomi and Sveva Magaraggia, 2023

Elisa Giomi and Sveva Magaraggia have asserted their right under the Copyright,
Designs and Patents Act, 1988, to be identified as Authors of this work.

For legal purposes the Acknowledgements on p. xiv constitute an
extension of this copyright page.

Cover design: Ben Anslow
Cover image © Broken glass over black background
(© Runrun2 / Shutterstock)

All rights reserved. No part of this publication may be reproduced or transmitted
in any form or by any means, electronic or mechanical, including photocopying,
recording, or any information storage or retrieval system, without prior
permission in writing from the publishers.

Bloomsbury Publishing Plc does not have any control over, or responsibility for,
any third-party websites referred to or in this book. All internet addresses given
in this book were correct at the time of going to press. The author and publisher
regret any inconvenience caused if addresses have changed or sites have ceased
to exist, but can accept no responsibility for any such changes.

A catalogue record for this book is available from the British Library.

Library of Congress Cataloging-in-Publication Data
Names: Giomi, Elisa, author. | Magaraggia, Sveva, author.
Title: Male and female violence in popular media /
Elisa Giomi and Sveva Magaraggia.
Description: New York : Bloomsbury Academic, 2022. | Series: Library of gender
and popular culture | Includes bibliographical references and index. |
Identifiers: LCCN 2021035056 (print) | LCCN 2021035057 (ebook) |
ISBN 9781350168756 (hardback) | ISBN 9781350293311 (paperback) |
ISBN 9781350168763 (pdf) | ISBN 9781350168770 (epub)
Subjects: LCSH: Violence in mass media. | Violence in men. |
Violence in women. | Violence in popular culture.
Classification: LCC P96.V5 G56 2022 (print) | LCC P96.V5 (ebook) |
DDC 303.6–dc23/eng/20211130
LC record available at https://lccn.loc.gov/2021035056
LC ebook record available at https://lccn.loc.gov/2021035057

ISBN: HB: 978-1-3501-6875-6
           ePDF: 978-1-3501-6876-3
           eBook: 978-1-3501-6877-0

Series: Library of Gender and Popular Culture

Typeset by Integra Software Services Pvt. Ltd.

To find out more about our authors and books visit www.bloomsbury.com
and sign up for our newsletters.

This book is dedicated to Frida Guerrera,
who hunts down men who kill women.

Contents

List of Tables

List of Abbreviations

ASA	Advertising Standards Authority
FBI	The Federal Bureau of Investigation
GBV	Gender-based violence
IAP	Institute for Self-regulation of Advertising
IPH	Intimate Partner Homicide
IPV	Intimate Partner Violence
MTV	Music Television Network
OTT	Over the Top
SVOD	Subscription Video on Demand
UCR	Uniform Crime Reporting
VAW/G	Violence against Women/Girls
VOD	Video on Demand
WHO	World Health Organization

Acknowledgements

We are in debt to those colleagues, friends and our partners who have assisted our work. We would like to thank Alberta Giorgi, Annie van den Oever, Arianna Mainardi, Barend van Heusden Chiara Ferrari, Cinzia Forte, Daniela Belliti, Daniel Morris, Daniela Cherubini, Diego Semerene Costa, Elia Cornero Mari, Flavia Laviosa, Harry Blatterer, Marina Calloni, Mary-Anne Frail and Quinn Winchell.

Elisa wishes to thank Diana, her strong and balanced little warrior, who has waited for her until now, and her step-sons Marcello and Giuliano, for becoming two amazing young men. Thanks, above all, to Emanuele, without whom this book, like a thousand other things, would not have been possible.

Sveva wishes to thank Deborah, for her persevering loving support.

Thanks to the contribution of UNIRE: 'Progetto realizzato con il contributo della Presidenza del Consiglio dei Ministri – Dipartimento per le Pari Opportunità'.

Series Editors' Introduction

At a time when we are becoming more aware of the effects of violence in society as found in mediated forms, this book offers an intriguing insight into the ways in which gender-based violence is represented in popular media. There has been substantial research into online violence, particularly the sort of abuse that is experienced by public figures on Twitter and Instagram. Gender-based violence has proven particularly prevalent. While these public forms of virtual violence are receiving the greatest attention at present, what this book does is argue that violence exists in many popular media forms and, as the authors explain, this is clearly gendered. As the authors of this book explore, since the 1930s in Westernized cultures there have been four distinct stages in which representations of violent women can be charted to mirror changes in gender roles in society, with female incursions into traditionally male domains being represented as a threat to societal order. Other books in this Library also explore aspects of this subject, such as Christelle Maury and David Roche's (2020) *Women Who Kill: Gender and Sexuality in Film and Series of the Post-feminist Era*. Their edited collection highlights the discourses surrounding appropriate gender behaviour. The collection of essays highlights how women who kill are frequently used as a measurement of normative behaviour to apply to women as a whole. They are either deviant and therefore monstrous and defeminized; or they are vengeful victims of patriarchal power, findings which are echoed here by Giomi and Magaraggia. Furthermore, in their exploration of male violence, Giomi and Magaraggia reinforce the arguments put forward by Lindsay Sternberg's (2021) *Are You Not Entertained? Mapping the Gladiator across Visual Media*. The potency of the hyper-masculine, powerful and violent gladiator and its resistance to challenges of gender equality mirror the representations of gender found across mediated texts, as Giomi and Magaraggia confirm. However, as books in this Library also show, there is a complexity to the figure of the violent, powerful actor that means it does not necessarily ennoble men or empower women. In drawing on a range of popular cultural texts, Giomi and Magaraggia's book cuts across the various subgenres in this Library. It covers representations of gender and violence that are both factual (news, print media, factual entertainment) and fictional (advertising, fictional entertainment in TV and film, music videos), offering nuanced readings that chime with findings in some of the Library's other books.

The conclusions reached by Giomi and Magaraggia reflect the continuation of the 'separate spheres' division of genders that is well established in Westernized societies. They show that violence by men on women known to them (as distinguished from 'strangers', which is discussed by the authors) across genres is an accepted practice. When it comes to good men versus bad men: the good men are those who suffer violence. Violence by women, conversely, is either framed as having a biological cause (triggered by the female sex cycle) or is used to highlight a deviant woman who is not sufficiently female.

While Giomi and Magaraggia's texts come from a wide variety of sources, mostly aimed at adults, their findings in terms of the gendered divisions are very much in line with Victoria Camm's (2018) *Girls Like This, Boys Like That*, where she surveyed the cultural tastes of contemporary youth. While books in this Library show that there are significant changes in gender relations in the twenty-first century, there persists a clear division in gendered representations, and as Giomi and Magaraggia explore here, this is most clearly seen in the case of gender-based violence.

Angela Smith and Claire Nally

Introduction*

Elisa Giomi

Sixteen-year-old Jules is reading Julia Kristeva having dismissed *The Catcher in the Rye* as a 'phallocentric piece of shit'. Later, she talks excitedly about the course on female violence in popular culture that she is following. We are not in a university cafeteria, nor a feminist collective. Actually, we are watching the second season of *Hanna* (Amazon Video 2019–present), and Jules is a co-star.

Female violence in popular culture is precisely the topic of this series. *Hanna* belongs to the sci-fi strand of 'young adult dystopia' that brings young female warriors combatting liberticidal regimes, deviant secret services and unscrupulous multinationals to the screen. However, whereas Katniss Everdeen of *Hunger Games* (Ross 2012; Lawrence 2013, 2014; 2016), Beatrice 'Tris' Prior from *Divergent* (Burger 2014; Schwentke 2015, 2016) or Cassie Sullivan from *The 5th Wave* (Blakeson 2016) find their enemies in adult women and their main ally in a boyfriend/mentor, elsewhere things are different. Sarah Manning of *Orphan Black* (Space/BBC, 2013–2017), Diana of *Wonder Woman* (Jenkins 2017) and Hanna succeed in their attempts to restore social justice thanks precisely to the protection of an older woman, a matrilineal transmission and above all the sisterhood. This change of course, we believe, can be read as an echo of the resumption of feminist mobilizations on a global scale, also thanks to campaigns such as #MeToo and #TimesUp.

But there is more. Young female warriors are not in fact an isolated phenomenon. An 'army' of criminals, prisoners, law-enforcement officers and fantasy world fighters permanently occupy sci-fi, crime, Western, superhero and other traditionally male genres (see Maury, Roche 2020 for an overview). Their presence, in terms of quantity and quality, is such as to classify the current moment as the fourth stage in the history of violent women and girls in popular culture narratives, which follows on from the 1930s and 1940s, the 1970s, the 1990s. These decades were characterized by rapidly changing gender roles, and, according to Neroni (2005: 20), the appearance of the filmic violent woman exposed the consequent tensions over gender issues. In fact, today, as in the past, other 'areas' of popular media culture appear engaged in a programmatic backlash (Faludi 1991). The same months in which Amazon Video made the first season of *Hanna* available, Netflix offered subscribers the second season of *You* (2018–present), where stalking and femicide become a source of entertainment; women, though educated and financially independent, appear naïve and vulnerable both online and offline. Female friendships are unable to offer any protection and the entire narrative is conducted from the killer's point of view, thus recentring the privileged subjectivity of white, heterosexual masculinity at a time when that subjectivity is being publicly challenged (Raijva & Patrick 2021). The acceleration of various media flows (Parikka 2015; Ramon et al. 2020) has made male violence against women even more widespread: murders and women's corpses populate a variety of products, ranging from advertising to music videos, television shows, films, online games: a real 'cadaverization', which has been occurring for years and which, according to Dillman (2014: 83), pursues a precise ideological project aimed at visually 'putting women back in their place and naturalizing their powerlessness in representations'.

Following this insight, we believe that in globally circulating media content the increase of violent women constitutes a symbolic transposition of the real and living bodies of women who have returned to occupy the public scene, intertwining their fight with other struggles and antiracist and queer/trans politics, whereas the increase in violence against women embodies their annihilation.

Therefore, the two forms of violence in media representation are strictly interconnected and need to be explored together. Thus far, however, all the existing contributions on the topic of gendered violence focus either on the representation of violent women (e.g. Early & Kennedy 2003; Inness 2004; Neroni 2005; Owen et al. 2007; Schubart 2007; Jones et al. 2014; Åhäll 2015; Brown, 2015; Gentry & Sjoberg 2015; Tasker & Steenberg 2016; Buonanno 2017; Maury & Roche 2020) or, more often, on the media's representation of violence against women (e.g. Projanski 2001; Berns 2004; Horeck 2013; Monckton-Smith 2012; Dillman 2014; Parikka 2015; Finley 2016; Moorti & Cucklanz 2016; Shoos 2017; Edwards 2020; Ramon et al. 2020). Among the few books that have analysed media depiction of both forms of gendered interpersonal violence (Wykes 2001; Boyle 2005; Burfoot & Lord 2006; Humphries 2009; Shepherd 2012; Jewkes 2015), only two (Shepherd 2012; Boyle 2005) adopt a comparative approach, which is the only way of revealing similarities and differences between female and male violence. Both books are thought-provoking and ground-breaking, but their scope is nevertheless limited to the representational level: the media coverage of men's and women's violence fails to be compared with the actualities of the two social phenomena (prevalence and incidence rates, patterns of victimization and offending, motives etc.).

Our book aims to rectify this omission by using a comparative analytical perspective that develops along two main 'vectors' – vertical and horizontal, so to speak – in an effort to establish multiple comparisons between the factual and the representational realms, between the material and symbolic dimensions of male and female violence.[1]

The concept of violence adopted here is as follows: 'any constraint of a physical or psychological nature which provokes harm, suffering or death of a human being' (Héritier 1996: 17). We limit our analysis to interpersonal violence, which manifests itself in individual behaviours. Although attention to the social and cultural components of such behaviour is a constant in this volume, forms of collective violence (war, military, political, institutional, etc.) are outside the perimeter of our exploration. Special attention is paid to intimate partner violence (IPV), with reference to heterosexual relationships. In the context of lethal interpersonal violence, the main cause of death for women over time and throughout the world is violence by their male partner. In view of the much lower incidence of violence by women, in order to be able to paint an accurate picture of this phenomenon and its media depiction, we decided to extend the analysis to multiple forms of interpersonal violence. Female-perpetrated violence against (ex) male partners remains, however, the investigation's main subject, both because, relatively speaking, it is one of the more widespread forms of female-perpetrated lethal violence and because it makes comparisons with male IPV possible.

Examining popular culture's depiction of men and women in their opposite, yet complementary roles of perpetrators and victims are also functional to this volume's second objective: to shed light on the under-investigated nexus of gender and violence, disclosing the configurations that it assumes in contemporary popular culture. In this aspect, the general theoretical framework of the book borrows from contributions originally developed within sociology (West & Zimmerman 1987) and criminology (Messerschmidt 1993). Our conceptualization of gender, violence and their mutual relationship can be divided into three propositions:

1. Gender and violence are 'performances'. Both are something that we 'do', that we perform;
2. At the same time, both gender and violence 'do' something: they have productive and normative effects;
3. These normative and productive effects are strictly intertwined: gender and violence 'do' each other; that is, they are mutually constitutive.

The specific, and the most original theoretical framework, stems from transposing such an analytical approach, based on the mutual constitution of gender and violence, to the field of media representation. In so doing, we follow a path traced by Boyle (2005) and above all by

Shepherd (2012), but extend their analysis to a larger number of media forms and compare them with statistics that relate to the two forms of violence.

Our research assumption is that the configurations of the nexus of gender and violence characterizing most contemporary global media are dependent on the politics of representation (Hall 1997) adopted by these media to portray male violence against women and female violence against men. The original features of these politics, we believe, were established in the United States, the UK and other Western European countries in the 1980s and 1990s, when popular culture became saturated with imagery linking intimate relations with extreme violence (Wykes 2001: 138): on the one hand, news and entertainment media started to pay attention to domestic violence and, on the other hand, to figures of violent women, in both cases as a response to the tensions over gender issues arising in the 1970s. For this reason we are interested in analysing the representation of gendered violence in professionalized and industrialized communication (Carah & Louw 2015: 39), rather than in social media or user-generated content. Therefore, these media products will be excluded from our investigation. We base this theoretical and methodological choice on the assumption that despite the rise of interactive technologies, the culture and media industries – either privately owned or state-licensed – are still central to controlling the production and circulation of meaning. Moreover, the boundaries between different media are increasingly blurred; digital technology has, on the one hand, allowed new players to emerge such as OTT (over-the-top) services and SVODs (subscription video on demand); on the other hand, 'traditional' media industries – linear television, broadcast radio, cinema, the printed press, advertising and music industries – convey their content trough digital practices on social media, video-sharing platforms and multimedia portals (Ramon et al. 2020). As a result, both female and male violence are experiencing an increased and more pervasive circulation.

In terms of the time frame, we focus on contemporary media products, that is, products still circulating and/or which were first released no more than ten years ago. In keeping with our research assumption, though, both theoretical and empirical chapters also include references to media artefacts dating back to the 1970s, 1980s and 1990s onwards, as those were the years when gender issues emerged and long-entrenched trends in representing the two forms of gendered violence under analysis originated.

The research questions guiding our exploration are the following: what are the features of men's violence against women and of women's violence against men? Are the respective media depictions faithful, as to the extent and causes of the problems, and also to victim and offender characteristics? Are these media depictions in line with the politics of representation that have characterized globally circulating media forms since the 1980s, or do they break from it? Finally, which gender imagery, which models of femininity, masculinity and gender relations do media representations of the two forms of violence draw on and simultaneously reproduce?

In the first part of the book, 'Theoretical Frames', men's violence against women and women's violence against men are illustrated, in Chapters 1 and 2, respectively, and compared in terms of their definitions, incidence, prevalence rates, motives, patterns of offending and victimization. Statistics from across the world are included, although the focus is on the United States and Western Europe, those being the countries where most of the media forms analysed in this study were produced. In Chapter 3, we present a survey of literature on violence, gender and the media, with regard to both factual (news, printed press, factual entertainment) and fictional (film, television series, advertising, music videos, etc.) genres. The review of literature from this field aims to offer a taxonomy of the most recurrent forms of representation of female and male violence. Each of the forms identified is compared with the picture of the two social phenomena presented by statistics, scholarly work and institutional definitions. This taxonomy will serve as a toolkit for empirical case analysis, which occupies the second part of the volume, 'Empirical Cases'. It includes four chapters, each dedicated to a different media genre: music (Chapter 4), advertising

(Chapter 5), factual entertainment (Chapter 6) and television crime series (Chapter 7). All of these media forms are under-researched, particularly concerning the representation of female violence against men. Compared to other media forms, music and advertising are also poorly covered in terms of male violence against women. This is worrying, considering that these are particularly pervasive genres, and that the few available contributions attribute a key role to them in the globalization of 'sexy violence' and rape culture (Parikka 2015; Finley 2016). As for the geocultural scope, the media products selected are from three types of countries: (a) those that have always been leaders in the international market (the United States and, to some extent, the UK as well); (b) those that have recently become producers and global exporters of a specific media form (such as the European crime series explored in Chapter 7); (c) countries whose media artefacts have rarely reached beyond national borders, but which offer particularly fertile ground for analysing the social problems being considered (the Italian pop songs analysed along with international hits in Chapter 4).

---

* Some of the ideas developed in this publication build on what was presented in the Italian book 'Relazioni Brutali. Genere e violenza nella cultura mediale' (Brutal Relations. Gender and Violence in Media Culture), published in 2017 by Il Mulino.

Male violence

Sveva Magaraggia

Gender-based violence against women and girls is one of the world's most pressing problems and one of the most prevalent human rights violations (United Nations Population Fund 2016). Furthermore, today it is still one of the principal risk factors for poor health and premature death in women aged 18–44 years (WHO 2013; Ayre et al. 2016). According to the United Nations, '[A]round one-third of women worldwide have experienced physical and/or sexual violence by an intimate partner; and 18 per cent have experienced such violence in the past twelve months. In the most extreme cases, violence against women is fatal: globally, an estimated 137 women are killed by their intimate partner or a family member every day' (UN 2020). These numbers have been validated by mirrored findings from a multi-country men's study, with 33 per cent of the men sampled admitting to the use of physical or sexual violence against their partner (Fulu et al. 2013: 29).

The recognition of the urgency to understand this pervasive social phenomenon has resulted in research proliferating rapidly. This has had positive outcomes for the prevention of intimate partner violence (IPV), but also confusion in its labelling and in the theoretical frames used to conceptualize it. A contested representation causes a cascade of confusion regarding the nature of the data collected as well as difficulties in measuring and comparing the prevalence of gender-based violence in different countries.

Given that the nominative processes create reality, this first chapter will delve into the debates around the terminology used when studying IPV and analyse the sociological debates about violence against women and investigate recent data. The goal is to conceptualize and measure gender-based violence with greater precision. It must be stressed that, in this volume, we do not read violence perpetrated by men against women as a residual phenomenon of our society, but rather a constitutive category of reality which functions to maintain a social structure based on unequal power relationships. To uphold that structure, it needs men to be in a condition of 'ontological primacy' and women in a subordinate, incomplete and dependent position. In addition, we read gender-based violence as a phenomenon that operates along a *continuum* (Scheper-Hughes & Bourgois 2004) which, as Bartholini (2015) points out, puts 'into play aspects that are structural (such as power and leadership), identitarian (such as the perception of self or those of gender, role or position)' (ibid., 72) as well as symbolic (such as the imposition of a world view or cognitive categories) and relational (such as emotional and affective investment). Gender-based violence is thus an explanatory category of interpersonal dynamics at the micro-social level and the gender order at large. It is a cultural problem related to women and men's roles and the relationship between them (Monckton-Smith 2012).

Nomen omen: Definitions and conceptual framework

Gender-based violence causes fear, pain and disability; it takes the voice and life away from an unimaginably high number of individuals every day and in every country. Nevertheless, it was only recognized as a social problem in the 1970s. Thanks to tireless feminist voices, it eventually stopped being treated as a uniquely private matter that did not warrant research or attention outside the family (Dobash & Dobash 1979). The women's political movement played a crucial role in the social construction and framing of the problem of violence against women, 'recognizing as social and systemic what was merely perceived as isolated and individual' (Crenshaw 1991: 1242). The very same definition of gender-based violence reveals the intent to stress the social roots of this phenomenon (Pitch 1998). It was in the context of the third World Conference on Women in Nairobi (1985) that it was formally recognized – through the approval of a specific Action Plan – that violence against women should be considered a public matter.

Since 1993, thanks to the Declaration on the Elimination of Violence against Women of the United Nations General Assembly, we understand it as a violation of human rights. This framing requires proactive approaches from national and international institutions (Latino 2019). In the European context, violence against women and girls 'has shifted from being framed as a health issue (Fernández de Vega et al. 2016) to more recently being framed as an equality issue' (Hearn et al. 2016: 554) understood as being both the cause and the effect of the inequalities between women and men.

This is the shared foundation from which the theoretical tools branch out in different directions due to the issue's interdisciplinary character. Gender-based violence (GBV) is the general term used to indicate different types of violence that occur 'as a result of the normative role expectations associated with each gender, along with the unequal power relationships between the two genders, within the context of a specific society' (Bloom 2008: 14). Sometimes it is used as a synonym for violence against women and girls (VAW/G), because the vast majority of GBV is perpetrated by men against women so that it has been defined as an 'almost routine violence' (Crenshaw 1991: 1241). However, these two terms are not equivalent (Bradbury-Jones et al. 2019). VAW/G is a prevalent part of GBV; however, men and boys can also be victims of gendered violence perpetrated by other men and boys or by women and girls.

The term 'VAW/G'[2] incorporates different types of violence perpetrated by an intimate partner or non-partner, as well as female genital mutilation, honour killings, trafficking of women, selective abortion, child marriage, stalking and, more recently, forms of technologically facilitated violence such as online harassment. Cyber Violence against Women and Girls came into use for the first time in an institutional context in 2015 (Schiavon 2019). Note also that in recent years a new way to destroy women has emerged with 'misogynistic terrorism' (Gentry 2020; Hoffman et al. 2020; Scaptura & Boyle 2020), a specific form of mass killings.

> Intimate partner violence[3] (IPV) is one of the most common forms of VAW/G. The term was introduced by the World Health Organization (WHO) in 2002 and is defined as [a]ny behaviour within an intimate relationship that causes physical, psychological or sexual harm to those in the relationship, including acts of physical aggression – such as slapping, hitting, kicking and beating. Psychological abuse – such as intimidation, constant belittling, and humiliating, forced intercourse and other forms of sexual coercion. Various controlling behaviours – such as isolating a person from their family and friends, monitoring their movements, and restricting their access to information or assistance.
>
> (Krug et al. 2002: 89)

In the last century, these same types of violence were defined as domestic violence, wife abuse or wife battering (United Nations 1980). Our suggestion is to modify Jeff Hearn's (2012) 'men's violence to known women' and use the phrase 'men's violence against known women' in conjunction with IPV. This terminological change permits a more direct identification of the subject that enacts the violence (i.e. men) while keeping open the type of relationship that ties the woman to her aggressor.

The gravest violence against women and girls is murder. Femicide indicates the homicide of a woman due to her being a woman. Originally, the 'use of the term "femicide" signalled political connotations. (…) this particular leitmotif originated in the mid-1970s with impetus from Diana E Russell, and was taken up in the 1990s by J Campbell in the USA, R&R Dobash in the UK, with an adaptation to the Mexican and Latin American context offered by M. Lagarde and J.E. Monarrez Fragoso' (Marcuello-Servós et al. 2016: 968). A useful cultural definition of femicide arises from an Italian debate during 2013, which considered the inclusion of this neologism in the Italian language. The Accademia della Crusca, the institution responsible for overseeing the Italian language, favoured the use of this term because it indicates an act that is based on 'a shared understanding of "female" as a social void. In short, it does not consider murder of a person who is female (...), but rather a crime that finds its deep motives within a culture that is hard to change, and within the institutions that still reflected it, at least partially' (Paoli 2013). So, the term 'femicide' indicates 'something more and something different (from homicide)'. Femicide is a social problem rooted in a cultural vision that sees 'the feminine (...) despised and disposable' (ibid.) and which legitimizes the masculine power of control over women. In fact, as proof of this, in most cases, femicide is preceded by episodes of psychological and physical violence (Mamo et al. 2015). The introduction of a specific term, in place of the generic intimate partner homicide (IPH), not only permits giving the phenomenon a name that would otherwise remain unspeakable, but also allows a nuanced conceptualization of a problem that was disregarded, if not ignored, and challenges the narrative of the inviolability of domestic space (McClain 1995).

The last type of violence that needs to be mentioned is symbolic violence. The social environment is, among other things, organized by way of exclusion, disempowerment and annihilation of certain social groups (McDonnell 2019). In these dynamics, symbolic violence, understood as 'a demonstration of power and an instrument of social control serving, on the whole, to reinforce and preserve the existing social order' (Gerbner & Gross 1976: 189), plays a central role. As Bourdieu (2004) has shown, symbolic and physical violence are the weapons that produce and incessantly reproduce the structures of domination. Singular agents and institutions such as families, the church, the educational system, the state and the media contribute to shaping categories, 'bodily emotions – shame, humiliation, timidity, anxiety, guilt – passions and sentiments – love, admiration, respect – constructed from the point of view of the dominant' (ibid., 341). Often this type of violence is invisible and may even appear to be benign and so not only does it often go unrecognized but it in fact becomes confused with something else. One of the instruments of symbolic violence is 'status degradation ceremonies' (Garfinkel 1956) directed towards women (see Chapter 4).

These types of violence should be questioned from an intersectional perspective, so as to understand the role of the interaction between different inequalities. It is a theoretical approach which is useful in interrogating how social categories 'intersect at the micro-level of individual experience to reflect multiple interlocking systems of privilege and oppression at the macro, social-structural level (e.g. racism, sexism, heterosexism)' (Bowleg 2012: 1267). GBV is 'democratic'. It is *the* social phenomenon that cuts across racial and socio-economic boundaries, as we will see throughout the book.

Semantic debates also surround the use of the term 'victim' to indicate women in violent relationships (Samelius et al. 2014; Pedace 2019). Concerns about an uncritical use of the term 'victim' are legitimate (Reich 2002) because within the semantic field of the term 'victim', diverse exceptions coexist, some of which are controversial. The risks are threefold, namely that it is a gendered term; it brings with itself an image of the 'good victim'; and it risks fixing a condition and status that are processual and temporary.

To understand the gendered nature of the term 'victim' we may consider contradictions inherent in feminists' discourses. As Wendy Brown (1995) and Nina Reich (2002) stress, 'wounded identities' and victim rhetoric were focal points around which feminists built alliances in the 1970s to make visible and demand recognition of VAW/G. This political strategy brought with it long-term problems, like ontologizing trauma and to 'produce a politics of recrimination and rancour with deep investments in victimization and suffering' (Phipps 2021: 83). In fact, to instantiate 'woman' as an identity based on injury (Brown 1995: 42) risks connecting 'women to victimisation, making the label victim a gendered term' (Reich 2002: 294), something that is constantly reinforced by news reports of sexual assaults that reiterate the belief that women are incapable of effectively defending themselves while men are described as being inherently dangerous (Hollander 2014). There are also institutional documents that contain a highly problematic interchangeability between the concepts of vulnerability and victimization (Abrisketa et al. 2015; Belluati et al. 2020). The gendered nature of the term has several consequences, not least among them the difficulties men encounter when claiming to be victims of violence.

Second, Sharon Lamb (1999) shows how, in order to be recognized (e.g. in court) as victims, women have to appear as a 'good' victim to fit the label, to seem not too self-reliant (Konradi 1996), to cry and to appear weak (Schneider 2000). Having to appear powerless to be believed increases the risk of reinforcing feelings of vulnerability as well as not matching the truth. Moreover, the process of blaming the perpetrator passes through a connotation of what constitutes an authentic or 'correct' victim, one that requires idealization: women victims are to be beautiful, affectionate and caring (Mandolini 2020).

Finally, in order not to victimize nor to shrink the complexity of our identities to just one dimension, we need to pose questions about how to do justice to the agency and strength of those who we label as 'victims', and how not to erase the complexity of their identities and the temporality of the situation they are in (Lamb 1999). These questions can help us not to fall into the trap of a dichotomy of victimization/agency and not to represent women in an acritical way as being particularly vulnerable because there is a risk of creating a descriptive norm, of reproducing or ratifying the problems described (Butler 2017).

Furthermore, not only do victims suffer consequences directly related to the crime, but the indirect consequences are often underestimated. The first can be traced back to the set of physical, psychological, economic, relational and social consequences directly due to the crime suffered. The indirect effects are a secondary form of victimization, i.e. those negative psychological, emotional and relational consequences deriving from the contact between the victim and institutions, including the justice system (Mendicino 2015; Simone et al. 2019; Gribaldo 2020) and the media. Secondary victimization has been described as a kind of 'second rape' (Martin & Powell, 1995; Campbell 1998) and assumes different forms, 'from minimizing the suffering, to blaming and devaluation, to the tendency to remove the problem' (Fanci 2011: 54), to attributing responsibility to the victim, and the sense of betrayal that 'comes from the survivor's expectation that she will be provided with belief, validation, and protection when she instead encounters victim-blaming attitudes' (Laing 2017: 1315). To avoid these pitfalls, we take up the suggestion offered by many abused women's centres, who work on empowerment and use the definition of 'women in temporary difficult situations' instead of victims.

Data

The importance of the gender dimension in criminal conduct is now a shared and consolidated fact in international criminological studies (Messerschmidt 1993; Gartner & McCharty 2014; Rinaldi 2018). Daly and Chesney-Lind (1988) define the gender ratio problem as the highest incidence of male crime in all types of crime. Global studies on homicide conducted over the years by the United Nations have found that the vast majority of homicide perpetrators as well as victims are men. If the majority of perpetrators are men, the gender of the victims changes depending on the place the murderous incident occurs: if 'roughly 80 per cent of all homicides committed globally have male victims and 20 per cent female victims', if we look only at 'victims of homicide perpetrated exclusively by an intimate partner (...) roughly 82 per cent were female victims while 18 per cent were male victims, a share that has remained quite stable since 2012. IPV continues to take a disproportionately heavy toll on women' (UNODC 2018: 19).

In 2019, in the UK, female victims (aged sixteen years and over) were more likely to be killed by a male partner or ex-partner (38 per cent, 80 homicides), while male victims were more likely to be killed by a friend or acquaintance (27 per cent, 105 homicides) (ONS 2020). In the United States, over 50 per cent of female homicide victims are murdered by former or current male intimate partners (Fridel and Fox 2019) while the percentage of male homicide victims killed by their partner is 5–8 per cent (Jack et al. 2018; Fridel & Fox 2019). Differences in the incidence of femicides are found in relation to ethnic groups. A recent study (Sabina and Swatt 2015) of data from sixteen US states spanning from 2005 to 2010 found that non-Latina Black women have the highest rate of femicide victimization, and Latinas, in turn, have a higher rate than non-Latina White women.

This trend is also confirmed in Italy (Giomi & Magaraggia 2017: 119; Giomi 2019) where, in 2019, men killed in the family or in an intimate relationship accounted for 27.9 per cent of the total murders of men and 83.8 per cent of the total murders of women. Men are killed mainly by unknown persons (43.1 per cent) or by unidentified perpetrators (21.1 per cent), while women are killed mainly by their partner or former partner (61.3 per cent). In particular, 55 murders (49.5 per cent) were caused by a man with whom the woman was in an intimate relationship at the time of her death (husband, cohabitant, boyfriend), 13 murders (11.7 per cent) by a former partner (Istat 2021).

The profile of femicide perpetrators differs from perpetrators who kill outside the family, as the former tend to be more 'conventional' than men who kill other men (Kivivuori et al. 2012), i.e. less disadvantaged with regard to employment, accommodation and criminal history than other types of homicide perpetrators (Liem et al. 2018).

Non-lethal IPV exists in all European member states and occurs at all levels of society (Council of Europe 2016). As Caroline Bradbury-Jones et al. (2019) highlight, an estimated one-fifth to one-quarter of all women have experienced physical violence at least once during their adult lives, and more than one-tenth have suffered sexual violence enacted by men (Council of Europe 2016). Forty-three per cent of women aged fifteen and over within Europe have experienced some form of psychological intimate partner violence, with 22 per cent of women having experienced physical and/or sexual violence by an intimate partner in their lifetime, and 10 per cent, aged fifteen or older, have experienced cyber harassment[4] (FRA 2014).

A recommendation that comes from several fronts (Walby 2005; Walby & Towers 2017; Bjørnholt & Hjemdal, 2018; Bettio et al. 2020) is to take into account also the frequency and severity of the violence, integrating the measurement scales used in the past with items able to measure mental, physical or economic damage (Marshall 1992; Straus et al. 1996). In doing so, it appears that the frequency and severity of violence enacted by male partners are much greater, and that an estimated three-quarters of women's violent acts are in self-defence (see Chapter 2). However, how this should be taken into account in the statistical surveys is the subject of an ongoing debate (Myhill 2017; Walby & Towers 2017; Bjørnholt & Hjemdal 2018; Bettio et al. 2020: 36).

Numerous studies agree on the serious consequences of IPV and unanimously highlight the major health problems (both physical and mental) it causes (Romito et al. 2005; 2013; Larsen 2016). Women in IPV situations suffer from multiple disadvantages. Living in a violent relationship is in all respects 'a corrosive disadvantage, because it acts on the weakening of protective factors and on the so-called guardians of resilience (family, school, society)' (Deriu 2016: 215). As Fiorenza Deriu (2016) points out, men who mistreat women deprive them of many of the capabilities central to human dignity listed by Martha Nussbaum (2000), such as bodily integrity, body health and emotions.

As Spangaro summarizes, consequences are not restricted to physical injuries, but encompass a broad range of impacts, including

> [h]igher rates of chronic pain, gastrointestinal and gynaecological problems, depression and anxiety (Rivara et al. 2007); levels of mental health functioning that are directly associated with the length of exposure to abuse (Bonomi et al. 2006); one and a half times the risk of contracting HIV (World Health Organization et al. 2013); a threefold risk of self-harm (Boyle et al. 2006); double the risk of access to contraception being prevented (Williams et al. 2008); 16 per cent greater chance of having a low birth weight baby than non-abused women (García-Moreno et al. 2005).
>
> (2019: 266)

The seriousness of these consequences means that gender-based violence can be considered a structural mechanism used to sustain male dominance and that there can be no real equality between women and men as long as women experience gender-based violence. Constructively framing the roots and causes of gender-based violence means focusing on the relationship between its actual practices and the social and cultural construction of masculinity (Connell 1995; Hearn 1998; Kimmel 2000). In the last several decades, the analysis has been broadened, the reading grids have multiplied, and more attention is paid to the intricate relationship between violence and masculinity in showing how often 'male identities are built through these acts of violence and through the narration of the same' (Arcidiacono & Di Napoli 2012: 126). In fact, the link between masculinity and violence is not random but profound and intimate. The different forms and manifestations of violence have their roots in the models of masculinity celebrated as ideals, which are desirable, in the normal ways and norms of what it means to be a man (Kimmel 2002a, 2013). We suggest that this theoretical awareness should also be reflected in the questions asked in international and national surveys on VAW/G.

Sociological debates

Jeff Hearn stresses the 'relative neglect of domestic violence in intimacy between known persons as a central concern in mainstream sociology' (2012: 153). This relative neglect distinguishes the whole history of our discipline from the classical sociologists up to today. The marginalization of this theme to a niche in family sociology is no longer sustainable, simply because of its relevance, proven by numerous national and comparative studies on IPV. Despite our discipline's reluctance, it is thanks to Feminist and Gender Studies that a rich theoretical corpus has developed, which is worth examining.

Simplifying a very articulate debate, it can be argued that there are two opposing theoretical perspectives on these issues: a feminist perspective and a family violence perspective. Feminist theorists locate the 'source' of violence in the dimension of gender, in social inequalities and in patriarchal domination, while family violence theorists locate it in family relationships, reading partner violence as a universal and inevitable aspect of the conflict that exists in families, as a 'normal part of family life in most societies' (Gelles & Straus 1979: 549). These perspectives differ so much that

> [e]ven deciding on the nomenclature for discussing the problem is fraught with difficulties, as the various terms for describing the problem reflect their underlying theoretical assumptions. The terms 'wife abuse', 'wife beating', and 'violence against women' all reflect a theoretical choice to frame the problem in gendered terms that reflect the fundamental assumption that gender is at the centre of the problem. Terms such as 'spousal abuse', 'marital violence', 'family violence', and even 'domestic violence' reflect the theoretical assumption that the problem is essentially gender-neutral and, therefore, should be studied and discussed in gender-neutral terms.
>
> (Lawson 2012: 574)

This shows that even the unit of analysis differs, being the gender order for the former and the family unit for the latter (Yllo 1993). For scholars positioned in the family violence perspective, to understand intimate partner violence means to understand why violence becomes a resource to resolve family conflicts.

Feminist perspectives, on the contrary, ground their analysis on reading male abuse in intimate relationships as an expression of male domination over women. The seminal work conducted by the British criminologist Russell Dobash and sociologist Rebecca Emerson Dobash (1979) was a milestone for this perspective and states that, even if within families, we can trace different types of violence (against elders or children), and that violence against wives is a separate unit of analysis that must be studied on its own, as it is explained by the dynamics of gender domination.

A more recent theoretical framework proposing an alternate reading of gender-based violence is 'gender symmetry', claiming that there is no gender difference in the use of violence in intimate relationships; according to this perspective, women equally perpetrate violence at the same rate as their male partners. This position is also linked to methodological controversies, as support for a symmetrical reading of IPV came from studies adopting the Conflict Tactics Scale (Straus 1979), now abandoned in favour of the composite abuse scale (Hegarty et al. 2005). This methodological shift combined with the strong criticism that this approach has and continues to arouse (see Kimmel 2002; Enander 2011) has contributed to correcting this (mis)reading (Salom et al. 2015; Spangaro 2019). As Kimmel (2002) stresses, the questions gender symmetry theorists pose the critiques they offer are unclear: 'Does gender symmetry mean that women hit men as often as men hit women? Or does it mean that an equal number of men and women hit each other? Does symmetry refer to men's and women's motivations for such violence, or does it mean that the consequences of it are symmetrical?' (Kimmel 2002: 1335).

We would argue that mainstream sociology needs to be interested in studying gender-based violence not merely because of its great prevalence, but rather because 'domestic violence is of sociological significance, as a paradoxical phenomenon, in its naming and framing, in terms of explanation and responsibility, and as embedded in hegemonic social formations' (Hearn 2012: 164). Studying this 'intimate terrorism' (Johnson 1995) can help us understand gender, the construction of intimacy and can restore sociology to its political aspiration, allowing it to 'make public issues out of private troubles' (Burawoy 2004: 5).

Gender equality and violence: What is the relationship?

A lively debate is animating the feminist perspectives regarding the reasons behind the failure to reduce IPV over the years. It often turns on the question concerning the relationship between the increase in gender equality achieved in recent decades and the constancy with which male violence against known women occurs. Put succinctly: do high levels of gender equality correspond to high levels of GBV, or is GBV reduced as gender equality increases?

One perspective in this debate uses the equation 'violence – power' to explain men's violence against women, in particular, IPV, as a result of women's emancipation movements and their denunciation of the asymmetric roles attributed to men and women in society and the family (Corradi 2011; Giomi & Magaraggia 2017; Giomi 2019). Another position in the debate no longer reads male violence as an explicit manifestation of patriarchy, but as a sign of its crisis, as a reaction to the overcoming of this order (Pitch 2008), a backlash due to the changes in the roles and authority of women. This second position appears capable of grasping recent social transformations as well as the contradiction inherent in IPV noted by Raewyn Connell: 'violence is a part of a system of domination, (…) but it is at the same time a measure of its imperfection' (1995: 84). Similarly, Kimmel, focusing on the micro-level, suggests that 'many men who assault their partners or ex-partners are using violence when they fear their control is breaking down, their ability to control their partners by the implicit threat of violence is compromised, and they feel compelled to use explicit violence to "restore" their control. Thus, men see their violence as restorative and retaliatory' (Kimmel 2002: 1352). For example, women who, in the name of their freedom, end a romantic relationship then go on to suffer violence at men's hands precisely because men perceive this freedom as dangerous and as a sign of their lost power.

Recent analyses (FRA 2014; Gracia & Merlo 2016; Bettio & Ticci 2017; Nevala 2017; Davoine & Jarred 2018; Willie & Kershaw 2019) suggest that, in order to understand the relationship between equality and gender-based violence, more precise questions must be asked and the complexity of our analysis has to increase by distinguishing between the different types of violence. By doing so, physical, sexual and psychological violence emerges as being 'higher overall in European countries with the lowest levels of gender equality. Which means (…) this does not apply to either non-partner violence or to sexual harassment (…). In the case of sexual harassment, the comparison between countries shows a positive and statistically significant association between equality indices and indices of violence' (Bettio et al. 2020: 53). As the authors explain, 'as women gain ground in the labour market, institutions, business and politics, violence "shifts" from the home to public areas – including workplaces – more so than increasing or decreasing everywhere' (ibid., 30).

From these recent empirical studies, it would seem vital to investigate gender-based violence's dislocation, its accelerating dispersal throughout the public domain, alongside its prevalence. The results of these studies must take us back to the origins of the conceptualization of GBV, namely to think of it as a structural phenomenon, as the result of a complex interaction between factors that cut across individual and family history, cultural and socio-economic context and the variety of social institutions. This means not to understand '"domestic violence" as specific behaviour, a "thing" to be explained, but as a deeply embedded political-economic-cultural phenomena with wider social formations' (Hearn 2012: 160).

To question and understand the thread that runs through the opposing readings of gender-based violence that we have illustrated, we might ask ourselves what cultural and structural tools gender violence can avail itself of to ensure its persistence. We adopt a multi-causal explanation and try to combine several realms, which may initially appear unrelated to IPV, such as labour market inequalities, lack of political representation, men's inability to fulfil caring duties, romantic love, and the construction of masculinity. We think that to combat gender-based violence, it is necessary to investigate these domains, disempower the inequalities that mark them, and question the connections between structural, cultural, symbolic and interpersonal violence.

Maintaining gender inequalities: Economy, politics and romantic love

The first tool used by gender-based violence is the maintenance of inequality in the public and private spheres. In the public sphere, examples include the gender pay gap or the glass ceiling found in working environments. In 2018, in Europe (twenty-seven countries), women's gross hourly earnings were on average 14.8 per cent lower than those of men (Eurostat 2020), meaning women earn 85 cents for every euro earned by a man, or in other words, on average, they work for free for about two months each year. Moreover, if we compare the data from 2010 when the gender pay gap in the European Union (EU-27) stood at 15.8 per cent, the reduction in the gap is derisory, particularly when considered alongside the fact that, in the last twenty years, women have exceeded men in the graduate population (in 2018, women accounted for 54 per cent of all tertiary students in the EU-27). In addition, the number of women employed in jobs decreases as we move up job hierarchies. The percentage of women occupying top positions is very low. In 2019, women account for just 27.8 per cent of board members of the largest public-listed companies registered in EU countries (European Commission 2020). The trends also apply to the political field. In European politics, female heads of national government account for 14.3 per cent; only 21.4 per cent of heads of state are women; and only 30 per cent of ministers in European countries (EU 27) are women (EU 2019). The European Parliament scores a little better, with 36 per cent of its members being women. Taken together, these facts contribute to maintaining the difference in the distribution of power between men and women and demonstrate an alliance between capitalism and patriarchy both of which are based on gender inequality (Fraser 2004).

Turning to the private sphere, we can see how inequality is nourished by the care gap, which is the unequal distribution of care work associated with traditional heterosexual family models. Across the EU, the bulk of unpaid care work is done by women (92 per cent) and a much lower proportion (68 per cent) by men. Similar inequalities have also been recorded for employed women, who do more than their fair share of unpaid care work. Across the EU, they spend ninety minutes more per day on unpaid care than employed men (Eige 2020).

These figures feed off a cultural climate that justifies fathers who do not actively participate in childcare. It assumes that women take on the bulk of the practical day-to-day management of the family and that care work is worth less than paid work. Thus, those who do it are also symbolically devalued. This is further evidence of a mechanism that marginalizes women, a devaluation that is a central antecedent of gendered violence.

Another is the inequality intrinsic to hierarchical relationships. As social scientists have abundantly shown, intergenerational power dynamics play a central role in the transmission of the grammar of violence. Thus, a large body of evidence indicates that exposure to IPV against one's mother is one of the most common factors associated with male perpetration and female experience of IPV later in life (Abramsky et al. 2011). Furthermore, growing up with a violent father has deleterious effects for the child (Øverlien 2010), including, as Spangaro (2019) summarizes: emotional and behavioural difficulties (Gartland et al. 2014), a threefold rate of conduct disorders (Meltzer et al. 2009) and increased exposure to the presence of other lifetime adversities (Holt et al. 2008).

In addition to the 'learned violence' from one's parents, the question also arises as to whether 'absorbed violence', that is, violence absorbed by the foetus during pregnancy, exists. In this context, the literature refers to the 'biographical body' (García-Moreno et al. 2005; Parker & Nelson 2005) and its susceptibility as prolonged stress can inhibit hormone production, fundamental for growth. Increasingly research shows that physical, sexual and psychological intimate partner violence against pregnant women is associated with higher levels of depression, anxiety and stress, as well as an increase in suicide attempts, a lack of attachment to the child and lower rates of breastfeeding (Zeitlin et al. 1999; Jasinski 2004; Martin et al. 2006; Bergman et al. 2007). The state of the mother's mood has a significant impact on foetal brain development and, therefore, on the child's behavioural development. Maternal antenatal stress can predict children's behavioural and emotional problems up to the age of four (O'Connor 2002; WHO 2011).

The consequences of witnessing violence in one's household are stressed in various studies, such as the quantitative research conducted by Diaz-Aguardo and Martinez (2015) which investigated types of dating violence against women by male adolescents. This study clearly shows the significant intergenerational impacts of violence. Violent boys who experienced violence in the home had lower self-esteem and were more inclined to justify male dominance and violence against women than those who grew up in non-violent families. Violence is learned and passed down from generation to generation.

Another discourse that produces gender asymmetries is the ideology of romantic love. Love should not be analysed as an emotion or individual psychological condition; instead, it should also be studied as a social fact (Alberoni 2008): the social, economic and cultural structure in which we live influences our ways of loving and the very sense we give to love. This perspective situates our idea about love in the social imagination and further implies a relativization of seemingly universal phenomena. There is no such feeling called love that crosses time and place; it is historically and culturally specific. For example, what Italian women and men mean by this word today depends on the society's cultural (patriarchal) and economic (neoliberal) structures. These structures determine the meaning we attribute to the sentimental experience and contribute to articulating the similarities and differences between men and women. As Illouz puts it, 'love contains, mirrors, and amplifies the "entrapment" of the self in the institutions of modernity, institutions, to be sure, shaped by economic and gender relations' (2012: 6).

The ideology of romantic love, by definition heterosexual, is instrumental in building well-codified power relationships and in defining oppositional genders (Evans 2003). Women appear as figures who, out of love, must be dedicated to a form of self-sacrificing altruism, so must victimize herself. The rhetoric of 'behind every great man there is a great woman' is an example. We must ask ourselves, with Bourdieu, whether 'love [is] an exception, the only one, but of the first order of magnitude, to the law of masculine domination, a suspension of symbolic violence, or is it the supreme – because the most subtle, the most invisible form of that violence?' (Bourdieu 2001: 109).

As Lea Melandri suggests, we can try to understand if 'romantic love is "harmony and reciprocity" or "bewilderment and self-sacrifice"' (ibid., 2011: 98). As long as romantic love means merging two beings into one 'almost as if they were two halves of a whole, it can only be experienced as a terrible necessity: a condition of survival for the woman, who is forced to borrow her own reason to live from the other sex; the exercise of power for the man, the sole protagonist of the world's fortune' (ibid., 54). Romantic love conceived in this way brings with it a violation of individuality, a threat of engulfment, a destructive potential: 'I love you to death', 'Crazy in love', 'I love you to pieces'. These expressions all signal the desire to possess, fuse and destroy (Ben-Ze'ev & Goussinsky 2008). The ideology of romantic love has incorporated these anxieties by promoting the idea that violence is a manifestation of passion and a measure of the intensity of a man's attachment, while the acceptance of violence – as we will see in the analysis of certain media representations (see Chapter 4) – is a sign of the woman's devotion.

Extreme emotions play contradictory roles in the ideology of romantic love: on the one hand they have become a measure of the authenticity of feelings; on the other they are considered capable of distorting the true nature of a person (he killed out of passion, not because of his own character or his own failings). The current configuration of the discourse on romantic love is based on extremely dangerous ambivalences and ontologically solidifies the link between love and violence.

Courtship and gallantry are closely connected to the ideology of romantic love. Goffman (1977) analyses the courtship system as a ritual that implies that the norms of sexual attraction affect the two sexes differently. The man's job is to be attracted, and the woman's is to attract. Traces of this division of roles can be seen in a magical rites study conducted in the 1950s by the Italian anthropologist Ernesto De Martino (1959). De Martino examined the different 'magical' rites women had available to them to make men fall in love. Not having the opportunity to ask for a man's hand directly, women organized themselves to make him ask for theirs. 'Due to being a traditionally passive element in the love affair, the woman relies more readily on the small world of love filters' (ibid., 21). These strategies remain dominated and have the (unwanted) effect of 'confirming the dominant representation of women as maleficent beings' (Bourdieu 2001: 32).

Today, the courtship system has clearly changed, but it still firmly rests on this cultural foundation. The courtesy system (gallantry) is an interpersonal ritual that constructs women as precious, fragile, inexperienced and unsuited to learning (e.g. incapable of changing a tyre or fixing a bicycle or household appliances). It follows that men must help and protect women. This obligation is also a privilege because the man can use it selectively (to define which women deserve his help or not). He can draw a subtle confirmation of his masculinity from the interaction itself. At the same time, the act of being gallant allows men to construct masculinity as being non-fragile and not in need of help. As Sassatelli highlights, 'unlike other disadvantaged groups, the latter (women) are held in high regard, but this is an ambiguous consideration, which denies them full recognition of their autonomy' (2010: 42). Thus, 'any benevolence that society shows towards women can be seen as a half-blessing in that it always seems to have the function of masking what might be considered a disadvantage' (Goffman 1979: 9).

The universal neutral is masculine

The protection of masculinity as the universal neutral is another tool that nourishes gender-based violence and can prevent the revelation of male partiality. The white, able-bodied, heterosexual male is the absolute signifier of a full and free social subject. He thinks and is thought of as a 'unique prototype of the human species' (Melandri 2011: 93), the citizen *par excellence*, while all others are minorities (Marchetti et al. 2012: 287). Linguistic structures also highlight how much men are the measure of things: in the Italian language, masculine is used as a universal neutral, reproducing a specific social order.

Historically, in distinguishing himself from the feminine, men have based access to full citizenship on the ability to 'liberate [themselves] from his own needs, [their] own emotions and affections' (Ciccone 2009: 176) on top of having exclusive participation entitlements in the public sphere. However, interpreting the break from primary care responsibilities as freedom, has 'mercilessly showed its inconsistency' (Melandri 2011: 96–7), revealing a backdrop of fragility and fear. By confining women to the role of mother, making them guardians of the house, childhood, and sexuality, men do force themselves to remain eternal children, establishing a *maternage* with their female partners. With these roles as prerequisites, being abandoned by a woman signifies dying. It means measuring oneself as being unable to provide for one's own survival. Losing the female gaze, which can nourish male narcissism, means losing one's sense of self, self-esteem, and freedom.

When 'love is experienced in terms of paternalism and shared identity, when separation is seen as loss of personal continuity, when masculine identity is defined in terms power and control, and when a rigid personal disposition accompanies the dangerous realization of Romantic Ideology's central theme – "without you I am nothing"' (Ben-Ze'ev & Goussinsky 2008: 109), building relationships characterized by this profound emotional dependence provides fertile ground for femicide.

Men's inability to accept abandonment is also closely linked to another aspect: difficulty in managing the most painful emotions due to the male stereotype that wants reason to dominate emotion. Emotions are denied and vented on the other, in a constant tension aimed at repressing vulnerability, the most human feelings. Emotional repression – not only of what one feels, but also of the need for attention from others – instils the germ of frustration in the foundations of the masculine construction.

This way of conceiving masculinity makes dependence on women essential and at the same time demeaning: making this need explicit corresponds to experiencing impotence and weakness, the humiliation of that same male identity that made it necessary. This profound short circuit, experienced by rigid identities – rigid because they lack an emotional grammar – finds easy answers in the ideology of romantic love, which legitimizes sacrifices and martyrs in its name.

These positions were taken up by Men's Studies, which highlighted how masculinity itself is inhibited by the symbolism inherent in heterosexuality. Men's Studies have brought to the fore the power relationships that exist between men. Its contribution has led to masculinities being discussed in the plural. It has revealed that men are forced to continually confront a hegemonic model, which is by its very definition unattainable. The imperative to achieve this ideal creates pressure, stress and anxiety for men as for women, recognizing this common frustration can be the basis for building strategic alliances.

These are just some of the many tools that male violence against women needs. They are some of the social and cultural forces that construct our gender order and shape how we read, interpret and act within the world. They are so invisible, so inherent to our being social actors that we can only perceive them with conscious reflection: a bit like eyelashes, they are too close to the eye to be seen. However, from the awareness of these mechanisms' pervasiveness and prescriptive strength, we can build interventions capable of speaking to those who experience intimate relationships based on violence and capable of breaking its intergenerational reproduction.

Female violence

Elisa Giomi

What we talk about when we talk about female violence against men: Data and their construction

Today, in the Anglo-American field, the analysis of interpersonal female violence is mainly found in the area of criminology. Many texts address it in relation to the role of gender in victimization and/or offending patterns, and sometimes in the context of a more general intersectional analysis of crime (Heimer & Kruttschnitt 2005; Heidensohn 2006; Morash 2006; Wykes & Welsh 2009; Barak et al. 2010; Britton 2011; Davies 2011; Walklate 2012; Renzetti et al. 2013; Fitz-Gibbon & Walklate 2018; Mallicoat 2014: 2019; Bernat et al. 2019; Belknap 2020). Explorations of the relationship between gender and interpersonal violence, including female violence, are also found in volumes with an interdisciplinary approach (e.g. Gartner & McCarthy 2014; Bahun & Rajan 2016; Marway & Widdows 2015; Silvestri & Crowther-Dowey 2016; Lombard 2018: Shepherd 2019). Other studies focus exclusively on women and girls as offenders and belong to the criminological domain (Cain & Howe 2008; Chesney-Lind & Jones 2010; Ness 2010; Sharpe 2013; Chesney-Lind & Pasko 2013; Naffine 2017), cultural criminology (Seal 2010), psychology (Motz 2008), human rights (Barberet 2014), or use multidisciplinary approaches within the social sciences (Jack 2001; Jensen 2001; Hird 2002).

It is significant that in none of these texts do we find the term 'female violence against (known) men'. There is no such phenomenon.

Or at least, it does not exist in the same terms in which the opposite phenomenon exists, namely male violence against (known) women. The term 'gender' now widely used in academic, legal and public discourses is 'one-way': it refers to a violative/anti-social conduct that sees men in the role of perpetrators and women in that of victims. This does not mean, however, that women do not commit violence, that theirs is not a form of violence as gendered as that of men or that there is no female-perpetrated IPV with specific characteristics. On the contrary, as we will show in this chapter, women are the authors of all types of crime committed by men, including violent ones, and the gender dimension affects not only the phenomenology but also the criminalization of such conduct. We will review the theories about interpersonal female violence that have followed each other over time. Far from providing a comprehensive overview, we are interested in highlighting the role and conceptualization of sex and gender in scientific discourse and legal discourse dealing with female violence. Finally, we will illustrate the specificities of women's violence within an intimate relationship, comparing it with that of men's and paying particular attention to the debate between proponents and detractors of the theory of 'gender symmetry' introduced in Chapter 1.

However, before starting this journey, it is important to clarify that if 'female violence against (known) men' does not define a concept with as much autonomy or immediate empirical evidence as that of 'male violence against (known) women', it is primarily because female and male violence – regardless of the gender of the victim or the type of violence perpetrated – have completely different prevalence and incidence rates. Table 2.1 was populated by processing the data provided by Uniform Crime Reporting (UCR) for the years 2017, 2018 and 2019. The UCR is based on arrests made by police, and the data are collected by the Federal Bureau of Investigation (FBI) from over 18,000 police agencies in the United States. In Table 2.1, the first column on the left shows the type of offence, the second column indicates the total arrests (of women and men) for each type, the third and fourth columns indicate the female and male arrests, respectively, and the fifth indicates the gender ratio, referring to the difference between the number of crimes committed by men and women. The average gender ratio (last line) – calculated based on the total number of arrests – is one woman for every three men. The data are ordered in descending order, i.e. starting from the type of crime in which the gender ratio is greater.

Table 2.1 Arrests made by police in 2017, 2018 and 2019 per gender ratio in the United States

Type of offence	Total F+M	Total F	Total M	Gender ratio
Rape	54,348	1,685	52,663	1:31
Sex offences (except rape and prostitution)	102,372	7,275	95,097	1:13
Weapons; carrying, possessing, etc.	366,928	34,493	332,435	1:10
Murder and non-negligent manslaughter	26,336	3,220	23,116	1:7
Robbery	198,591	30,013	168,578	1:6
Burglary	412,625	81,048	331,577	1:4
Arson	20,599	4,398	16,201	1:4
Gambling	6,894	1,507	5,387	1:4
Drunkenness	762,031	159,703	602,328	1:4
Aggravated assault	883,578	207,289	676,289	1:3
Motor vehicle theft	198,692	45,140	153,552	1:3
Stolen property; buying, receiving, possessing	212,497	46,955	165,542	1:3
Vandalism	413,541	94,602	318,939	1:3
Drug abuse violations	3,595,428	890,123	2,705,305	1:3
Driving under the influence	2,170,046	556,576	1,613,470	1:3
Disorderly conduct	740,129	218,813	521,316	1:3
Vagrancy	52,767	12,581	40,186	1:3
All other offences (except traffic)	7,219,760	1,936,251	5,283,509	1:3
Suspicion	1,446	381	1,065	1:3
Larceny/theft	2,037,554	849,985	1,187,569	1:2

Other assaults	2,360,239	684,010	1,676,229	1:2
Forgery and counterfeiting	114,157	38,699	75,458	1:2
Fraud	267,788	97,966	169,822	1:2
Offences against the family and children	195,821	59,085	136,736	1:2
Liquor laws	404,665	123,243	281,422	1:2
Curfew and loitering law violations	51,379	15,808	35,571	1:2
Embezzlement	33,813	16,775	17,038	1:1
Prostitution and commercialized vice	72,204	45,220	26,984	2:1
Total	**22,976,228**	**6,262,844**	**16,713,384**	**1:3**

Source: The Federal Bureau of Investigation (FBI) (www.fbi.gov/services/cjis/ucr/).

Table 2.1 confirms what are today 'the few undisputed "facts" of criminology' (Heidensohn & Silvestri 2012: 336): the first, which is quantitative in nature, is that men commit many more crimes than women. Or, to put it another way, female crime has a much lower incidence than men's (Walklate 2004: 5). The second figure, to which we referred above, is qualitative: women, although to a much lesser extent, are present in all types of crime committed by men, from the most to the least serious. This evidence is the source of questions that have always accompanied sector studies. The first concerns the existence of typical crimes for men and women. The lack of differentiation between female and male criminal conduct, at least in terms of quality, would seem to rule out the existence of typical crimes. The second question, strictly linked to the first, concerns the relevance of the gender variable in reading crime. As is well known, attention to this variable made its way into criminology in the 1970s, thanks to second-wave feminism, starting with the works of Carol Smart. The initial approach, typical of white liberal feminists, 'focused only on gender and did not include discussions that reflected a multicultural identity' (Mallicoat 2018: 2). Later, thanks to third-wave feminism, an approach was established that explored links between criminology and intersectionality (Barak et al.

2010: 22), looking at the interplay of multiple axes of social inequality (e.g. age, social class, race, in addition to gender).

However, there appears to be very precise gender patterns in offending, which allow us to outline a substantial difference between male violence and female violence. Looking at the table of arrests from the United States, what we see first is that the gender gap (the gender ratio in committing crime) is wider in cases of serious or violent crimes and narrower for crimes such as property and drug-related offences. Also, the crimes in which the gap between men and women widens the most, with the greatest divergence from the average gender ratio (1:3), belong to two types: (a) sexual violence (rape is committed by one woman for every 31 men, and sex offences by one woman for every thirteen men); (b) murder and non-negligent manslaughter (1:7). Possessing and carrying weapons, although certainly much less serious, also relates to the sphere of violent crime against a person and appears to be a significantly more masculine than feminine crime (1:10). The only type of crime in which the gender ratio is unbalanced in favour of women is prostitution and commercialized vice (2:1). It should be noted that most people arrested for this type of offence are the trade workers and not the traffickers or customers associated with these crimes (Mallicoat 2019: 139). This overshadows the fact that the majority of prostitutes or sex workers are women, and the majority of clients are men:[5] it is therefore in male sexuality that a crucial area in the deconstruction and interpretation of this crime – as well as in sex offences – should be found.

We now quickly consider different geographical contexts. Since 2010, the reports by the Criminal Justice System Statistics Quarterly about people in prison in England and Wales (published by the Ministry of Justice), no longer differentiate according to the type of crime. However, we know that the gender ratio of the total prison population is 1:4, therefore in line with that of the United States. Table 2.2 refers to crimes reported to police forces in 2017, 2018 and 2019.

Although these are different datasets and contexts, many similarities with the United States emerge.

Table 2.2 Crimes reported to police forces in 2017, 2018 and 2019 in England and Wales

Type of offence	Total F+M	Total F	Total M	Gender ratio
Sexual offence	8,740	280	8,400	1:30
Burglary	4,660	590	4,030	1:7
Harassment	5,440	800	4,610	1:6
Possession of a firearm	670	90	580	1:6
Breach court order	9,490	1610	7,840	1:5
Possession of an offensive weapon	4,520	700	3,780	1:5
Robbery	1,540	240	1,290	1:5
Unknown	22,150	3,290	17,340	1:5
Criminal damage	9,200	1640	7,530	1:4
Drug offences	4,880	990	3,860	1:4
Murder	800	160	640	1:4
Vehicle crime	1,130	210	900	1:4
Theft	10,240	2,810	7,370	1:3
Violence against the person	38,820	9,740	28,900	1.3
Other	11,130	2,920	8,130	1:3
Arson	990	280	710	1:2
Fraud and forgery	890	330	550	1:2
Motoring offences	6,150	1750	4,350	1:2
Public order – nuisance	11,590	3,320	8,190	1:2
Total	**153,020**	**31,710**	**119,000**	**1:4**

Source: Office of National Statistics, CSEW – Crime Survey for England and Wales (https://www.ons.gov.uk/peoplepopulationandcommunity/crimeandjustice)

Again, the largest gender gap is found in sexual offences (1:30) and harassment (1:6), but also possession of firearm/offensive weapon (1:6 and 1:5, respectively). Unlike in the United States, lethal violence against the person, i.e. murder and manslaughter (1:4), is in line with the total gender ratio (1:4).

Finally, with regard to the Italian context, we have the gender ratio relating to the crimes reported by the police to the judicial authority over the three-year period, 2017, 2018 and 2019.

Table 2.3 Crimes reported by the police to the judicial authority in 2017, 2018 and 2019 in Italy

Type of crime	Total F+M	Total F	Total M	Gender ratio
Sexual assault	14,257	279	1,3978	1:78
Motorcycle thefts	2,091	41	2,050	1:50
Bank robbery	2,497	60	2,437	1:41
Voluntary homicide mafia type	740	25	715	1:29
Moped thefts	1,424	56	1,368	1:24
Car thefts	9,092	412	8,680	1:21
Robberies in post offices	876	42	834	1:20
Sexual acts with underage	1,850	93	1,757	1:19
Mafia-type association	7,248	417	6,831	1:16
Attempted murders	5,959	345	5,614	1:16
Muggings	25,835	1,691	24,144	1:14
Attacks	497	33	464	1:14
Smuggling	1,531	114	1,417	1:12
Drug law	216,028	16,091	199,937	1:12
Damage by fire	3,733	304	3,429	1:11
Child pornography and possession of child pornography	2,284	186	2,098	1:11
Theft of works of art and archaeological material	226	21	205	1:10
Burglaries in parked cars	13,094	1,272	11,822	1:9
Voluntary homicides for the purpose of theft or robbery	153	15	138	1:9
Corruption of minors	467	46	421	1:9
Theft (bag snatching)	5,775	655	5,120	1:8
Shoplifting	13,029	1,505	11,524	1:8

Extortion	29,310	3,106	26,204	1:8
Kidnappings	4,701	515	4,186	1:8
Intellectual property infringement	2,152	250	1,902	1:8
Arson	1,367	162	1,205	1:7
Burglary	6,035	760	5,275	1:7
Premeditated murders	160	20	140	1:7
Receiving stolen goods	83,237	9,821	73,416	1:7
Manslaughter by car accident	3,781	556	3,225	1:6
Counterfeiting of industrial brands and products	20,197	3,105	17,092	1:6
Criminal damage	75,536	11,120	64,416	1:6
Mass murder	54	8	46	1:6
Infanticides	6	6	0	6:0
Total	**2,606,323**	**464,568**	**2,141,755**	**1.5**

Source: Istat database (http://dati.istat.it/Index.aspx?DataSetCode=dccv_delittips)

Given that there are 50 types of crime recorded in Italy, due to space needs, the table shows only those with a gender ratio higher than the average gender ratio (1:5), which is slightly more pronounced than in the other two countries (US 1:3 and England and Wales 1:4). Despite the diversity of legal systems, the snapshot is superimposed on that of the United States and the England and Wales: the first positions in the 'ranking' are occupied by sexual violence (1:78), theft (1:50), robbery (1:41), murder (1:29).

The data from the three countries confirm the results of previous studies: sexual violence and serious interpersonal violence are the most gender-differentiated areas, and in these areas gender is undoubtedly 'the' variable (for US, see Britton 2011: 27 and Mallicoat 2019: 8; for UK, see Davies 2011: 27; for Italy, see Giomi & Magaraggia 2017: 12). The only exception is infanticide, a crime in which women largely exceed men in the role of perpetrator. However, some caution needs to be taken in terms of the reliability of the data reported. As stressed in Chapter 1, many of the victimization experiences of women, such as intimate partner abuse and sexual assault, are significantly underreported and therefore do not appear in these statistics. This means that the gender gap in this type of crime could be even more pronounced in favour of men. The second clarification concerns statistics *per se*. Critical criminology warns about the socially constructed nature of deviance and the mechanisms of its production and is wary of looking at crime as an ontological category (Dal Lago 1981; Pitch 1987). Among the mechanisms of deviance production we can also certainly include structural gender biases and beliefs about gender and gender differences, which greatly condition the attribution of responsibility and therefore the processes of criminalization and social control (Gartner & McCharty 2014: 3; see also Marway & Widdows 2015: 4). For example, until the first half of the twentieth century, in many Western countries the crimes which women committed were not related to the economic-political sphere but to the violation of the patriarchal society's rules, linked to the field of sexuality, affectivity, care, that is, prostitution, adultery, abortion and infanticide. Depending on the time and society, in short, there are great differences in the criminalization and discipline of both acts in which women outnumber men as perpetrators and those in which they are predominantly the victims (marital rape, which is also legal and culturally condoned in much of the world, represents the most striking example, Torres & Ylló 2021).

The Chivalry hypothesis constitutes another example of the role gender norms play in the process of criminalization. Elaborated in the 1950s by Otto Pollak, it remains the subject of renewed discourse. According to this thesis, the number of women among the offenders recorded in the statistics would be very under-represented: the judicial system's male and sexist matrix would, at all levels, result in milder attitudes, of clement superiority (chivalric, precisely) towards women, who would receive more lenient sentences, even when convicted of violent crime (Fridel 2019) or even avoid incarceration (Butcher et al. 2017). However, it has been shown that this gender leniency only applies to defendants who conform to traditional femininity, which, as we noted in Chapter 1, is a fundamental requirement in order to be recognized as victims, even in court. For example, the 'chivalry' does not act when violence affects a couple of homosexual women (Romain & Freiburger 2016): the criminal justice system, as an 'official agent of social control', responds not only to crime but also to transgressions of gender norms (Barak et al. 2010, 18). This is precisely the premise of the Evil Woman hypothesis, which is opposite to the Chivalry hypothesis, and suggests that women are treated more harshly than their male counterparts, even when charged with the same offence, for the very fact of being women (Nagel & Hagan 1983). Finally, chivalry is also strictly conditioned by the intersections of gender with race and ethnicity: some studies indicate that women of colour are treated more harshly than white people, and other researchers have found that indigenous women are treated in a more lenient fashion (Mallicoat 2019: 162).

Research into crime and violence against women has been undertaken for a century and a half. In this time some theses tend to recur cyclically. In the next paragraph, we will show how biological determinism is one of these, and it is difficult to liberate the field from it, both in the scientific and legal discursive order. In the following paragraph, we will pay particular attention to more recent contributions, of a sociological and/or feminist nature, which have dealt with female violence through a gender lens, or by investigating the salience of this variable.

Etiologies based on biological determinism and sexuality: How (and why) to exorcise female violence

The *Oxford Handbook of Sex, Gender and Crime* (Gartner & Jung 2014: 9) brings together a set of contributions under a label of 'psycho and sociobiological perspectives', which, despite the diversity of approaches, highlight factors such as the greater heritability of aggressive traits in males than in females, the role of hormones in the greater expression of violent behaviour in males than in females. Though still not sufficiently supported by empirical data, this approach reveals the existence of the belief that violence, crime and anti-social behaviour have biological origins and that they are typically male characteristics. This belief originated in the 1800s. Gilbert (2002: 1285) traces the historical roots of social stereotypes about violent women, highlighting the commitment of scientists of that time – sociologists, biologists, doctors, endocrinologists, including Darwin and his followers – in demonstrating the correlation between the assumption of masculine traits and the gradual tendency to bisexuality, sexual excess, perversion of maternal instinct and finally crime. The most significant contribution in this direction comes from the father of positivist criminology and criminal anthropology, Cesare Lombroso. In 1893, together with Guglielmo Ferrero, in *La donna delinquente, la prostituta e la donna normale* (Criminal Woman, the Prostitute and the Normal Woman) they argued that the criminal was closer to the normal man than to a 'normal' woman, sharing with the male numerous psycho-physical traits: more pronounced intellectual activity and sexual ardour. Those who most manifested an exaggerated and continuous libido, according to Lombroso and Ferrero, were both 'born-criminals' and 'born-prostitutes', and their lasciviousness mixed with ferocity and made them more similar to men (Lombroso & Ferrero [1893] 2009: 408). With Lombroso and Ferrero, the two-pronged process of 'masculinization' and sexualization of female crime began. It was destined to influence the perception of female crime over the centuries. In criminology, the relationship between the lack of development of an 'appropriate' femininity and a propensity for anti-social behaviour was explored by Glueck and Glueck (1934) and Cowie et al. (1968). In more recent times, the assumption of male psychological traits has been used as a key to reading female IPV (see Dietz & Jasinski 2003). In law, and often (as we will see) in media coverage too, the masculine woman's stereotype is frequently mobilized when the offender is lesbian. Like the Lombrosian prostitute, her sexuality is believed to be 'deviant' and active and thus male. 'Perverse sexuality', the 'dominant' temperament, a physical appearance far removed from the female aesthetic canons, greatly helped guide the verdicts against the protagonists of cases that had a significant impact in the 1970s, 1980s and 1990s, namely the English Rose West and the American Wanda Jean Allen and Aileen Wuornos (the last two being sentenced to death). West raped and sexually abused children and adolescents together with her husband Fred; Allen killed her (female) partner and the prostitute Wuornos, known as the 'first female serial killer', killed seven clients over the years (see Hart 1994; Ballinger 2000; Morrissey 2003; Seal 2010).

The belief that crime is a male attribute means that 'female criminals are perceived as being either "not women" or "not criminals"'. This famous formulation by Worrall (1990: 31, in Davies 2011, 95–6) indicates two great threads in reading women's crime which have unravelled through the centuries: with 'not-women' the gender affiliation of crime and violence perpetrators is denied (they are not, in short, real women); with 'not criminals' it is denied that the crime committed by women is 'real crime'. We will start with the first.

Alongside masculinity as an argument for criminal women not being 'real women', is the concept of wickedness. The archetype of the witch has very distant roots but, in the 1990s, the first theory of the 'gangsta girls' emerged which labelled them as 'wild and ruthless' (Kruttschnitt et al. 2008: 10) and guilty of contravening the innate female tendencies of discipline and goodness. Evil is an explanation still adopted in popular publications (e.g. Alt and Wells 2000) and in Italy it even appears in university manuals: violent women may be rarer exceptions, but more astute, subtle and devious than men (Costanzo 2015: 265–7). The 'unnaturalness' of masculine women, sexually deviant women (e.g. 'exaggerated' or non-hetero-normative) and 'diabolical' women is considered an 'explanation for the unnaturalness of the weaker and gentle sex committing violent crime' (Barak et al. 2010: 123). Some of these figures are doubly unnatural. Lesbians, for example, are 'others' within a group that is already considered 'other' by the patriarchal society – that is, the group of women – and lend themselves to exorcizing the otherness of violence.

But why is this exorcism necessary? Why is female violence so disturbing and destabilizing to the symbolic order? An initial, elementary answer lies in the essentialist vision which considers biological peculiarity as an element capable of determining not only the physical identity of a woman but also the psychic one. 'To be able to give life excludes, in ambiguous parallelism, the ability to take it' (Sarra 2011: 108). From this perspective, the ability to be able to generate life automatically implies pro-social attitudes, an emotional capacity, a predisposition to care and motherhood, all qualities at odds with violence. Lloyd (1995) effectively described this concept when talking about a 'double deviance' of female violence, which transgresses the social norms and the gender norms, penal law and presumed natural law. 'Presumed' is the key word here: the deep reason why female violence has the impact it does is that it undermines socially defined certainties about gender (Jack 2001: 30), which identify the primary difference between men and women specifically in aggression and violence. But even more so, the inherent threat in female violence is 'to expose the constructed nature of gender' (Boyle 2005: 95). If anyone can be violent, irrespective of gender, the essentialist argument that gender and sex are indissolubly linked falters, as does the whole hierarchy of relationships on which this argument is based and reproduces.

It is precisely for this reason that we believe biological determinism plays a central role in many interpretations of female violence. It allows the essentialist argument, which is called into question by female violence, to be reaffirmed. In some of the cases examined so far, this argument is reaffirmed by postulating that criminal women deviate from their biology (that is, theorizing that they are 'unnatural' women). In other cases, the reaffirmation works in the opposite way, namely by pushing violent women back within the limits of their biology and drawing an explanation of violence that rests within these limits. This is what happens in the second 'thread' identified by Worrall: women's crime is not real crime. This means refusing to acknowledge that the subject acted responsibly, consciously, intentionally or autonomously due to psychic abnormalities. In the past, said abnormalities have often been attributed to (dis)functions related to sexuality, therefore confirming sexuality as being central in the underlying causes of women's crime and violence. Between the end of the nineteenth century and the beginning of the twentieth, both physiology and psychiatry explained the murder of a lover or husband, respectively, as the result of neuropathic disorders with their roots in sexual development or emotional disorders precipitated by hysteria (Marotta 2011: 116–17). Over the same period, this was also true in a judicial context, as documented by Frigon's meticulous study of the trials of 28 women in Canada who had murdered their husbands. The defence cited abortions and menopause as being responsible for causing functional disturbances that made women incapable of control, while hysteria was considered a condition of permanent 'mental instability'. The tendency to pathologize the female sexual cycle continues to the present day. Even in the 1980s, homicide trials in different countries identified premenstrual syndrome as a factor limiting mental faculties (Seal 2010: 50).

The legal systems reflect certain theories and their biological and psychic determinism: in the 1938 version of the English law on infanticide *(Infanticide Act)*, a lighter penalty was established for a mother who kills her child within the first year of life, if, at the time of the act her mental equilibrium was disturbed by the effects of childbirth or breastfeeding. As noted by Motz (2008: 132–3) – and this also applies to the previous paragraph – while it appears to take a sympathetic approach to women, it is the legacy of an ancestral fear. It is based on a primitive image of the woman, viewing her as a passive creature, moved by mysterious biological forces and at the mercy of her hormones. Infanticide is so devoid of any moral agency – it is 'not true crime' – and the motivations, even if they are rational ones, that in particular circumstances can dictate this gesture go unrecognized. Even in cases of filicide, the response of the judicial system often appears to be marked by an essentialist view. The woman who kills her children represents a contradiction in terms. It is the perfect embodiment of that short circuit between giving life, which in an essentialist vision defines a woman, and taking life that is incompatible with it. The only explanation for the short circuit produced by such a conception of women and motherhood is madness. In the court psychiatric reports on women for the trials held in Italy, the expectation of mental illness is so high 'that it is difficult for both parties, including the public prosecutor, to accept a report that excludes them' (Fariello 2012: 21–2). The same occurs in other geocultural contexts. Compared to other perpetrators, mothers who (attempt to) kill their children are most likely to be diagnosed with a mental disorder and legally excused based on insanity (Scott 2014: 382). Once again, a woman's self-determination is denied, and the complexity of the factors in play in such a gesture is overshadowed. The act is thus denied the status of a 'real crime'.

Categories such as 'madness' and 'wickedness' are symptomatic of an approach that trivializes female violence, yet the terms occur with such frequency that they constitute a 'celebrity couple': 'Bad and Mad'. Their use is not only confined to public opinion and public discourse (Gilbert 2002: 1272; Saavedra et al. 2015), but they appear in academic discourses (Farrell et al. 2011: 232–3), and also in legal rulings against different types of female offenders (Wilczynski 1997; Ballinger 2000; Scott 2005). They even appear in the portrayal of women who have been raped (Wykes & Welsh 2009: 161). 'Not real women' or 'not real crimes'; 'mad' or 'bad'; victim or executioner; virgin or whore: these are all dichotomies resulting from an essentialist view of femininity, a view that produces two-dimensional figures and reduces the complexity of acting to two options, allowing only a binary reading of a complex phenomenon such as violence.

As we shall see in the next paragraph, the use of the analytical category of 'gender' allows the complexity to be kept together and offers a much more promising prospect to interpret women's crime and its prevention. Nevertheless, we will also find some of the 'biases' that we encountered in this section, here too.

The contribution of sociology and feminist criticism: The gender lens and the deconstruction of the male as the norm

When investigating the sociocultural factors underlying deviant conduct, sociology is perhaps the one discipline that has contributed most to exporting the heuristic category of gender from the analysis of sociality to that of antisociality. The first important example is constituted by emancipationist theories on women's crime elaborated during the impulse of second-wave feminism and the liberal principles that distinguished it. Pioneered by sociologists Freda Adler (1975) and Rita J. Simon (1975), these theories identified men's economic and social oppression over women as a deterrent to female crime. With the success of emancipation policies, female crime was expected to grow and become similar to male crime, including the most severe types and, above all, violent crime. This thesis fell into disuse in the 1980s but, in the following decade and even more recently, it found new empirical support in the eyes of some, precisely due to the increased presence of women in violent crimes and crimes related to the drugs market (Davies 2011: 97), and more generally in the awareness that female conduct can be as violent as male conduct, as demonstrated by girls being involved with gangs.

In a similar vein we find the power control theory by Hagan et al. (1987), which, like the previous one, brings the difference in the social distribution of delinquency between males and females back to a disparity between the sexes and, more precisely, to the different models of socialization. In turn, these models vary according to the family's social class and the children's gender. The markedly patriarchal structure of disadvantaged families translates into less freedom for and greater control over girls and women, who are thus kept away from crime. Both Hagan and Adler read the lower incidence of women behaving delinquently as a result of women being in a socially inferior position while attributing it to different causes. Therefore, their predictions are similar: the progressive crisis of the patriarchal family model and the emancipation of women in many areas of economic and working life should produce a more equal distribution of crime between genders. However, despite this simplicity, it should be emphasized that the social control theory has the merit of insisting on the critical role socialization plays and its centrality to a sociological reading of gender deviance and aggression in particular. Gender socialization leads girls to internalize models and norms that prescribe censoring aggression in order to avoid social sanctions and to behave in ways that safeguard the introjected image of themselves as weaker and more vulnerable people (Pitch 2002: 179–81). Of course, this hypothesis is also not without contradictions. In the context of feminist criminology, various exponents have asked why some women do not conform to the cultural stereotypes of 'femininity' despite being socialized to them (see Jewkes 2015).

Finally, an additional common feature of Adler, Simon and Hagan's theses, which is of particular interest here, is the use – albeit in a more advanced form – of the assumption encountered in the previous paragraph: crime is a characteristic of men, and female delinquency necessarily implies the homologation of girls and women towards the male model (as a confirmation, in addition to being referred to as the Emancipation Theory, Adler's thesis is also known as Masculinization Theory). In other words, these theses look at women's crime by erasing gender differences and using the same conceptual categories used for male crime, which is why the theses are ineffective in deconstructing and critiquing male as a norm.

Critiquing this norm was the main contributor of the tradition of legal feminism that was taking shape in Italy at the same time, between the 1970s and 1980s, when the debate promoted by second-wave feminism first cut across practice and then legal reflection. This tradition brings together the originality of the Italian feminist idea (the 'idea of sexual difference'), generating a radical and incisive criticism of the patriarchal order and criminal law, which until the 1970s was directly derived from that order.[6] A key concept in this sense is that of 'deviance': 'during the development of feminist movements, female conduct that had been traditionally stigmatized, started to be valued as practices of freedom' (Verdolini 2019: 72). One of the leading exponents of Italian legal feminism from a differentialism perspective is the anthropologist and sociologist of law Tamar Pitch (1975). Pitch argues that the development of the concept of deviance, being intrinsically linked to power, social control, forms of standardization and labelling, presents a parallel with the history of social control over women, which is very deep-rooted and has always accompanied criminology and sociology of criminal law. For this reason, deviance lends itself well to being re-signified and appropriated by feminists in a positive, transgressive way, as a gesture that ruptures the entire system of moral norms and legal codification that are at the base of social control over women. This re-signifying and appropriation is well illustrated by the symbolic overthrow of the witch archetype, which become an icon for the 1970s feminist mobilization ('tremble, tremble, the witches are back' was a slogan they used).

In Pitch's view, both the criminalization processes which led to the codification of illegal conduct and the processes by which women, minors and the mentally infirm were disciplined are based on the construction of exceptions, of 'deviations' from a norm. This norm is precisely embodied in a white, bourgeois, heterosexual adult male (today we would add 'able-bodied' and 'cisgender'). Therefore, identifying with the label of deviance permits a break from this norm, permitting women's subjectification and liberation. The result of this reflection became visible, for example, with the activists' commitment to decriminalize abortion and, arguably, most importantly, in the approach to the 'female criminal question'. This term was also new to the discourse.[7] In the 1970s in the United States, as we have seen before, there were arguments that women's emancipation would reduce the gap between male and female crime rates and incarceration. These hypotheses have never been proven (women continue to be significantly under-represented in both criminal statistics and the prison population), but the line of inquiry into the reasons for low female crime rates, as noted in the first paragraph, has continued to this day. Posing the question in these terms can indirectly help reproduce maleness normativity and conceive female difference as something negative, as a 'gap' to be filled with respect to the male standard. Using the 'criminal question' approach, Pitch twisted the paradigm, putting the opposite question at the centre: Why are male crime and incarceration rates so high? This theoretical and political gesture reveals all the power, held by the feminism of difference, to deconstruct the patriarchal order.

The commitment to deconstruct male normativity and a strong constructivist trait are also found in the last approach that we present here, and which is the basis of this volume. Again, it comes from sociology and is structured around a theoretical construct that has also proved very useful in criminology, that of 'doing gender' (West & Zimmerman 1987: 135). It led to a body of studies in which crime was considered a gendered social practice, 'which draws on and reproduces existing assumptions about masculinity and femininity' (Britton 2011: 21). Despite the belief that crime was 'a male thing' which has characterized criminology since its inception, it was only from the 1990s, largely thanks to Messerschmidt's contribution (1993), that the links between masculinity and violence came to the fore.

The basic idea is that women and men 'do gender' even when they are involved in criminal conduct. On the female side, this approach has been used mainly to study female juvenile delinquency (MedaChesney-Lind's work has been ground-breaking here). Crime is not only a 'masculine-validating resource' (Messerschmidt 1993: 83): equally for girls participating in gang violence and using drugs can be a means of constructing an alternative, 'bad girl' femininity. Nevertheless, Miller (2014: 24) warns that interpreting the gender performance produced through the practice of crime and violence in terms of femininity 'variants' compared to the dominant view is likely to validate the idea of criminal women as doubly deviant (from social norms and gender norms). So, once again, a more complex approach is desirable: one that explores the gendered nature of crime, going beyond simple reflection on the regulatory dimension of gender identity, but which considers other axes of power/inequality – race, class, sexual orientation, etc. – that intersect with it. Attention to sex and gender and the peculiar forms of women's involvement in crime have also been incorporated into studies of organized crime, corporate/white-collar crime (Davies 2011), political violence (Sjoberg & Gentry 2007; Åhäll & Shepherd 2012; Gentry & Sjoberg 2015; Åhäll 2015) and state violence (Collins 2017).

As far as interpersonal violent crime is concerned, in addition to infanticide and filicide, IPV is the most studied in terms of gender. However, at least for non-lethal IPV, the forms, motives and even the extent of female involvement are subjects of dispute.

Women's IPV

Non-lethal female-perpetrated IPV

In the previous chapter, we cited the debate between proponents of the VAW/G approach. We argued that domestic violence is asymmetrically gendered, and criticized the Family Violence approach (Dobash & Dobash 2004), according to which men and women are equally likely to both use violence and be victims of it in their intimate relationships. Johnson's studies (1995, 2006), Johnson and Ferrero (2000) and Johnson and Leone (2005) tried to make sense of the IPV research's conflicting findings and identified four subtypes of IPV. They suggested that different samples will have a different proportion of each subtype IPV.[8] 'Intimate terrorism' is the type of violence most commonly committed by men, and includes various forms of psychological violence, economic subordination and threats towards a non-violent or non-controlling partner. 'Situational couple violence' typically originates from conflicts occasionally getting 'out of hand'. It leads to 'minor' forms of violence and rarely escalates into serious or life-threatening forms of violence. This is the most common form of intimate partner violence in the Western world and involves men and women at relatively equal rates. Offensive conduct in which women outnumber their male partners is defined as 'violent resistance' and occurs when a victim of intimate terrorism responds to their partner's controlling tactics with violence (Johnson 2006: 10060) to protect themselves or others. It can become fatal if the victim feels as though their only way out is to kill their partner. There are now numerous studies showing that women carry out more violent resistance than men. This is the type of violence most commonly practised by women in the context of intimate relationships (for a recent illustration cf. Boxall et al. 2020; Mackay et al. 2018).

Conversely, comparative research developed under the gender symmetry approach questions self-defence as a motivating factor underlying more female than male-perpetrated IPV, thus confuting theoretical perspectives of female IPV specialization (Wolbers and Ackerman 2020). Anger and coercive control (Langhinrichsen-Rohling et al. 2012), communication difficulties and self-defence (Elmquist et al. 2014), retaliation/getting back at a partner for physical or verbal abuse are underlined as the most frequently endorsed motive categories for both men and women (Leisring & Grigorian 2016: 949)). Despite an emerging realization within the IPV literature that findings based upon one sub-population cannot be readily generalized to others because of the many differences among types of couples, empirical studies aligning with gender symmetry keep focusing primarily on samples of younger and unmarried couples, which differ from the general population in important aspects. When populations other than students are sampled – such as persons arrested for IPV – the gender symmetry of IPV is put down to intergenerational transmission of intimate partner violence into adulthood for both men and women (e.g. Straus 2015) or abusive partners presenting with borderline traits (Bernardi & Stein 2019).

At the basis of this reading, which pathologizes and degenderizes IPV, there is a very elementary notion of 'gender', which coincides with biological sex, rather than with a social and cultural construction. But, in our opinion, even the examples of research that correctly highlight this notion in the interpretation of IPV show an interesting asymmetry. As we saw in Chapter 1, the influence of gender norms is now widely considered in analysing male-perpetrated IPV against known women.

On the victimization side, a gendered approach has long been used to analyse the perception and consequences of IPV on women (e.g. Dobash et al. 1998; Tarzia 2021) and, more recently, also on men (Bates & Weare 2020; Dim 2020). In the latter case, it has been shown that forms of hegemonic masculinities restrict how male victims of domestic violence and abuse can understand, experience and respond to it (Williamson et al. 2018). Interestingly, femininity and the social and cultural construction of it are only referred to when exploring the experience of girls and women as the object, not the subject of IPV.

Lethal female-perpetrated IPV

Unlike non-lethal forms of IPV, for lethal forms, at least quantitatively speaking, there is no room for disputes over findings which appear incontrovertible. As we saw in the first chapter, the risk of victimization with fatal outcomes in the context of intimate relationships is infinitely greater for women than for men. In the United States, former or current intimate partners are responsible for more than 50 per cent of women's murders and only 5–8 per cent of the murders of men (Fridel & Fox 2019). In Europe, the gender ratio calculated on the total number of IPH victims in 2017, 2018 and 2019 is one man for every four women. However, there are significant variations, ranging from Switzerland (1:41), followed by Italy (1:10); the Netherlands (1:8); Spain (1:7); Croatia, England and Wales and Sweden (1:6); Germany (1:5). All other countries have ratios of 1:4 or less. The narrowest ratio is in Iceland (0:1).[9]

Intimate relationships represent not only the context in which women run a greater risk of incurring fatal incidents but also the context in which the majority of female-perpetrated homicides take place. Compared to killings by males, a larger proportion of murders by females involve intimate partners (Gartner & Jug 2014: 431). In any case, according to Stöckl et al. (2013), globally, men outnumber women as perpetrators of IPH by a 6:1 ratio. Unfortunately, not many empirical studies return qualitative data. From those available, however, significant differences emerge between femicide and female-perpetrated IPH: compared to men, women are more likely to be unemployed, to have suffered from a substance abuse disorder, to belong to the most marginalized segments of generally disadvantaged groups (Caman et al. 2016; Vatnar 2018) and to have endured previous IPV at the hands of their victim (Enander 2011), which is consistent with motives linked to self-defence being more common in female rather than in male perpetrators (e.g. Caman et al. 2016; Liem & Roberts 2009). Its incidence and prevalence, though, vary according to the woman's identity: for instance, the intersection of race/ethnicity, class and gender that defines the specific condition of Latinas in the United States accounts for their being less likely than Black and White women to commit self-help IPH (Harper 2017). Vatnar and colleagues (2018) confirmed that fear was a motive more common in female than in male IPH perpetrators: additional data in support of the ongoing and systemic nature of IPV suffered by women and terror as a tool to control them (Enander 2011: 111–12). On the contrary, it is now clear that motives (jealousy, separation/divorce) and types of crime common among men belong much less to women (Wilson & Daily 1992), and some types of lethal crime are practically uniquely male: 'mercy' killings, family massacres are very telling of the gendered dimension of lethal violence, being often the acts of men who perceive themselves as the arbiters of the life and death of their relatives (Giomi 2013).

Among the causal models developed within different theoretical perspectives to explain female-perpetrated IPH, a reaction to an abusive partner prevails. In the detailed review by Graham et al. (2020), self-help/self-defence theory is presented as the only feminist theory that explicitly focuses on describing why women might perpetrate IPH against men. Although its strength is taking into account the role of gender in reading IPH, this theory fails to do so when addressing IPH among people who do not identify with the male-female gender binary. Among the theories that fall into the sociological/criminological group, only one addresses female-perpetrated IPH, that is, the already mentioned social control theory. Like feminist self-help/self-defence theory, social control theory looks at female-perpetrated IPH as an extreme means for women to survive/exert control over their lives in a context of restricted access to legal means, lack of social bonds, and fear. The general strain theory of IPH also belongs to the sociological/ criminological group. It is also based on social control theory and applies to both genders. It asserts that different constellations of strains, negative emotions and conditioning factors help explain male- versus female-perpetrated IPH. Among the examples of the sources of strain that lead to negative emotions and therefore, potentially, to IPH perpetration by men, relationship separation is quoted. In contrast, for women, the example provided is witnessing her children's abuse by an IPV perpetrator (Graham 2020: 11).

Although self-defence prevails over other motives in female-perpetrated IPH, other motives exist: preservation of respect, jealousy, self-help and retaliation has all been found to motivate violence by both sexes. It is worth noticing that 'lethal violence by females, as well as males, typically is the intentional behaviour of a self-conscious agent, albeit one whose choices and circumstances are constrained by power disparities and gender inequality' (Gartner & Jung 2014: 432). However, the theories presented betray the difficulty of thinking of women as executioners and reading their conduct as an expression of self-determination: admitting the possibility of female violence only in the guise of self-defence or the traumatic response to experiences of victimization, in fact, means endorsing the idea that female crime is not 'real crime'; it means legitimizing that binary logic according to which criminal women are either guilty executioners or innocent victims (who kill their partner to protect themselves and their children) (Ferraro 2015: 180–210). As we shall see in the next chapter, media discourse often proceeds along similar dichotomies.

Male and female violence in the media

Elisa Giomi

This chapter presents a taxonomy of discursive macro-configurations that occur more frequently in the media's representation of male and female violence according to the theoretical and empirical literature. Such discursive configurations transverse media genres, forms, geocultural contexts and, in some cases, even epochs. They are powered by elements related to both the narrative and visual dimension, which have different 'extension', ranging from the single lexicon to entire discursive repertoires, news values, frames and narrative patterns, along with single framing and entire visual styles. We are interested in highlighting how many of the rhetorical and aesthetic devices that are most widespread in globally circulating media products have cemented a 'regressive' type of representative tradition for both types of violence. However, occasionally, we also emphasize the forms that break with tradition and introduce alternative and progressive perspectives.

The macro-configurations that we will present are often strongly intertwined because many have their roots embedded in the vast themes of guilt and responsibility, which are central to both types of violence. Thus, the two sections – the one on male violence and the one on female violence – follow a similar pattern. For each configuration, we illustrate their basic operation and provide examples from different media forms, prioritizing journalism. It aims to represent factual reality and therefore offers a terrain that is well suited to assessing the consistency of media depictions of male and female violence against their actual features emerging from the data provided in the two previous chapters. With regard to the forms of violence considered, for male violence, IPV is our main focus. For women, where IPV has fewer incidents, and subsequently the media coverage is less extensive, it is necessary to broaden our scope to include other types of violence as well.

Male violence in the media

De-responsibilizing the perpetrator

In this section we review the narrative forms of intimate violence perpetrated by a man on his female companion that are used to mitigate his responsibility or even suggest that his actions were legitimate.

Framing violence

The first narrative form relates to the overall key that is chosen to recount violence (whether it is a chronicle of facts or a fictional story). In this regard, news-making theories distinguish between 'episodic' and 'thematic' frames (Iyengar 1994): the first takes the form of a case study or report focused on the event (an event-oriented report), it dwells on the description of individual events and their dynamics, it amplifies the incidence of subjective factors and specific circumstances. Therefore, similar events are made to appear as isolated, non-connected episodes. The thematic frame highlights their interconnections and facilitates the reading of events as an expression of a wider phenomenon, providing context information and describing the general aspects through data, statistics and in-depth analysis.

The episodic frame risks directing the reader towards an individualized interpretation which ascribes the problem to the specific person: the protagonist of the case or to the group to which they belong. On the contrary, thematic frames make it possible to focus on the social and cultural factors that determine the problem and thus identify wider responsibilities, for example, institutional and political ones, and responses in terms of prevention rather than cure. Studies on the coverage of IPV in the American press (Carlyle et al. 2008; Sims 2008; Taylor 2009; Sutherland et al. 2015: 12–13), Canadian press (Lee & Wong 2020) and other contexts (Rollè et al. 2020) show that the episodic frame is much more widespread than the thematic one, with the result that it overshadows the specificity of IPH as a crime largely preceded by abuse and instead treats it as just like 'any other' homicide (Lee & Wong 2020: 219). On television, the episodic frame mainly prevails in short formats, which favour headlines over deeper analysis, such as breaking news (Wozniak & McCloskey 2010) and news (RAI, 2020), even though in countries like Spain, the news has definitively moved from the framing of violence against women as a private issue to a public problem (Comas-d'Argemir 2015: 129).

Excusing the perpetrator (and blaming the victim)

Highlighting the perpetrator's characteristics and his situation at the time of femicide can feed the episodic frame, shifting attention to subjective factors and peculiar circumstances. Some examples: personal loss of control or a moral breakdown by the perpetrator (Gillespie et al. 2013; Richards et al. 2014) such as 'a moment of passion', 'a moment of madness', being taken over by anger, despair, or the effect of drugs or alcohol; mental problems, physical problems or, financial problems (Meyers 1994; Taylor 2009; Richards et al. 2011; Carlyle et al. 2008; Wong & Lee 2020). The de-responsabilizing effect is noted in the news reports of IPV cases involving not only ordinary people, but also celebrities and royals (Lloyd 2020: 80). Finally, a form of excusing the perpetrator common in both news and entertainment genres is the 'frame of romantic love' which brings violence back to the perpetrator's 'torments of love'. We will return to this extensively in the next sections. Here we simply note that the emotional dimension is also stressed in the coverage of the so-called 'mercy killings'. These involve very elderly and sick women who are no longer independent, and are usually followed by the suicide of the perpetrator, who is culturally unprepared to look after his partner, due to – as a gender (and power) reading would suggest – the inadequate socialization of males to care work.

In addition to factors specific to the accused, one of the reasons suggested as to what influenced the accused's behaviour was the conduct of the victim. They are often portrayed as being the one who 'triggered' the outburst or caused the perpetrator's loss of control. Victim-blaming, as it is called, transfers the responsibility from perpetrator to the victim (see Chapter 1). It is a phenomenon long detected in media accounts of gender-based violence and it can be either direct or indirect (Meyers 1997; Taylor 2009; Gillespie et al. 2013). Victim-blaming also affects genres and forms of entertainment: television series and films, music, advertising and celebrity culture (Boyle 2005; Finley 2016; Shepherd 2019; Ramon et al. 2021), and even comic books (e.g. Garland et al. 2016). In the cases of sexual assault, the false belief, often fed by popular culture narratives, is that victims could avoid rape by changing their conduct (i.e. job choice, dressing provocatively, being out alone, being intoxicated). An indirect and very common form of victim-blaming is what Berns, in her study of US magazines and talk shows, defines as 'the victim empowerment perspective'. While adopting a sympathetic attitude towards the victim, this perspective places responsibility on the woman to end the abuse and therefore it fits into a frame of 'individual responsibility' (2004: 78). Many Hollywood domestic violence films also express this perspective, calling on the protagonist to renounce her 'victim' status and stand up to her abuser on her own, absolving society at large of responsibility (Shoos 2021: 111).

Blaming or excusing the couple (but not the victim)

According to Berns (2004: 67), even the narratives that focus on the couple fall into a frame of 'individual responsibility', because they can suggest that femicide depends on peculiarities in the dynamics of the couple involved. An initial example is provided by accounts that focus on conflict, which can offer excuses similar to the loss of control by the perpetrator: consider expressions such as 'femicide occurred at the height of/during a quarrel' (Gius & Lalli 2014; Giomi 2015b) or references to arguments that preceded the violence

(Sutherland et al. 2015). In both cases, the effect is to distribute the blame between victim and perpetrator (it takes two to tango!). At other times, conflict is presented as an actual feature of the relationship ('they always quarrelled'), conveying a sense of mutual combat and downgrading the violence from a crime to a relationship problem (Easteal et al. 2015: 111).

A characteristic of the couple who are opposed to conflict and who are often emphasized in reports of femicide is what we propose to call the 'quiet couple' theme. References made to this include phrases such as 'they never quarrelled'. It is a counterfactual representation, because we know that men's violence against the partner tends to have a systematic and continuous characteristic, and that the fatal incidents are preceded by a whole history of the victim being mistreated (see Chapter 1). Just as with the use of the episodic frame, the 'quiet couple' theme produces a mystification of femicide as an 'isolated event' which occurs out of the blue and is difficult to predict and so to prevent (Gillespie et al. 2013: 227).

Minimizing and normalizing violence

In this section we include discursive constructions that diminish the gravity of the event and contribute to determining the social acceptability of male violence against women, presenting it as an ordinary (even 'routine') and inevitable part of couples' relationships, masculinity and the entire social reality.

Male IPV normalization: Conflict and romance

The first and most basic form through which IPV and even femicide normalization can occur is the selection of news. According to Surette's 'Law of Opposite' (1998: 47), the types of crimes, the perpetrators and the victims that are considered most newsworthy are those that the viewers are at least at risk of experiencing. For example, in 2006, Italy's prime-time news (Giomi & Tonello 2013) and press (Giomi

2015a) consistently presented a disproportionate number of items about women killed by an unknown person, compared to IPV. In the media, this disproportion is by a factor of ten. The coverage of femicides committed within stable/cohabiting/married couples is lower than that of femicides committed within extramarital relationships, despite these being less common (Lalli 2020: 41). In short, the 'normal' – statistically speaking – male-perpetrated domestic violence does not make news. At the same time, poor news coverage contributes to its routinization and to a reproduction of its ordinary, 'normal' character. The same applies to other types of violence: literature from the sector has long highlighted that a disproportionate emphasis is placed on certain types of incidents, such as murder or rape, at the expense of other and far more common offences, such as battery, sexual assault and sexual harassment (Carter 1998: 228), while emotional abuse is practically relegated to invisibility (Sims 2008). This trend endures over time, as shown by the over-representation of femicide at the expense of other forms of abuses in 2020 in Italian public service television (RAI, 2020).

From a qualitative point of view, one of the most common forms of standardizing IPV is, once again, the pattern of conflict. Information such as the 'victim and perpetrator always quarrelled' risks minimizing the violence because it makes it appear like just another clash between the two, only with worse consequences. This helps to reproduce the widespread myth that much of what is referred to as intimate partner violence is a normal reaction to relationship conflict (Peters 2008; Worden & Carlson 2005). Thaller and Messing (2014: 633) identified this myth in the lyrics and video '*Love the Way you Lie*', by Eminem and Rihanna.[10] Although the song lyrics culminated with the threat of one-sided fatal violence (he threatens to set her on fire), the couple's conflict is initially presented as mutual, and violence is presented as the natural outcome of a relationship characterized by highs and lows. These emotional extremes are in turn presented as 'normal' ('maybe our relationship/Isn't as crazy as it seems').

Factual entertainment is a particularly significant case because it occupies a large part of television's representation of male violence against women and because it brings 'real' people and relationships on stage, and therefore has more pronounced role-modelling power. US programs such as *Jersey Shore* (MTV 2009–2012), *Real World* (MTV/ Facebook Watch 1992–present) and *Teen Mom* (MTV 2009–present) transform troubled romantic relationships and scenes of physical violence into a source of entertainment, and even humour (McDonnell 2019: 195), so that the public struggles to recognize the violence for what it is (Liebler et al. 2016: 19).

Romanticization appears both in this paragraph and in the next because it is a significant component of the media depiction of male-perpetrated IPV. Here we will show how its severity is decreased and its acceptance favoured by deploying a romantic frame. As for news media, an example consists of depicting femicide as a 'couple' problem, where love in a relationship has broken down creating the dynamics for male sexual jealousy, depression and anger (Monckton-Smith 2012: 63). Research analysing the Italian press from 2012 to 2017 (Gius & Lalli 2014; Giomi 2015b; Lalli 2020) showed how the romantic frame is practised systematically and finds its leitmotif in jealousy. It minimizes the aggressor's responsibility, firstly because, as a passion, it is believed to act as an irrational and irresistible force, but above all because it appears to be a natural component of a romantic relationship, functional to its protection. The iconic code plays a fundamental role in the production of the romantic frame: our research, which has not yet been published, compared the images used in English and Italian online newspapers and their accompanying articles on similar cases of gender-based violence that happened in the two countries in 2018. It found that photographs depicting victim and perpetrator together, smiling affectionately, were frequently used and showed complicit attitudes. The combination of these photos often with sensationalistic titles ('slaughtered', 'torn to pieces', etc.) risks conveying the ambiguous message that violence, even extreme, is compatible with love, as if love and violence are inseparable: two sides of the same coin (see Chapter 1).

Moving on to entertainment, the same message is at the centre of many vampire stories. Vampire stories are a worldwide cult phenomenon and perhaps the most striking case of IPV normalization through the romantic lens that popular media culture has ever produced. The TV series *The Vampire Diaries* (The CW 2009–2017), *True Blood* (HBO 2008–2014) and particularly the *Twilight* film saga (Hardwicke 2008; Weitz 2009; Slade 2010; Condon 2011 and 2012) bring girls involved in sentimental relationships with vampires to the screen (in the case of *Twilight*, with werewolves too). These are creatures that instinctively harm humans, so the link between violence and love is presented as an inevitable component of a romantic relationship ('You have to learn to love what hurts you', Bella's father says). Heroines, in fact, strive to keep the relationship in place at all costs (Franiuk & Scherr 2013: 20) and even go so far as to blame themselves for the violent conduct of their loved ones: 'I wouldn't let you lose control', Bella tells Jakob. 'I would remind you how extraordinary you are'. Here is another victim-blaming myth: men who use violence do so because their companions don't encourage their self-esteem.

Stalking and behaviours aimed at monitoring/controlling a female partner are among the behaviours that pop culture tends to recode the most as romance. For example, in *There's Something about Mary* (Farrelly 1998), the protagonist hires a private investigator for over ten years to spy on the object of his affections, Mary, who had rejected him. It is stalking but the audience does not perceive it as such because it is presented as courtship and a sign of the protagonist's unwavering affection (Lippman 2015: 9). In the same vein, in the previously mentioned vampire stories, alarm-generating behaviours such as spying or eavesdropping on conversations are viewed by the protagonists as an expression of emotional attachment (Taylor 2014: 391). A recent and noteworthy case is the television series *You*, referred to in the introduction. The central male character Joe preys upon innocent girls and women. But Joe is at the same time represented as a caring and devoted partner, so that the compatibility of violence and love is reiterated. A key role in the normalization of gender violence in this series is executed by the humorous register and the decision to narrate events from Joe's perspective. According to Raijva and Patrick

(2021), Joe's ironic season-long voiceover constitutes a sort of 'gender ventriloquism' that invites viewers into the emotional landscape of a stalker and serial killer of young women, erases victims' voices, and reasserts masculine narrative authority. However, shifting between points of view is not an antidote to the normalization of gender-based violence either. On the contrary, in the television series *Stalker* (CBS 2014–2015), there is a risk of transforming male violence against women from an objective social problem to a relative concept: when detective Beth Davis's point of view dominates, we sympathize with her storyline, which is marked by stalking and abuse, but when the perspective is that of detective Jack Larsen, who persecutes his wife, who left him taking with her his little son, we are led to think that understandable motives for harassing a woman do exist.

Normalization of violence as a male characteristic: Naturalization

Violence is often normalized as a typically male behaviour. A striking example is naturalization, that is, presenting violence as an expression of a principle of nature, but which only affects men. In *Natural Born Killers* (Stone 1994) Mickey and Mallory Knox have a history of family violence, yet this biography works completely differently: it explains Mallory's transformation from a good family girl to a ruthless assassin (an effect of her father's sexual abuse), marking her actions as unnatural and pathological. Conversely, Mickey is positioned in continuity with the men in his family, as if violence were an expression of a genetic factor: 'It's in my blood'. My dad had it, his dad had it. It's my fate'. Mickey, and only Mickey, is a natural born killer (Boyle 2005: 152).[11] The idea of the patrilineal transmission of violence endures over the decades: in *Killer Instinct* (Fox 2005), for example, one wonders if the leading detective, Jack Hale, will end up following the footsteps of his father, a confessed serial killer. In the award-winning *Zodiac* (Fincher 2007) murder is represented, more generally, as an irrepressible compulsion, that 'people have in their blood'. They say 'people' but again the serial killer is male. More recently, the television series *Breaking Bad* (AMC 2008–2013) is another interesting example of double standards. While the male central character undergoes a complete biosocial transformation into a violent offender, the show's female characters are unable to do so (Wakeman 2017).

Looking specifically at male violence against women, its 'normality' is indirectly reproduced in various forms, e.g. reinforcing the assumption that men have violent tendencies and are always ready to explode (Wong & Lee 2020: 226) or omitting from news reporting the motives of aggression, as if women were so 'natural' for men that it does not deserve explanation (Carlyle et al. 2014: 10). The frame of naturalization can be found in the series *Angel* (The WB 1999–2004), in which violence is presented as the result of primordial misogyny lodged in men's blood (Shepherd 2013: 732), and in the vampire stories. If the protagonists fall in love with their vampires, it is precisely because, unlike the others, they fight against the desire for blood, and repress their instinct to kill. But presenting them as heroic because of this means that, once again, the idea 'that males are all "naturally" violent is reiterated and such impulses are "endemic" to masculinity' (Durham 2012: 293). Masculinity, therefore, is built as a binary opposite – 'good' men who repudiate their innate predilection for violence and 'bad' men who succumb to it.

The normalization of female victimization: Between double standards and denied agency

In the first paragraph, we analysed the criteria of newsworthiness and narrative formulas which under-represent and 'routinize' violence against women by their partners, helping to normalize it. But the same outcome can also come from the opposite phenomenon: hyper-visibility. A considerable amount of literature has highlighted the inflation of brutalized female bodies and corpses in global popular culture's imagery (Dillman 2014; Parikka 2015; Finley 2016; Ramon et al. 2021, just to name the most recent). This imagery can corroborate the idea that female victimization is an ordinary, structural fact of social reality. Analysing the narrative level, this idea is fuelled by two phenomena in particular: the systematic association between femininity and sexual vulnerability and depriving women of agency. As to the first one, the 'double standard' of male and female vulnerability is very evident in the opening scenes of *Travelers* (Netflix 2016–2018): despite the death of four people happening simultaneously and performing the same narrative function, only the two female characters die due to the will of male subjugation (including sexual). Depicting female victimization mostly in terms of sexual vulnerability contributes to what Boyle (2019b: 105) defines as the 'universalizing narrative (…) consistently presenting rape as the worst possible thing that could happen to a woman': this is simultaneously an individualizing narrative, with personal and psychological – not social, political, cultural – solutions. Sometimes it is the female police officers themselves who become victims: a way to remind them that they belong to a vulnerable gender (De Tardo-Bora 2009).

The second form of female victimization normalization passes through the cancellation of the agency. Analysing the dead woman's appearance in the nineteenth-century visual arts, Bronfen (1992) notes that being deprived of the possibility of seeing, the dead woman is subject to absolute domination by the male spectator/subject, whose gaze falls upon the woman and meditates on femininity and death, the two great puzzles of Western discourse, from a safe distance. An interesting case of the deprivation of agency is that of murdered women who have a 'post-mortem' life because they remain at the centre of news stories due to ongoing investigations or are phantasmagorian presences in fictional works. According to Dillman (2014: 10), these 'dead-but-not-gone' women are de-subjectified subjects having pseudo-agency: they are ultimately contained and reinscribed in an androcentric order that refuses to accept responsibility for the injustices and powerlessness that women collectively endure. We also find this trope in contemporary and progressive products in the representation of gender-based violence, such as the television series *13 Reasons Why* (Netflix 2017–2020) or *Hotel Beau Séjour* (Eén/ Netflix 2017–present).

Another example of the normalization of female victimization consists of a type of image that is widespread in Italy and accompanies press articles and news broadcasts on episodes of gender-based violence and even awareness campaigns. They portray girls or women in poses of self-defence, huddled in a corner, with their hands covering their faces. A man's silhouette or a man's clenched fist looms over them. Recalling Hollander's remarks (2014) cited in the first chapter, these images reinforce the belief that women are incapable of effectively defending themselves. According to our unpublished research, this type of image is completely absent in the English press, while it characterizes 13 per cent of Italian press. When it comes to rape, the protagonists (invariably young and white) are also fetishized by poses and clothing that amplifies the idea of their sexual predability.

However, the most radical form of erasing women's agency in popular media culture is dehumanization. In advertising, the symbolic mutilation of the female body is very common and normally only the woman's head is severed, or the lower part of her face is saved at most. The eyes are what are always missing, perhaps because the face is covered, or the image is shot from behind. It is a device that is also consistent with the economy of vision that assigns power to the masculine gaze and places the female in the role of object, unable to return it. Reification is a 'literal' variant of sexual objectualization (Vance et al. 2015): pieces of female body are transformed into objects: breasts like airbags, legs and torsos like scissors or can openers, buttocks like bowling balls – every-day utensils, or objects with vicarial functions, or supports for product exhibits: a bust-frame in which a perfume is set in place of the sexual organs, a back acting as pedestal on which a bag dominates. These women's bodies are reduced to low value objects and they are entirely in tune with the discourses of neoliberalism and globalization, which wants women to be a 'disposable' resource, renewable and replaceable. Furthermore, it is a policy of representation that authorizes violence in several forms. Firstly, if women are 'less than human' it becomes possible to treat them accordingly, secondly, the female body, when so dismembered, plasticized, reified, appears to be a non-sentient body, which can therefore be disposed of at will, and subjected to manipulation and violence without any resistance or reaction at all: precisely as with all objects. Empirical studies have, in fact, shown that objectification of women mediates the relationships between media use and attitudes and behaviours that support violence against women (e.g. Seabrook et al. 2019). The phenomenon also affects rap and hip-hop music, as we will see in Chapter 5.

Spectacularizing violence: Eroticizing and anaesthetizing

Here, we will briefly treat narrative and visual forms that can have opposite effects to the ones previously discussed: not to minimize/ normalize but instead to enhance/spectacularize. In the press, the main form of spectacularization consists of sensationalism produced, in turn, by the newsworthiness criteria such as those examined in the previous pages, which favour more striking but less common forms of violence, or by a 'bombastic' style that over time has also crept into IPV coverage in high-quality newspapers, as a result of tabloidization (Smith et al. 2019).

In the previous section, we noticed how the use of the romantic frame can de-rubricate stalking, control and other violent conduct to 'ordinary' behaviours. Now let us illustrate another aspect of how these frame works: violence is presented as violence, but it is celebrated. To underline the difference, we will return to the media products already mentioned. For example, in *Love the Way You Lie* (2010, Eminem feat. Rihanna),[12] violence is not only normalized but praised as a sign of passion ('Maybe our relationship/Isn't as crazy as it seems/Maybe that's what happens when a tornado meets a volcano'). Rihanna's verses mirror Eminem's: they call violence by its name ('Just going to stand there and watch me burn') but they recodify it as a pleasant experience ('But that's alright because I like the way it hurts'), which in the video seamlessly evolves into erotic scenes. The *Twilight Saga* books and films conflate Edward's craving for Bella's blood with his sexual longing for her; the desires work in tandem so that sex is inseparable from violence (Durham 201: 291).

The visual eroticization of male violence against women affects many forms of media and violence, including lethal violence. It is surprizing how many television series, like *Travelers*, open with an erotically connoted female corpse. The phenomenon is particularly pronounced in crime series where real tropes originate: the 'white female victim', a 'gateway body' that invites audiences into the opening season (Klinger 2018: 522). From *CSI* (CBS 2000–2015) onwards even a 'necrophilic' look has been normalized: the viewer is positioned in order to take pleasure from the 'carnographic revelation' produced by shots of bodily organs (Tait 2006: 50). Once again, a 'double standard' is at work: the female corpses remain connoted in an erotic sense even after death, due to the alternation between autopsy scenes and the flashbacks of the lethal incident, with all its spicy details. A central aspect in the spectacularization of violence against women in contemporary pop culture is precisely what we propose to call *an-aesthetizing* (Giomi & Magaraggia 2017): violence is sanitized, its consequences (pain, suffering, transfiguring of the body) are removed, to be able to recode it as a pleasurable spectacle. In advertisements, female faces exhibit bruises and streaks of blood, and yet they smile and wink at us; they show no suffering even during the act of sexual brutalization. The labels of '*torture chic*' and '*bondage chic*' for the literary trilogy *Fifty Shades of Grey* (Brown 2014: 1127) testify to the spread of this phenomenon, which in more recent times has returned to the fore with the Netflix production *365 Days* (Białowąs/Mandes, 2020).

Exorcizing violence: Othering and erasing

Here we present two macro-configurations that have the common, possible effect of removing, even 'exorcizing' violence. The first is othering, which contrasts with normalizing: violence, instead of being presented as a routine of social reality, is confined to a social 'otherness'. The second strategy, erasing, is opposite to the spectacularization examined in the previous section, and consists in making violence invisible.

Othering violence

As with normalization, in othering, which is the reverse, the main factor is the choice of news. The tendency to 'select single events, that favour incidents or extreme violence or other markers that supposedly make the event unique' (Cucklanz 1995: 337) can lead to the assumption that those who enact violence, those who suffer it, or both, are 'abnormal' (Sotirovic 2003; Sutherland 2015: 15), inherently different from other people. Many forms of de-responsabilization of the perpetrator (financial difficulties, depression, mental illness, alcohol or drug addiction) can also become forms of otherization if they serve to emphasize his atypicality. Elsewhere, the perpetrator is marked as 'different' because of his belonging to a social or ethnic group which is constructed as 'other' from the point of view of dominant groups. An example of the former is the myth-based belief that IPV can only occur in dysfunctional or low-income neighbourhoods. It is replicated by the newsworthiness criteria that reward the spectacular value of degradation, but also by other media forms, such as in the video *Love the Way you Lie*: the couple is depicted as working class, with a dirty apartment, work boots, tattoos, constant boozing, bar fights and unapologetic criminal behaviour (Thaller & Messig 2014). The ethnicity of the perpetrator is emphasized predominantly in interracial assaults: research that today is now considered a classic (Benedict 1992; Moorti 2002; Stable 2006) show that offences against white females by non-white perpetrators, unlike those committed by white perpetrators, are explicitly linked to race and represented as emblematic of their entire community. The press from different European countries tends to 'other' non-white men in terms of abusive behaviour in order to mask the fact that in those countries, the majority of sexual and physical abuse is perpetrated by white men (Giomi & Tonello 2013; Gill & Day 2020). Race-based bias was also found in long-term research of US newspapers' coverage of serial rapists (Wright 2017) and in news media portrayals of celebrities perpetrating IPV (Pepin 2015).

However, the most literal way in which violence is exorcized is to attribute it to men who are 'other' by definition: strangers. The trend becomes greatest when dealing with sex crimes, and the most significant contribution to the reiteration of 'stranger danger' (Greer 2003: 100) comes from novels, television series and films centred on serial killers (Soothill & Walby 1991). Stranger danger goes hand in hand with the construction of public space as unsafe places, which affects a plurality of media forms, often indirectly. For example, in both the Italian and English press, images depicting places (the crime scene, or urban streets) are used only in articles of femicides and rapes that took place outdoors. Domestic spaces, where most of the violence takes place, are completely removed from the press's visual landscape. Fictional and factual tales, in short, cooperate to limit the spaces and times that women can move freely, acting as cautionary tales that prescribe appropriate behaviour for women, in pain of being attacked (Boyle 2005: 94–122). Even campaigns against online harassment act as cautionary tales potentially limiting women's presence in the public digital realm (Karaian 2014): they represent it as yet another public place full of dangers for women, who frequent it at their own risk (Vitis & Gilmour 2016: 5).

The othering also involves victims, and in their case the main criterion is nonconformity to gender norms. The re-victimization discourse distinguishes between innocent victims and victims who deserve their fate, and this is amplified by social networks (Willem, Araüna & Tortajada, 2019: 12; Dragotto et al. 2020). Its underlying message, once again, is that it is women who must change their behaviour to avoid abuse: on the one hand, pop culture denies women agency, on the other it also attributes it in excess when it comes to preventing violence at the hands of men.

Erasing violence

The regime of visibility of gender-based violence is perhaps the longest debated and most controversial issue among scholars (Shoos 2010: 115). By 'visibility' we do not only mean iconic, but, more generally, we mean representation. Some ways of recounting and depicting male violence against women – romanticization, eroticization, anaesthetization –

encourage it, yet, according to some critics, it is the very act of representing it that is problematic. It can help to produce or reproduce the conditions of violence, to be in 'itself' a form of violence (Burfoot & Lord 2006: XV). The omnipresence of sexual/sexualized violence against women in contemporary media culture should be taken into consideration when deciding to produce other such representations. Regardless of the aesthetics adopted, there is a risk of saturating an already crowded environment.

The frequent contradiction between the narrative and visual levels that characterize popular culture, further complicate matters. For example, Stieg Larsson's trilogy, *Millennium*, is appreciated by many feminist critics because it conceptualizes gender-based violence in appropriate terms (DeWelde 2012), but there are numerous acts of brutalization of women and they are graphically described, so much so that Ferber (2012: 331) wonders why we cannot challenge rape culture without reproducing its disturbing and violent imagery. O'Neill and Seal (2012: 61) believe that, if we consider the entire trilogy, similar descriptions are relatively few, and to sugar-coat or omit serial rapes and killings would have been just as problematic. Higgins and Silver (1991) illustrate this aspect well in *Rape and Representation*, an anthology in which they examine historic and contemporary rape stories in myths, oral culture, literature and films. They put forward famous examples such as the narration of Clarissa's rape, in Samuel Richardson's (1748) novel of the same name and Adela in *Passage to India* (Forster 1924), underline how many cultural forms there are in which sexual violence, the subject of 'an obsessive inscription and an obsessive erasure', constitutes at the same time both a 'structuring device and a gaping elision' (Higgins & Silver 1991: 2–3). This also occurred in Hollywood in the 1930s and 1940s: as a result of the Production Code, which prohibited explicit representations, films alluded to rape obliquely but nonetheless 'systematically depend on rape to motivate narrative progression' (Projansky 2001: 27). Removing the representation in its whole, though, often means removing the problem (precisely an exorcism). Replacing the 'elliptical' references to rape sedimented by the literary traditions of Richardson and Forster becomes essential to restore public visibility to an act that, in line with feminist conceptualization, must not remain confined to the silence of the private sphere (see also Laviosa 2011).

Female violence in the media

De-responsabilizing the perpetrator and minimizing violence

Compared to the literature available on male IPV, the literature on female IPV is very limited. News reporting studies show both similarities and differences between the two types. As for analogies, the comparative study by Sellers et al. (2014) into newspaper articles shows that for both male and female perpetrators, incidents of IPV were overwhelmingly framed as a private matter, whereas larger societal and cultural factors were rarely discussed. Carlyle et al. (2014) show that the loss of control due to passion acts as a mitigating factor for female violence too. Women are often portrayed as being overly emotional and acting violently 'in the heat of passion'. According to the authors, such reasoning can serve to excuse violence in the same ways that some forms of male violence are rationalized with 'boys will be boys'. However, in our opinion, gender differences persist in reporting: the cause that precipitates the violent tendency of men to explode is often identified in the behaviour of the partner, while the innate emotionality of women that determines loss of control is not represented as being triggered by partners. More generally, in news reports on female violence, de-responsabilizing the perpetrator and minimizing the violence are never accompanied by victim-blaming. In addition, some of the factors most commonly used by the media to excuse men who use violence (drugs, alcohol, mental illness, jealousy, etc.) are the same factors that the media use to blame women for the violence (Sutherland et al. 2015: 19) or at least they are presented as aggravating circumstances.

As we saw in Chapter 2, violence is the intentional behaviour of a self-conscious agent, albeit one whose choices and circumstances are constrained by power disparities and gender inequality. A review of the literature on the news coverage of the female perpetrated IPH made by Easteal et al. (2015) and Rollé et al. (2020: 258), found that the prevailing media representations of women who kill their violent partner depict them as lacking agency and promote a collective understanding of the battered woman as a person whose identity is predominantly that of a victim. Someone who acted out violent behaviours as a consequence of their mental instability due to previous abuses suffered at the hand of their partner. The 'battered woman syndrome' (which is the only case of 'victim-blaming' in the representation of female-perpetrated IPV) constitutes a variant of the 'madness' we encountered in Chapter 2. 'Bad and Mad' is among the most established standard narratives used to depict women who use violence in legal discourse and in the media too, although recent studies suggest that this applies to a much narrower set of cases than found by previous research (Pelvin 2019). This narrative either denies women's femininity (bad) or neutralizes their culpability in the violence, claiming that violence committed by women is not a 'real crime' (mad). To ascribe violence to the loss of control, self-defence, or 'madness' are all ways to deny female self-determination, the woman's intentionality to commit it. It constructs offenders as 'non-agents' (Morrissey 2003). As in the media representation of female victimization, agency and femininity thus return to being intertwined, and even if the roles are reversed (the woman is perpetrator and not victim), the same rule seems to apply: little agency = a lot of femininity. Venäläinen's study (2016) comes to the same conclusion by analysing an extensive body of Finnish tabloid articles: female perpetrators are alternately represented either as 'violent women' (with a lot of agency) or as 'feminine women', equipped with little agency, who find themselves carrying out violence for causes outside their control. It is precisely this 'sensationalistic dichotomy' that neutralizes the threat to the order of gender relations posed by women's violence.

The last theme that determines the partial or total excusing of women's violence as 'not real crime' is that of mothers acting to protect their children. It is a widespread theme, not only in IPH, because it has very ancient roots: according to Gentry and Sjoberg's enlightening analysis (2015: 71) even Medea kills as a mother, that is, finding in her role the tools to retaliate against her husband.

Now let us turn to fictional genres. Giomi (2017: 112) proposed calling a set of different textual strategies *Excusatio*. These are strategies that are intended to provide justification for the female (anti)hero featuring in typical male popular culture genres/roles/contexts, and, most importantly, exercising violence. Among these strategies, once again we find maternity, with the heroine 'acting to protect her children, either biological or adoptive' (Tasker 1998: 69): the trope characterizes the first action heroines, as it features in *Aliens* (Cameron 1986) and *Terminator 2* (Cameron 1991). Since it is a motivating factor that falls within the scope of defensive violence, it is a form of reducing agency, and also carries a precise ideological implication: women are allowed to be aggressive, violent and transgressive only in the name (and within the limits) of their biological functions. Over the last few years, in the audiovisual narratives, this trope has been weakened, or, as in the case of *The Walking Dead* (AMC 2010–present), has been reworked in ways that challenge patriarchal notions of femininity and offers alternatives to hegemonic discourses (Suarez 2020: 167). In any case, rarely does the male action hero need to justify what he is or does in the name of his offspring (the implicit idea of the 'normality' of violence for men returns).

Another narrative theme widely used in popular culture to justify the subversive and/or violent nature of the heroine is that of the father. In 'classic' Hollywood films, it refers to the centrality of oedipal scenarios, as Pravadelli explains (2015: 2173–80). Female heroism, Tasker (1998: 69) observes, is often legitimized in relation to the beloved or lost father, from whom the protagonist inherits a sense of justice, her craft/mission, and often the skills, including that of fighter. Think of characters such as Clarice Starling in *The Silence of the Lambs* (Demme 1991), a police officer who is the daughter of a police officer, or Katniss Everdeen of *The Hunger Games*, who is an archer like her father. The heroine's assumption of male traits such as violence is explained by its excessive identification in the father but is further justified by the absence of a maternal figure, and therefore of a female role model: according to

Owen et al. (2007: 15), at least this is a derogation in the dominant trend of heroines obsessed with their father, who in this, betray the desire to join the patriarchy.

We now come to Excusatio's third motive. The theme of revenge has always justified a protagonist's violence in the most diverse range of media genres, be that against either a single or collective antagonist, human, animal or robot. In the case of women, however, this device also knows a 'gendered' variant: '*rape-revenge*'. It was a feature of the first violent women in the 1970s and 1980s, such as *Lady Snowblood* (Fujita, 1973); it occurs in particular in *blaxploitation*, low-budget action films centred on Black characters (e.g. actress Pam Grier), and in horrors, such as *The Last House on the Left* (Craven, 1972) or *I Spit on Your Grave* (Zarchi 1978). The victim-turned-avenger is perhaps the figure that has increasingly catalysed the contradictions of violent female characters and the discordant judgements of feminist critics (see Clover 1992). More recently, the debate has been reopened with *Millennium's* Lisbeth Salander, for both the novels (see Åström et al. 2013; King & Lee Smith 2012) and the film adaptation. While the US version (*The Girl with the Dragon Tattoo*) (Fincher 2011) is accused of 'pornifying' Lisbeth, the Swedish original (Oplev 2009) more closely follows the source and creates an innovative figure: it is realistically constructed, in a context in which the majority of revenge/violent figures remain artificially constructed 'beauty queens' (Brown 2015: 860), embodies a 'physical feminism' in which the body transforms from a source of vulnerability and sexualization into a tool for resistance and weapon against sexism and rape culture (De Welde 2012: 471). Such heroines, however, could generate a 'guilty pleasure' (O'Neill & Seal 2012: 62) because together with the fantasy of revenge against male violence, they express that of 'punishment', which is contrary to the aim of a certain type of feminism: to reduce violence. The victim-turned-avenger idea does not stop at novels, as television series and films and even essay films also use it. For example: *Revenge* (Fargeat 2017), *The Nightingale* (Kent 2018), *A Vigilante* (Daggar-Nickson 2018), *Promising Young Woman* (Fennell 2020), the last hailed as a response to the #MeToo movement.

On the one hand, these films – all four directed by women – promote female agency and a cathartic revenge fantasy; on the other hand, the protagonists are now fetishized, now traced back to the cliché of the pathological and sacrificial heroine (in *Promising Young Woman* the protagonist even dies). Moreover, they are all post-feminist in their emphasis on individual solution to GBV rather than on a collective struggle and political transformation. Alternative narratives come from recent television series that, while not fully part of the rape-revenge genre, have trauma and abuse in their main themes: *Jessica Jones* (Netflix 2015–2019), *Big Little Lies* (HBO 2017–2019), *13 Reasons Why*, *Quicksand* (Netflix 2019), *I May Destroy You* (HBO/BBC One 2020) break with the Hollywood paradigm and a lot of television, representing violence not as the problem and responsibility of victim/survivors but of the wider community, enhancing alliances with other women and with non-heteronormative people. Thanks to an intersectional reading, some highlight race and class as additional factors of oppression, while others debunk the myth-based belief that IPV can only occur in dysfunctional or low-income neighbourhoods (Shoos 2021).

Normalizing violence and normalizing the perpetrator

We include under this section two vastly different phenomena, one concerning violent female action and the other concerning the agent. The first phenomenon is similar to the 'normalization' of those types of femicide that receive less visibility because they are more common: in one recent study of Canadian newspapers, the female-perpetrated killings that received no or limited coverage shared precise characteristics, constructing a picture of the typical woman who kills as one half of a working-class or unemployed couple involved in an argument that escalated into lethal violence, often after a night of drinking (Pelvin 2019: 263). Those crimes do not make headlines because they mirror the individual and situational characteristics of a large portion of women's IPH (see Chapter 2). They are 'normal crimes', which do not upset a generally accepted understanding of violence between intimate partners, therefore an explanation is not needed.

Women's violence is highly destabilizing to the order of gender relations: it cannot be normalized as an element of the daily media landscape, not as much as its male counterpart. An attempt is therefore made to normalize women who practise violence, to 'domesticate' them, by pushing them back to normative femininity. In fiction genres, this is especially true by transporting violent heroines 'out of the narrative' (Schubart 2007: 529). In some cases, they die, and are therefore turned from combatant heroines into sacrificial figures (Crosby 2004): for example, *Xena The Warrior Princess* (Syndication 1995–2001) and *Buffy The Vampire Slayer* (TheWB/ UPN 1997–2003), but also Tris from the *Divergent* saga. At other times, it is the heroines themselves who spontaneously abandon their role or mission. This choice identifies the large group of narratives that Schubart believes are based on the archetype of the 'daughter', in which a young woman is transformed into a deadly assassin/spy/criminal/fighter by an older man (*Nikita*, Besson 1990; *Léon: The Professional*, Besson 1994); by her father (*Hanna*, Amazon Video 2019–present); by her lover (Beatrix Kiddo in *Kill Bill*, Tarantino 2003); or by an entire male system, such as the Secret Service for Sydney Bristow in *Alias* (ABC 2001–2006) or the perverse *Hunger Games* reality show for Katniss Everdeen. The process that makes these heroines professional assassins, paradoxically, takes place in parallel with their transformation from 'tomboy', non-gender-conforming girls, into 'real women'. For the tomboy, undergoing the Oedipal trajectory means developing appropriate femininity, growing and accepting limits and responsibilities defined within the terms of heterosexuality, overcoming their immaturity and entering the symbolic order of the father. The subversive potential of tomboy – and the associated practice of crossdressing – is so contained, even overturned, by the narrative of the Oedipal journey at the end of which the heroine disfavours the male traits to assume her 'true identity': it coincides with a conventional gender identity, which – this is the message – is not compatible with the exercise of violence.

Motherhood, however, remains the most powerful standardization strategy, which also arises where we would not expect it: Kate Austen in *Lost* (ABC 2004–2010) is a fascinating woman who murdered her father and who has a failed marriage behind her because of her incompatibility with the role of wife and mother. However, her moral ambiguity is offset by becoming the loving adoptive mother to her friend Claire's son.

Sexuality is another highly effective device in diluting the subversive traits of the anti-heroine and relocating them in line with traditional gender expectations. In *Lost*, Kate's choice of Jack as a partner, and the consequent interruption of the love triangle between them and Sawyer, 'could be interpreted as an acceptance that ultimately heterosexual monogamy must prevail as an ideal' (O'Neill & Seal 2012: 53). If hacker Lisbeth Salander's open bisexuality in *Millennium* amplifies the deviant profile of a turbulent young woman with antisocial traits, the love affair with journalist Blomkvist relocates her in the more consensual role of fragile, vulnerable female. However, *Millennium* (especially in the literary text) can also be interpreted as being critical of monogamy and heteronormativity, because the relationship between Lisbeth and Miriam Wu appears just as significant and fulfilling as that with Blomkvist (Schippers 2012: 1231). Similarly, Shepherd's analysis (2013: 38) of *Buffy The Vampire Slayer* shows the complexity of a series that at the same time reproduces and questions moral and sexual codes through the depiction of violence. On the one hand, the subversive potential of the protagonist is mitigated by a conventionally pleasing appearance and heteronormative schemes; on the other hand, there is a systematic construction of heterosexuality as inherently violent: almost all the sexual intercourse Buffy has during the series produces insecurity and fragility, and are emotionally and physically harmful. Lesbian bonds, on the other hand, are presented as positive and saving, capable of resisting patriarchal 'divide and rule' and feed 'mutually beneficial heroism' (Ross 2004: 238).

Exorcizing violence: Othering and pathologizing

Othering

Similar to male-perpetrated IPV, for women the first and most widespread form of 'exorcism' consists of othering the perpetrator. It is worth noting what it is considered 'other'. A first indication comes from the newsworthiness criteria. Although female-perpetrated IPH is a rare, or at least less common, phenomenon than femicide (at European level the gender ratio is 1 to 4), this is not enough to ensure media coverage. A first explanation is proposed by Pelvin: 'normal crimes', which do not gain visibility, involve working-class/unemployed couples and circumstances that can be represented as 'degradation'. This is enough to push women's violence into a kind of social 'otherness', making other explanations superfluous. Also, as for male violence, we also find ethnic/racial otherness: news stories about white female offenders are more likely to contain excuses for their alleged or actual offences than stories about 'minority' female offenders (Brennan & Vandenberg 2009).

However, the otherness in which violent women are more often confined, is defined in relation to their gender; in short, the 'not real woman' returns. The Carlyle et al. study confirms that when the perpetrator was a female, her criminal history was reported more frequently than for male perpetrators. This could be interpreted as a tendency to explain her aggressive behaviour by establishing that she is not a 'typical' woman (2014: 17). Also, according to Easteal et al. (2015: 26), this happens more frequently in cases of women killing their husbands or children. Those homicides take place in the sphere in which women *naturally* reside more, increasing the necessity to distance these women from 'ordinary/normal' women and suggest that we need not bother ourselves with their stories and motivations. Two opposite assumptions – that violence is natural/normal for men and unnatural for women – generate the same result: the inability to effectively investigate the reasons lying behind their conduct.

The tendency to exorcise female violence as a product of 'not real women' also characterizes media coverage of women's violence against victims other than their partners or children. Naylor's now classic study (1995) analyses the English press and identifies six types of narratives more common in news media coverage of violent women, later increased to eight by Yvonne Jewkes (2015). Almost all of them are related to the 'bad' family. Unlike madness or victimization/self-defence, it recognizes the agency of the woman who commits violence. When the standardized narrative of the bad woman is mobilized, in short, her violence is presented as a 'real crime'. For this reason, it becomes important to frame perpetrators as not 'real women'. This occurs in different forms.

The 'bad mother' narrative – a missing and defective woman *par excellence* – is culturally so widespread that it applies to virtually all women guilty of crime, whether or not they are mothers, and even if their crimes do not involve children (Jewkes 2015). Conversely, if they involve them but the perpetrators do not have children, the media treats them as if they did, or should have had them ('crypto-mothers'), according to Boyle (2005: 117), precisely because of the automatic tendency to bring femininity and motherhood together. The result, once again, is that the crimes of these women appear worse than those of their possible male accomplices. Even in fictional narratives, the bad mother's trope is a form of amplification of the transgressive character of the violent/lawbreaking woman. In recent years, however, a trend has been established that confirms the ability of popular culture to challenge rigid gender ideologies: the emergence, especially in television shows, of 'aberrant mothers' like Nancy Botwin in *Weeds* (Showtime 2005–2012), who unapologetically live their non-normative and even dysfunctional mothering (Walters & Harrison 2014: 48).

The figure of 'evil manipulator' has always been widely used when women act together with their partners. We find it in the media coverage of famous cases for example that of Rose West and Karla Homolka, and in that of Myra Hindley, who in the 1960s was accused, together with her partner Ian Brady, of sexual abuse and the murder of many children and young people. Although these women were not the material executors of the crimes, or had a less decisive role than their companions, the three were the centrepieces of news media attention, which presented them as the real leaders morally, because they had not shown the compassion that one would expect from a woman for the victims, nor had they been able to moderate their men, as one would expect from good companions/wives (Jewkes 2015). Homolka's case also illuminates another of the most recurrent behaviours in the media: reflecting the uncertainty in the numerous psychiatric reports, in one moment, the news reports present the woman as the actual perpetrator, and in another as a passive inspiration for crimes and victimized in the same way the girls were raped and killed, forced to participate by her abusive companion. Seal calls this dichotomy 'Mastermind/Muse' (2010: 38). In news reports, the two narrative options were mutually exclusive, betraying the cultural inability to think of criminal women as executioners and victims at the same time. But keeping this duplicity together would have made it possible to understand their gestures. Thus, Boyle (2005: 102) comments that when the narrative of the victim prevails, attributing the role of executioner becomes simply unthinkable: Homolka is portrayed by the media as an automaton, subject to the will of her boyfriend. But if it is the role of executioner that predominates, then those who interpret it cannot be simultaneously positioned as a victim: Rose West comes from a long history of physical, psychological abuse and, from the age of 13, sexual abuse too (by her father). However, the newspapers minimize or even use her story as support for the sexual deviance of the woman. It is undoubtedly an effect of the binary logic that we mentioned in the previous chapter, and of the inadequate exploration of the relationship between *victimization* and *offending*.

The 'mythical monsters' narrative – based on the notion of 'monstrous feminine' elaborated by Creed (1986) – refers, in particular, to monsters of myths and legends, and is based on images from different traditions (pagan mythology, Judaeo-Christian theology, classical art and literature): gorgons, witches, Satanists, vampires, harpies, diabolical temptress, fallen women and sinners. All these figures are used to emphasize the violent woman's marked contrast with traditional femininity. Sternadori (2014) compares two cases of multiple murder, committed by two university professors, a man (George Zinkhan) and a woman (Amy Bishop). The American press describes George Zinkhan, as a poor Othello in the grip of passion, who jealously kills a woman. Amy Bishop received much less supportive treatment: her actions were motivated by a malaise for the obstacles placed in her career, and the nickname of 'witch' ascribed to her in the tabloids, confirms that female ambition and greed are treated harshly. In fact, there is even widespread resistance in criminology to attributing economic crimes or even just instrumental economic rationality to women (Davies 2011: 96). Myra Hindley, who abused and killed children, was described as Medea or Medusa (Birch 1993; Naylor 1995). Australian Tracey Wigginton, guilty of the death of a stranger who she lured into a sexual trap, was renamed the lesbian vampire-killer, while her three heterosexual and pleasant-looking accomplices, attracted little attention; only she, a lesbian and with robust features, became the focus of the story.

As noted in Chapter 2 regarding the aetiologies of female violence, the sexual history of criminal women is widely used by news media to argue their evil nature. References are so frequent that they create a standard narrative called, precisely, 'sexuality and sexual deviance' (Jewkes 2015). In figures such as that of Rose West, whose sexual deviance was covered by the tabloid press in salacious detail, Jewkes notes a contemporary incarnation of criminological positivism's 'born female criminal'. In the fictional domain too, a deviant sexuality is used as an explanation for the 'unnaturalness' of women who conduct themselves antisocially or increases the transgressiveness of their character. We have observed this in Lisbeth Salander, but lesbians and bisexuals also populate the 'women in prison genre' (consider *Orange Is the New Black*, Netflix 2013–2019). They play assassins (*Basic Instinct* Verhoeven 1992), fraudsters (*Bound* Wachowski 1996), drug dealers (*Weeds*) and criminals (*Mafiosa, le clan/Mafiosa* Canal+ 2006–2014). In these last two series, the parallelism between social deviance and gender deviance is marked by the expedient of 'double baptism' (Giomi 2017: 116–17): the moment when the protagonists assume their new roles, that of drug dealer and boss, is sealed by 'transgressive' sexual intercourses.

The sexual order is so pervasive in the cultural construction of the feminine that it is not surprising that it recurs in different narrative typologies. Physical appearance is also an area of obsessive interest for the media. Jewkes calls it the narrative of '(lack of) physical attractiveness': it overlaps with that of the 'monstrous feminine', as the lack of the woman's attractiveness functions to produce this when the protagonists do not conform to hegemonic aesthetic canons. Physicality also plays a central role in fostering more lenient attitudes on the part of judges and journalists, but to benefit from it, it is not always necessary to be beautiful: in the case of a Finnish multiple murderer it was precisely the woman's ordinariness, and anonymity, combined with her resigned posture, that pushed forward the label of 'poor thing', and the case was dismissed as a 'sad' result of individual pathology (Berrington & Honkatukia 2002).

Pathologizing

In this section we illustrate a strategy opposed to the normalization of the heroine: it consists of representing the violent woman as pathological. We do not consider it among the forms of violence minimization based on 'madness' because the 'pathology' in question is not directly related to the violent act of the female offender. Instead it serves more generally to explain an atypical, transgressive character, and therefore to exorcise not only the act perpetrated by the violent woman, but her entire persona as an exception. From this point of view, pathologization can be considered a further form of othering. Pathologizing is often derived from other narrative reasons, such as in the case, just analysed, of sexual deviance or the dysfunctional relationship of the heroine with her father or mother. The theme of rape-revenge can also go in the same direction: Veronica Mars' toughness, for example, is pathologized as a result of the trauma she suffered (Sibielski 2010: 331), which resonates with the cases of rape on campus which Veronica investigates. The same is true of the female police officers in *Top of the Lake* (BBC UKTV/ BBC Two 2013–2017) and *Happy Valley* (BBC One 2014–present), although in the latter case it is her daughter who was raped, and who later committed suicide. More generally, in crime series, there is a widespread presence of heroines who are emotionally disabled or have experienced abuse (often echoing those of the victims of the cases they are investigating). Coulthard et al. (2018: 510) refer to this as the tropes of 'broken bodies' and 'inquiring minds'. Among the pathologies, we find bipolarity (*Homeland*, Showtime 2011–2020), amnesia (*Marcella*, ITV/Netflix 2016–present), hyperthymesia (Carrie Wells of *Unforgettable*, CBS/A&E 2011–2016), and especially Asperger's syndrome: Lisbeth Salander, Temperance Brennan (*Bones*, Fox 2005–present) and Saga Norén (*Bron/Broen* detective (SVT1/DR1 2011–2018), which retains this feature both in the US remake (*The Bridge*, SVT1/DR1 2013–2014) and in the Franco-English adaptation (*The Tunnel*, Canal+/Sky Atlantic 2013–2018). Moreover, disorders placed on the autism spectrum have the effect of compromising interpersonal and empathic skills, thus undermining the specifically feminine traits: in short, the 'not real women' returns (see McHugh 2018 for further study).

When pathologizing does not operate upstream, as a device to explain (or amplify) the protagonist's deviance, it operates downstream, as a price to be paid for entry into professional ranks and male media genres. Little has changed since the days of ambitious policewoman Christine Cagney in *Cagney & Lacy* (CBS 1982–1988) and similarly Jane Tennison in *Prime Suspect* (ITV 1991–2006): both were 'punished' with sentimental instability, loneliness and a descent into alcoholism (Thornam & Purvis 2005, 118). According to Gilchrist (2020), by portraying the single female detective as socially dysfunctional, vulnerable or deviant in series like *The Bridge*/Broen, *The Good Wife* (CBS, 2009–2016), *Fargo* (FX 2014–present) and *Unbelievable* (Netflix 2019), the patriarchal discourse of heteronormative coupledom is reinscribed and renders the single woman a threat to femininity. This same backlash value is seen in young adult dystopian narratives, with the antagonists to the heroines we mentioned in the introduction. According to Boutang (2020), the figures of President Alma Coin and Jeanine Matthews, from the *Hunger Games* and the *Divergent* saga respectively, of Sergeant Reznik from *The 5th Wave* and Marissa Wiegler in the first season of *Hanna*, represent negative caricatures of second-wave feminism because their position as a leader, a typically male role, is associated with the overall denial of (normative) femininity: the absence of emotional ties and children, a lack of empathy and morality, and even sadism (they all commit the most 'unnatural' crime for women, namely killing children and adolescents). Once again, violence is marked as the conduct of masculinized and pathological women. But beware: in the next paragraph we will show how the opposite configuration, of hyper femininity and eroticism, can produce the same pathologizing effect and the same outcome of the backlash to feminism.

Spectacularizing violence: Eroticizing

Unlike male violence, female violence is the subject of strong ambivalence: it is offered as a cautionary tale about the elision of gender difference on the narrative level, but also as an attraction on the level of spectacle (Neroni 2005: 20). One analogy, however, is that the spectacularizing of female violence also stems from the forms examined above, especially those emphasizing its abnormality. Without doubt, however, the longest-running strategy is to charge it with erotic appeal. In this sense, all the violent women in popular culture have a debt towards the 1930s and 1940s noir femme fatales. She was rarely depicted, however, as violent: she was never filmed in the act of killing, and in any case, she used a gun. This allowed her to retain rather than break away from her femininity. Today, the femme fatale still remains an archetype through which to read the depictions of violence perpetrated by women, real or imaginary, who, unlike the monstrous feminine, present a destabilizing dichotomy between charm and danger. Simkin (2014) examines the media coverage of the case of Amanda Knox, accused (and later acquitted in the highest court) of killing Meredith Kercher along with her then-boyfriend Raffaele Sollecito and a third (Black) man, Rudy Guede, who was the only one convicted. Amanda Knox would have all the attributes to qualify as a classic evil manipulator who instigates the crime and mesmerizes accomplices; someone unscrupulous, self-confident, cold and controlled – like a man. However, at the same time she is beautiful and hyperfeminine so she cannot be exorcized as a 'monster' nor as an aberrant form of 'faux masculinity', that is, a woman whose violent conduct can be explained on the basis of her homologation to men. Neither evil manipulator nor 'monster', therefore: the combination of beauty and coldness earned Knox the nickname of femme fatale by the press.

According to Neroni (2004), between the 1970s and 1980s, violent heroines became more numerous, although they were still predominantly concentrated in two fairly marginal, or at least not always mainstream, genres: horror, where female protagonism was inaugurated by Marilyn Burns from *The Texas Chain Saw Massacre* (Hooper, 1974), and 'Blaxploitation'. These years are also characterized by the appearance of female figures who were more generally identified, if not by violence, by a common subversive/aggressive quality and protagonism in male genres, such as *Wonder Woman* (ABC/CBS 1975–1979) or *Charlie's Angels* (ABC 1976–1981). On the one hand, these heroines were at the centre of action narrative but, on the other hand, they were re-coded as objects of erotic contemplation through fetishizing conventions and forms (e.g. the dominatrix) (Inness 2004). This ambivalence would continue over the coming years.

It was in the 1990s that the presence of violent women became widespread and cross-media: action (*Terminator 2*, Cameron 1991), thriller (*The Silence of the Lambs*, Demme 1991), road movie (*Thelma and Louise*, Scott 1991), western (*Bad Girls*, Kaplan 1994), war (*Soldier Jane*, Scott 1997). At the same time, we witnessed the debut of a new femme fatal figure with a wave of 1980s and 1990s 'erotic thrillers' defined as 'neo-noirs' (Letort 2020, 24): *Fatal Attraction* (Lyne 1987), the aforementioned *Basic Instinct*; *Body of Evidence* (Edel 1993); *The Last Seduction* (Dahl 1994). The beautiful and sensual protagonists of these films, named "super-bitch killer beauties" (Faith 1993: 265) or 'deadly dolls' (Holmlund 1993), act with lethal violence against their (ex)lovers and constitute the fictional counterpart to the figures in news reports, who were equally young and beautiful, and who turned the spotlight on women's violence: the American, Lorena Bobbit, who emasculated her husband, Karla Homolka, and also the 'ladette', were at the centre of a moral panic spread by the US news media for the increase – completely disproved by the data – of the participation of young women in gangs (Kruttschnitt et al. 2008: 10–11). But above all, deadly dolls are an expression of the backlash because they represent career women who lack stable ties or a family in the derogatory fashion of violent psychopaths. Letort (2020: 38) offers a more nuanced view and interprets the neo-noir femme fatale's concomitance between agency and sexual commodification as a sign of the emerging postfeminist culture: by killing the male, these women achieve liberation from masculine domination and heteronormative conventions, including their own sexual reification. On the other hand, as alluded to in the previous paragraphs, the femme fatale's excessive sexuality is a metaphor for her killing instinct, creating a pathological framework for the understanding of female sexual emancipation. The protagonist of *Gone Girl* (Fincher 2014) is one of the few exceptions and constitutes a complex character: she appears as a 'hypersexualized' neo-noir femme fatale, but is then de-eroticized, thus becoming an ironic product of post feminism (Maury 2020: 109).

Finally, a profound difference emerges in respect of male-perpetrated IPV. There is a total absence of romanticization. In the cases of neo femme fatales, who frequently take revenge on men who reject them (consider *Fatal Attraction* or *Disclosure*, Levinson 1994), the romantic motivation does not provide any kind of excusing or mitigation, on the contrary it helps to demonize them.

'Singing with a different voice?': Transition towards hegemonic masculinity in Italian top charts songs

Sveva Magaraggia

This study is based on a qualitative content analysis of the lyrics of the most played songs in Italy between 2018 and 2020. The analysis aims to understand the role that (intimate partner) violence plays in constructing the gendered imaginary presented in these songs and its role in shaping male and female profiles and interpersonal relationships. The key theme running through our reflections in this section is the politics of representation of intimate partner violence.

Popular music is an interesting case study, as it has become an inextricable part of how identities are produced and reproduced in contemporary societies (Bennett & Rogers 2016), including in the ongoing work of doing gender.

A sociological approach to music

Music is a social fact both because there is no society without music and because music accompanies many moments of our daily lives. To confirm this, each time I presented an analysis of song lyrics conducted a few years ago (Magaraggia 2017), I found myself involved in lengthy discussions, followed by messages and emails with suggestions for other songs to include in future analysis. As Tia DeNora (2000) points out, the reactions that music studies arouse 'point to music as a dynamic material, a medium for making, sustaining and changing social worlds and social activities' (ibid., X). Looking at music from a sociological perspective therefore means trying to understand how embedded music is in social relationships, how functional it is to the construction of our personas and our social worlds. Once again, Tia DeNora (2000), in their analysis, notes the existence of 'a range of strategies through which music is mobilized as a resource for producing the scenes, routines, assumptions and occasions that constitute "social life"' (ibid., XI). From this perspective, therefore, music becomes the expression of shared social meanings.

How to study its effects is much debated, and for analytical convenience we can identify two main positions within this lively debate: on the one hand, there are those who study music as an object and, on the other hand, there are those who analyse it as an activity (Roy & Dowd 2010).

Considering songs as an object is to examine them as a written text. Here, music lyrics are interpreted both as a mirror of society and means 'able to construct the people' (Frith 1987: 137), able to recreate gender, class but also phenomena like romantic love, sexism, racism and homophobia (see, for example, hooks 1994; Anderson et al. 2001; Thaller & Messing 2014; Bal 2020). As the feminist textual turn shows, reality is discursively constructed and 'language is a constitutive force, creating a particular view of reality of writing as of speaking, and as true of science as of poetry. (…) A disclosure of writing practices is thus always a disclosure of forms of power' (Richardson 1991: 174). As bell hooks highlights, language is also a place of struggle and a map of sense shaped by power. Studying song lyrics means understanding the coding of the world and the common sense they (re)propose.

Other scholars argue that the musical object can only be understood if, along with the words, the music's structure is also analysed, as 'musical and textual meaning are interrelated, [and] co-productive' (DeNora 2000: 28). Research positioned in this theoretical framework includes one conducted by Robert Walser (1999), which shows how the musical structure (rhythm and sound) of heavy metal promotes specific models of masculinity, and one by Susan McClary (1992) who shows how music contributes to the process of making sense of the words to which it is attached.

The second position sees music as a social activity, which can only be understood by studying the context in which musical use occurs. As Paolo Magaudda and Marco Santoro (2013) recall,

> the practice of listening and the influence of musical technologies have been problematized (…) also in various pages of Adorno (1941; 1945; 1962) or in the early sociological research into music by Simon Frith (1978; see Ribac 2006). In any case, at least until the end of the seventies, for social and cultural studies, research into sound coincided above all and mainly with the study of music's social and cultural implications.
>
> (ibid., 4)

Therefore, the focus is on the listeners, and it is assumed that the relationships created at the moment of its use are decisive in attributing meaning to what is heard. To use DeNora's (2000) words again, which express this perspective in a fruitful way, 'the focus is directed at the question of how particular actors make connections or, as Stuart Hall later put it, "articulations" (1980, 1986) between music and social formations' (2000: 6). It is in the relationships of the audiences that the meaning lies. Thus, for example, from this perspective to understand whether music inspires violence or helps to vent it peacefully does not depend so much on the lyrics of the songs, but on how they are used, on what the listeners do with the words they hear (Binder 1993; Cobb & Boettcher 2007; Wright & Centeno 2018; Coffey-Glover & Handforth 2019). The meaning is created through a set of activities; it has a contingent nature in which the social status of the listeners influences the final result

Music and misogyny

This subdivision – music as an object or as an activity – is also a useful compass to orient ourselves among the numerous studies that have dealt with stereotypical or misogynistic representations or even those depicting GBV.

Considering songs as an object means examining it as a written text, and the methodological rationale that guides this perspective is twofold: on the one hand, the analysis is conducted for individual musical genres, on the other hand, it is conducted by starting with singles and albums charts or with the most listened to or watched videos in a country over a defined period of time.

In general, research analysing songs at the top of the charts has recorded an increase, since the late 1950s, in sexualized lyrics of both male and female artists (Bretthauer et al. 2007; Hall et al. 2012). This is not surprising given the radical transformation of cultural norms that has affected most societies. However, the sexual liberation that began with the movements of 1968, is accompanied by an increase in women's sexual objectification and by a lack of agency and individuality of the person being objectified (Nussbaum 1995; Fredrickson & Roberts 1997; Andsager & Roe 2003; Bretthauer et al. 2007; Papadopoulos 2010; Tolman & McClelland 2011; Lynskey 2013; Murphy 2014; Silvaggi et al. 2016; Karsay et al. 2018). It is a phenomenon similar to that observed in Chapter 3 regarding the fetishization of violent or 'tough' female figures since their inception in the 1970s in response to feminism's demands.

In music, this trend shows specifications that depend on the musical genre referenced (see Finley 2018 for an overview). Rasmussen and Densley (2017), for example, found an increase in female objectification in country music songs, while pop music is less objectifying but more inclined to propose stereotypical and idealized models of heterosexual romantic love (Ryan & Peterson 1982; Agbo-Quaye & Robertson 2010; Grönevik 2013), and rock music to depict sexual experimentation (Agbo-Quaye & Robertson 2010).[13]

Certainly, the most studied genres of music with a gender perspective is rap (with a heated racialized debate on gangsta rap) and hip-hop (Johnson et al. 1995; Armstrong 2001; Kubrin 2005; Kistler & Lee 2009; Hill 2009; Oware 2011; Fearing et al. 2018), since these are the genres that contain the most degrading sexual references (Primack et al. 2008; Herd 2009; Wright & Centeno 2018). Extreme use of vulgar and explicitly violent terms referring to women, and in particular towards women of colour, for the purpose of ridicule or subordination (Collins 2000; Adams & Fuller 2006; Ling & Dipolog-Ubanan 2017; Bal 2020), and of representing them only as sexual objects, as prostitutes/sex workers (van Oosten et al. 2015) who have no reason to exist other than for the sexual satisfaction of men (Kistler & Lee 2009), who are celebrated as pimps. A sense of distrust 'and several specific reasons to be suspicious of women, who are seen as prone to entrap, betray, exploit, or destroy men' is another recurrent theme found in rap/hip-hop songs (Weitzer & Kubrin 2009: 16). In these genres, the combination of sexuality and violence is also celebrated (Rhym 1997; Oliver 2006; Rebollo-Gil & Moras 2012). Violence, which is presented as appropriate and acceptable, often becomes an ingredient 'to assert masculinity and personal prowess through bragging' (Herd 2009: 400). Violence is one of the means of eliciting respect from others. It is the main tool for the assertion of hegemonic masculinity.

Songs written by female musicians show a wider range of subject matters in the context of abstract virtues, greater gender equality, themes of female agency (Andsager & Roe 1999; Haugen 2003; Oware 2009; Krause & North 2019), but a tendency to self-objectify is also present accompanied with the denigration of other women (Guevara 1996; Aubrey et al. 2011), as is a tendency to represent women as gold diggers, ready to entrap and betray, interested solely in exploiting men (Pough 2004), and references 'to the fraudulent nature of masculinity; men are not to be taken seriously but to be laughed at' (Skeggs 1993: 308).

A body of work analysing music videos content has been consolidated since their appearance at the beginning of the 1980s on the Music Television Network (MTV). An analysis by music genres has shown that, for example, the majority of rock music videos (Vincent et al. 1987; Alexander 1999) and of country music videos (Andsager & Roe 1999) presented women in a devaluing, condescending manner and that only one in ten videos presented women as fully equal to men. Interestingly, while 8 per cent of rock videos displayed male violence against women, none of the country music content did (Vincent et al. 1987). Aubrey and Frisby (2011) observed that 80 per cent of pop videos do not depict women as purely decorative elements, unlike hip-hop/rap and R&B.

Analyses of music videos occupying the different national top chart positions reveal that women are predominantly portrayed on the basis of negative stereotypes and as sexual objects, more or less complacent victims of male attention and violence (Alexander 1999; Andsager & Roe 1999; Arnett 2002; Haynes 2009; Aubrey & Frisby 2011; Wallis 2011; Karsay et al. 2019). Furthermore, contemporary music videos not only objectify women but often enforce racial boundaries (Gordon 2008; Berberick 2010).

There are two criticisms to these studies which can be useful to recall: firstly, what bell hooks (1994) said in the heated debate that took place in the early 1990s, when reminding us that rappers (who are predominantly Black) reflect the dominant values of a society, and rather than criticizing them as a pathologized group, it is the norm that requires criticism, thus drawing attention to the systemic nature of violence of which rappers are just an expression.

The second criticism is recent and isolated, but no less useful, because it highlights the risk of producing a 'paranoid reading' of musical lyrics, 'rapey songs can thus be read as BDSM fetishized performances, where pleasure is cultivated through exaggerated roles and violent motifs' (Khan 2017: 26). While not sharing Ummni Khan's point of view, it is useful to remember that an excessively literal and reductionist approach to interpreting lyrics may amplify moral panic.

Studying the reception of music and music videos is complex, as they are 'correlational in nature, causal direction cannot be established with certainty' (Hansen 2007: 632). However, there are a number of consistent results that show that exposure to 'misogynistic' music and music videos has predictable effects on behaviour that result in greater affinity for and acceptance of socially negative values (Hansen & Hansen 1990; Rubin et al. 2001; Huesmann et al. 2006; West 2008; Kistler et al. 2009; Aubrey et al. 2011; Burgess & Burpo 2012; Van Oosten 2015).

Before moving onto the analysis of musical lyrics, it is important to recall that the music industry (Katz & Earp 1999), as well as the music charts, are still dominated by male singers, composers and lyricists (Weitzer & Kubrin 2009; Flynn et al. 2016; Krause & North 2019). This is also true in Italy (Campus 2015; Giomi & Magaraggia 2017; Burgazzi 2021).

Methodology

This chapter examines popular music and its lyrics as the locus for analysing discursive strategies. It deals with the music's intention rather than with audience responses. It analyses popular chart music, and not a specific pop music genre. Some of the predominant themes in popular music will be analysed through a qualitative content analysis of the top three songs of the weekly Italian charts between 2018 and 2020. These themes will relate to the social construction of genders, particularly the role that violence plays in constructing masculinities and femininities, as well as the relationships between them.

Each song was listened to at least three times in its entirety while simultaneously reading the lyrics, and at least once, the song's music video (if it existed) was watched. The lyrics were obtained online and were analysed using an inductive approach. The online *Urban Dictionary* was consulted in cases of uncertainty regarding the meaning of slang terms or phrases, and ATLAS.ti was used in the coding and analysis process.

The sample is comprised of 119 songs – the majority in Italian, but also some in English and Spanish – some of which remained in the top positions for many weeks, others only for one. Of these, 86 were written by male lyricists, 4 by women lyricists and 29 by mixed groups (each comprising an equal or greater number of men). The pervasiveness of male authors and their epistemic power corresponds to a predominance of singers of the same gender. In total, of 119 songs, 91 are sung by one or more boys or men, 10 by one or more girls or women, and 18 by groups of men and women. This disproportion can exist without any need for excuses, since 'the strength of the masculine order is seen in the fact that it dispenses with justification: the androcentric vision imposes itself as neutral and has no need to spell itself out in discourses aimed at legitimating it' (Bourdieu 2001: 9). We can say that, even today, the definition of the framework of meaning used to read reality is firmly in male hands.

Trap and hip-hop/rap is the musical genre that dominates the charts and which represents 56 per cent of all the musical genres in them (in absolute numbers 67 out of 119). Its specific motifs are no longer sex, drugs and rock'n roll but can be summarized succinctly in: success, competition and drugs. It would be trivial and unfair to an entire generation of artists and audiences, those of GenZ (Scholz 2014), not to go between the lines of these performances where the unspeakable symbolic universes, fears, anger and desires nestle. Our analysis focuses on the gendered symbolic representations and the role that violence plays in constructing masculinities and femininities. Given the proportions and characteristics of the musical genres, we first analysed the trap and hip-hop/rap music and then all the other musical genres, ranging from pop to the singer songwriter genre, passing through electronic music.

It's a man's world: Homosociality, success and bitches

The great diversity in the representation of men compared to that of women in the songs we analysed emerges because of the labels used in the lyrics. Men are often called 'bro', or one of its Italian synonyms (*Brothi, frate, fra, frero, amico*), by their professions 'trap boy, Rockstar, paparazzi, sheriff, Superman, rapper, boss', or by name. Sexual epithet is limited to 'Daddy and *papito*' and those derogatory terms like '*scemo* (fool)'. Women are often called '*tipa* (chick), baby, mademoiselle, *amore* (love)' or, more rarely, by name, or even 'bitch' (which does not necessarily need to be read as a derogatory label), but also 'escorts, *troia* (sluts), *puttane* (whores)'. Further, they are defined by their aesthetics '*cavalla* (horse), *rimastona* (airhead/bimbo), *gnocca* (babe), *cesso* (toilet)', and as sexual objects '*gafi* (slang for pussy), punani (slang for vagina, pussy), *figa* (pussy)' and racialized '*pussy nera* and *pussy gialla* (black pussy and yellow pussy)'. It should be remembered that terms like 'bitch' and 'ho' can be used in rap music without diminishing women (Kitwana 1994: 25; Keyes 2002), rather to metaphorically indicate sexually free women. A positive re-appropriation of a term's meaning that patriarchal language has always used to stigmatize women who do not conform to the ideals of normative femininity, similar to that mentioned in Chapter 2, is the term 'witch', found in the feminist movements of the 1970s, and equally centred on the positive reversal of the category of 'transgression'. Not ambivalent are the objectifying terms that do not represent a person in their entirety, but as a body part considered an instrument of male pleasure and desire (Fredrickson & Roberts 1997). Another form by which female objectification is evident in music is that of vulgar appreciations of the body. This introduces 'an asymmetry between those who enjoy the prototypical quality of the human and those who are considered lacking' (Silvaggi et al. 2016: 6).

The analysis of the most listened-to songs in Italy in 2018, 2019 and 2020 shows a specific pathway towards hegemonic masculinity regarding trap and hip-hop/rap songs. The similarities amongst the narratives contained in these songs build a map that shows how to find and interpret the 'practices that institutionalize men's dominance over women' (Connell 1987: 185) within the contemporary gender order. In other musical genres, however, different hegemonic narratives emerge.

The thresholds of the transition towards hegemonic masculinities narrated in the symbolic world of trap and hip-hop/rap songs include (a) the affirmation of one's own heterosexuality, (b) 'status degradation ceremonies' (Garfinkel 1956), (c) self-celebration, (d) being emotionally detached, and (e) the display of the will to do violence.

The construction of masculinity, and therefore of manhood, is characterized, and must constantly be certified, by real rites and tests aimed at strengthening male solidarity. Failure to overcome these thresholds leads to the fear of being excluded and relegated to a degraded status. Male privilege also ends up being a trap that forces each man to continually show and prove his manhood to other men (Kaufman 1999).

The affirmation of one's own heterosexuality

With regard to the first aspect, literature has widely shown that the unequivocal affirmation of one's own heterosexuality is the first step towards achieving hegemony (Connell 1987; Kimmel 2005; Pascoe 2007). This is still true in these lyrics, especially those of trap and hip-hop/rap, and it takes place through an emphasis on one's sexual performance and through the display of continuous risky behaviours (demonstrating one's manly courage) as clearly can be seen in the lyrics in the song 'Tesla', which describe speeding in a car with a woman in the passenger seat:

'Head to tail, I'm with my chick on a Tesla / A hundred and eighty, shift into sixth / She tells me to slow down (skrt, skrt)' (2018 04 28#1[14] Tesla, Capo Plaza ft. Sfera Ebbasta and DrefGold).[15]

Heterosexuality is also (re)affirmed in other musical genres but in a less obsessive and a more playful way and is done in at least two ways. Through well-known sexualized behaviours: 'Do it slowly / I put on some reggaeton so you can turn off that body for me' (2019 01 19# 3 Calma (remix) Pedro Capó ft. Farruko)[16] and in less stereotypical imaginary such as in this pop song: 'Well, I found a woman, stronger than anyone I know / I found a love, to carry more than just my secrets / To carry love, to carry children of our own' (2018 01 06#1 Perfect, Ed Sheeran).[17]

Status degradation ceremonies

The second threshold is the 'status degradation ceremony' (Garfinkel 1956) directed at women and at 'subordinated masculinities' (Connell 2005). The ritual destruction of women is constant in trap and hip-hop/rap music. Sexual objectification, which transforms women into disposable products, and that erases their agency and personhood (see Chapter 1) takes various forms. Women might be treated like food items: 'Every day Bitches won't leave me alone (no) /I order them from home like on Deliveroo' (2019 02 02 #2 TVTB, Fedez and Dark Polo Gang).[18] Alternatively, sometimes, objectification takes on the literal variant of reification, and the parallels between consumerism of goods (shopping) and sexual exploitation of women: 'Pink Pussy, pink shocking / Your [girlfriend] is with me shopping / G-U-E, you know I keep it dipped / I fill her like her Gucci pouch' (2018 09 22 #1 Borsello, Guè Pequeno).[19]

Another typical example is one where women are turned into rewards and prizes for achieved success: 'Bros, then I piss on the heads of those who challenge us / These perfect chicks are the reward' (2019 06 15#1 Veleno 7, Gemitaiz, MadMan).[20]

These forms of dehumanization are 'propaedeutic' to violence, which can also pass through the representation of the female body as a 'plastic' body, fake and artefact, therefore not sentient: 'Tell these phoney bitches "beat it"/With that Photoshoppin', body Adobe, help me' (2020 02 05#2 THE SCOTTS, Travis Scott, Kid Cudi). Finally, women are represented as spaces that are available to anyone (Jhally 2009), which in the philosophy of the disposable culture do not belong to anyone and can therefore be temporarily crossed by everyone: 'This city is like a beautiful woman / Just waiting for someone to do her' (2019 07 13 #2 YOSHI, prod. Massacre).[21]

As found in other research based on content analyses of song lyrics (Weitzer & Kubrin 2009; Aubrey & Frisby 2011: 124), women are part of the narration in order to be sexually used as object of a *rite de passage* for men's empowerment. Women, especially in trap and hip-hop/rap songs, are present only as tools for the affirmation of masculinity. They fulfil their aim, which is to assume, through objectification, a 'negative symbolic coefficient' (Bourdieu 1998) that is necessary for the male gender to represent itself as a full and worthy subject.

Status degradation ceremonies against subordinated masculinities show some innovative aspects. In the songs, a close bond with one or a few real friends emerges ('*bro*', '*fra*', '*frero*', which are all synonyms of 'brother'), a bond where understanding is total, replete with homoerotic nuances: 'I know you know the rest (yeah) / That I write to you today too / I wonder where you hang out / What will you do next, Let's go out? / … And pick me up / In the middle of the dust / Remember? There was no money, it was you and me' (2018 04 28#3 Davide, Gemitaiz ft. Mr Coez).[22]

In songs we hear about fundamental, solid and long-standing friendships: 'I wouldn't change my brother, we were separated at birth' (2019 10 12#3 Gigolò, Lazza)[23] in which the cultural imposition of hegemonic masculinity goes uncontested (Kaufman 1999), as the space of conflict and degradation are reserved only for others, enemies that are diminished through competition: 'Your time is already up / You are out of fashion like your bag, damn' (2018 09 22#1 Borsello, Guè Pequeno)[24] and through the conquest of 'their' partners: 'Your b-b-b, says, "Yes, yes, yes"/But who knows what it's like, when she's with you she says, "No, no, no"' (2020 11 28#2 Tik Tok RMX, Sfera Ebbasta (ft. Marracash, Guè Pequeno[25]).

An unprecedented and certainly significant aspect is that there are no disparaging references to homosexual men in hip-hop/rap trap, who are not represented in these narrative repertoires. Also, in these contexts we can hear an echo of the configuration of practices of 'inclusive masculinities' (Anderson & McCormack 2018), namely more inclusive behaviours in male peer group cultures. The only reference found is an artist joking about himself and his own way of dressing: 'Oh yes, I put on furs like a pussy (Oh yes)/Uzi, me and the gang have the same taste' (2020 05 16#2 Pussy, Dark Polo Gang ft. Lazza e Salmo).[26]

The singers' own (hyper)heterosexuality is asserted by objectifying women and pointing out supremacy over other men but without offending gay men, and not even lesbian women.

Other musical genres present in the charts also revealed different models of masculinity, showing 'men's agentive and emotionally reflective engagement with masculinity' (Waling 2019: 90). We find representations of men encouraging their companions to be free: 'Marlena, you win the evening /Strip off black, take everything that makes you comfortable and sincere /Open the sail, come on travel light' (2018 03 31#2 Morirò da re, Maneskin);[27] and of men who talk about their fragility:

> I hate these scars because they make me feel different / I can hide them from everyone, but not myself (...) Every wound is a path leading to our best side /Because through them you can look inside me /Feel what I feel, understand what I feel.
>
> (2020 04 04#3 Fiori di Chernobyl, Mr. Rain)[28]

In addition to these cultural innovations we also find narratives that recall the traditional codes of gallantry (see Chapter 1) instrumental in depicting men as protectors of fragile women: 'No, don't be afraid / When you go to sleep alone / If the room seems empty (...) / I'll take care, I'll take care of you' (2019 10 05#2 Non avere paura, Tommaso Paradiso).[29]

Self-celebration

Self-celebration primarily attributable to financial success is the third crucial threshold one has to overcome to become a hegemonic man. In line with generational dictates, in which GenZ are to be 'entrepreneurs of themselves' (Dardot & Laval 2013), cars, branded clothes, luxury and women are quoted to show off. They are used to stress a distinction from 'subordinate masculinities': 'Now the whole of Italy knows my name /I want a Panamera /Now I pay for my mother's cruise /Now, I have new shoes every day. /And a different chick from yesterday' (2018 09 15#2 Trap Phone, Guè Pequeno).[30]

For these singers 'success and self-realization are narrated through a chronicle of goods, trophies, outfits, status symbols, trademarks, and thanks to a ritual count, the women possessed, the marijuana smoked, the number of sold out concerts, views and gold records achieved' (Carozzi 2019: 55). Economic success, in addition to marking membership of gender hegemony, is also what allows us to undertake an accelerated parable of social mobility (class) and transition to adulthood (generation) (Cuzzocrea & Benasso 2020). These lyrics tell of rapid transitions from one extreme of the social order to the other. Between the lines of this claim there is an emancipatory potential, as it is 'producing paradoxical minoritarian universalism, that could, if we understand the universalization of a dream of individual success' be 'an implicit request for egalitarian society' (Jernej 2019: 23). This behaviour can be seen as a mere celebration of the material world, as hedonistic materialism, but the fact that it is taken to excess, makes it grotesque and makes internal contradictions visible. Between the songs' lines, we also glimpse the efforts and commitments needed to achieve the goals they have set for themselves.

Social mobility is expressed, for example, by pointing how music has been crucial for escaping peripheral and rundown neighbourhoods: 'I still think without rap, three on a motorbike / (...) Like when they were looking if I was driving around the block / But I was in the studio to get myself out of the block' (2020 02 01#2 Calmo, Shiva ft. tha supreme),[31] while concerning the transition to adulthood speed is emphasized: 'You don't know what I went through, I saw the chasm as well / (...) We are young, but grew up early, yah, yah' (2020 06 13#3 Powder (ft. Cape Plaza) – Tedua feat).[32]

Economic success is necessary, sought and celebrated as a marker of hegemony, but at the same time, it is represented as damaging one's integrity: 'These roads are cold but / I have a new Vuitton jacket, ah / You don't know how much it costs to be free /Much more than these machines, than this ice' (2019 10 12#3 Gigolò, Lazza),[33] as a cause of the loss of friends or reason for being envied and opposed 'It's not easy to be famous / Because when you make it, you've got everyone against you' (2020 22 28#3 Hollywood, Sfera Ebbasta).[34] The theme of success is only told so explicitly and persistently in the trap and hip-hop/rap genre.

Being emotionally detached

The fourth threshold that leads to hegemonic masculinity is the ability to withhold expressions of intimacy, to be emotionally detached, as the contrary equates to reveal vulnerability and weakness: 'I am a rockstar, rockstar / it won't be a bitch that kills me / My heart is cold (...) And if you try to warm it you risk melting it' (2018 02 27#2 Rockstar, Sfera Ebbasta).[35]

These lyrics evince a short-circuit, namely the desire to show awareness of one's real vulnerability in the face of strong emotions, which goes hand in hand with the fear of being fragile, because this emotion still does not have the full right of citizenship and must be concealed. 'She says, "Do you love me?" I tell her, "Only partly" I only love my bed and my momma' (2018 03 17#2 God's Plan, Drake).[36] Giving expression to one's emotional world means risking losing control, and crying is tantamount to losing sanity: 'They ask about our love, (…) I lost my reason, the reason is you / That you make me go crazy' (2018 11 24#2 Il cielo nella stanza, Salmo ft. Nstasia).[37]

An interesting space for agency also emerges in this fourth marker, since some trap and hip-hop/rap songs talk about one's pain, and emotional presence without losing hegemony: 'I cried too much for us, but all the tears I have / I gave you everything, you no, you were Crudelia De Mon' (2019 11 09 #3 Crudelia – I nervi, Marracash).[38]

Drugs are a constant presence in trap and hip-hop/rap songs, and they are praised not only as a tool for having fun or for amplifying reality: 'cherry red eyes / from the roof, Milan seems like Las Vegas to me' (2020 04 04 #3 le feste di Pablo, Cara ft Fedez)[39] but also as tools to stop conflict: 'Make a joint, and like that it passes/This fighting does not make us talk (no, no)' (2020 06 20#3 M' Manc Shablo, Geolier, Sfera Ebbasta);[40] to stop feeling, to protect oneself, to feel emotions: 'At school I had lean in my backpack, lean/I worried about uncertainty and embarrassment/I embarrass myself when I think of you' (2019 11 09#2 Supreme – L'ego, Marracash);[41] to stay calm: 'I smoke this missile that could pierce the marble/It's my secret to stay calm (babe)' (2018 04 28#3

Davide, Gemitaiz ft. Coez);[42] and to not suffer and not feel anxiety: 'Ay, you are already stoned and in any case breathe /Anxiety ate me, now no (now no) /I take two or three draws, Bro' what's up?' (2019 09 28#2 Fuori e Dentro, Gemitaiz e Madman).[43]

Emotional detachment evoked in trap and hip-hop/rap song, contrary to what is highlighted in classical literature (Chodorow 1978) is not about the relationship with the mother, still evoked as a reference figure and as a witness to their success: 'Look mum, no hands, I am a rock star /Mum you know that apart from you I don't love anyone else' (2018 02 27#2 Rockstar, Sfera Ebbasta);[44] 'The lyrics are true, you know mum is proud' (2020 04 04#2 Blue Car, Shiva feat Eiffel 65 Prod. Adam11).[45]

However, in the songs from other musical genres, representations of men who find the strength to call themselves fragile and intimidated openly are to be found. For example: 'I'm falling / In all the good times I find myself / Longin' for change / And in the bad times I fear myself" (2018 10 20#3 Shallow (A star is born), Lady Gaga and Bradley Cooper)[46] or in this Italian pop song in which it is permissible to cry because of love: 'A salty tear wets my cheek while / She caresses my face gently' (2018 10 06#1 Torna a casa, Maneskin)[47]; there are also representations of men who do not hide their vulnerability: 'And deep pain / Look how it overwhelmed my life / I will click my fingers and still find myself / To talk to you with my heart in my hand' (2019 09 07#3 Chiasso, Random).[48] As highlighted in the first part of this chapter, pop music genres display a wider repertoire of gender models.

The display of the will to do violence

The final marker frequently evoked in representations of hegemonic masculinities is the display of the will to do violence.[49] Sometimes, in general terms, it is a question of violent action, at other times of intimate partner violence. In the first case, the rhetorical apparatus of loss of control occurs, but it does not merely justify the violence and make those who act responsible for it, but it becomes an integral part of a mythopoeic construction, as emerges from these words: 'I enter into a cinepanettone, [comical Italian farce film] mhh / With a buckshot rifle, I am a madman, now I explode / I am under the tree of your chick, I give her cock with a bow' (2019 12 14#3 Charles Manson (Buon Natale 2), Salmo).[50] Violence is celebrated as an instrument of a male antihero against mass culture and its rituals ('Cinepanettone',[51]), who desecrates what have become empty symbols with his irreverent but performative sexuality (and therefore in line with hegemonical masculinity).

In other cases, the lack of rationality is again called into question, but the violence appears even more gratuitous: 'Bad vampire with fang, I sharpen it / See a dot you are on target / I kill you because I aim at you (...) / Don't Fuck with me, I'm crazy' (2019 06 15#1 Veleno 7, Gemitaiz, MadMan).[52]

The playful approach and the narrative of the point of view shot, reminiscent of the gamer's perspective, contribute to making male violence accepted even if not always acceptable (Hearn 2012). A significant aspect is that elsewhere attention is paid to the pervasiveness of violence in social reality, and is denounced by way of counterpointing normalization: 'Swimming among sharks for reward / Outside you only find free weapons and violence / Nothing that tells you about the consequences' (2019 12 07#3 Soldi in Nero, Shiva e Sfera Ebbasta).[53]

When control and violence inhabit intimate relationships, they are sweetened by the romantic frame. The reference to states of alteration here is presented as a justification of the desire to control his ex-girlfriend: 'There's a storm in my head / And this storm is not temporary / It's a mistake to call, a mistake who to love / (...) / And maybe I'll sound like a total idiot / When I send you this voice message / You never answer me' (2018 01 06#3 Irraggiungibile, Shade ft. Federica).[54]

The story told in this song is self-absolving and tends to normalize anger and emotional upset as answers to the partner's lack of reciprocity ('it is not temporary'), which is veiledly victim blaming ('You never answer me'). Certain cultural encrustations die hard. Even when the narrative is not re-victimizing, and therefore violence is not attributed to her conduct, the narrative is always denying responsibility:

'And it is not your fault / If all these right hand punches, right hand punches, right hand punches, to the wall do not make us return there / To those moments there / A when everything went full sail' (2020 10 24#2 Destri, Gazelles),[55] which is presented as being caused by jealousy: 'And I would fill that old boyfriend of yours with punches / (…) / And I would punch the guy who hits on you (...) / And there is a part of you that is part of me' (2020 09 19#3 Superclassico, Ernia).[56]

The violence here is even personified, has its own agency and so is externalized ('the right hand punch' that goes to the wall alone), and in any case it is justified in the name of jealousy. Jealousy, as widely shown in the literature (Magaraggia & Cherubini 2013; Giomi 2015a; Flood 2019; Cook & Walklate 2020; Lalli 2021), is capable of providing mitigating factors because, as a passion, it can be represented as an irrational and irresistible force and is positively connoted in our culture (see Chapter 3).

A notable point is that the number of songs that explicitly evoke violence is marginal (out of 119 songs, only 14 did this, so less than 12 per cent), and those that did offer a much less brutal narrative than emerged from previously conducted analysis (Magaraggia 2017). We cannot know what prompted these trappers to mitigate their violent rhymes. Perhaps it was the public discourse that increasingly criticized the songs and the more aggressive and humiliating lyrics, or it might have been a growing awareness amoung these singers and songwriters. This element is undoubtedly worth highlighting and observing in the years to come.

In other musical genres, there is no call for violence against women or other men. In the top of the charts over the last three years, there was just one song denouncing a story of abuse suffered by a little girl: 'At school she hid her bruises / Sometimes he [her father] beat her and yelled at her with satisfaction / Linda shivered when that worm came home drunk / And the first thing he would take off was only his tie' (2019 02 16#3 La ragazza con il cuore di latta, Irama).[57]

Women narrators and narrated women

The female models found in the analysed songs correspond to those highlighted by other research: in addition to the objectification of women is ubiquitous, to their use for men's sexual pleasure, to their description with derogatory statements as being disposable and discardable we also find references to women causing 'trouble' for men, to women as 'users' of men (as Adams & Fuller 2006), and to women portrayed as needing to be saved by men (Bal 2020).

Furthermore, there are women represented as being guilty of making their partners callous through their own infidelity:

'I'll stay alone, I don't give a damn about your problems / that time I introduced you to my parents as my girlfriend / but you are so fake / too fake' (2019 11 16#2 blun7 in swishland, tha Supreme).[58]

In other musical genres, we find women represented as indispensable, as a reference point capable of giving strength to the male protagonist: 'And I said, ooh, I'm blinded by the lights / No, I can't sleep until I feel your touch / I said, ooh, I'm drowning in the night /Oh, when I'm like this, you're the one I trust' (2020 02 08#1 Blinding Lights, The Weeknd).[59] This feminine indispensability is problematic, as it brings the couple dangerously close to a conception of love as bewilderment and self-sacrifice rather than as harmony and reciprocity (see Chapter 1). In addition, in order to become indispensable in heterosexual romances, women must be dedicated to a form of self-sacrificial altruism. In order to create indispensable links with the women who have to take care of them, men must delegate the dimensions of care and emotion to the feminine. Doing this means relegating yourself to a position of emotional addiction, which is essential and demeaning at the same time (Melandri 2011).

In the few songs written by a female songwriter or a group of male and female songwriters, we find tales of women who sit outside stereotypes, and it is interesting to see how rhetoric turns on being 'mad or bad'. We have women who recount themselves like a 'Bad Guy' 'I'm that bad type/Make your mama sad type/Make your girlfriend mad tight/ Might seduce your dad type/I'm the bad guy, duh' (2019 05 11#2 bad guy, Billie Eilish).[60] The term 'guy' is interesting: it signals the centrality of the discursive repertoire of masculinization to describe a transgressive woman. She disregards (feminine) gender expectations because her behavior causes discomfort in others or because of sexually inappropriate attitudes. The rhetorical procedure is reminiscent of what violent women are subjected to and what is said of them, namely, that they are 'not real women'. The alternative, as we know, is to argue that what they have committed is 'not a real crime'. This happens on the following track, 'She'll make you curse, but she a blessing/She'll rip your shirt within a second/You'll be coming back (...) you'll play along' (2019 02 09#2 Sweet but Psycho, Ava Max). In reality, the strongly eroticized figure of the femme fatale is mobilized here, which brings back female violence in the form of male desire and arousal.

However, there are also cases where mental illness is narrated with great authenticity and without any stereotypical reduction. 'And I try to tell it in every song / But people always think "you talk about other people" / But how cute you are / With this child's face (...) But the little girl grew too fast / Between the walls of a bedroom that began to be too small' (2018 12 01#3 Cherofobia, Martina Attili).[61]

Or again, we find women who play with their own desire: 'Hola little daddy, I don't speak Spanish / How cool you are, you understand that I say / You will be a tattoo that I will regret' (2018 07 07#2 Da zero a cento, Baby K)[62] and who talk about their erotic power: 'When I think about you I smile / And after that I don't care about anything / If my dress falls you lose yourself completely' (2020 07 25#3 A Un Passo dalla Luna, RoccoHunt e Ana Mena).[63]

In conclusion, this analysis shows the 'fine-grained production and negotiation of masculinities (and femininities) as configurations of practice' (Connell 2005, 840) in the most popular songs in Italy. The five thresholds of the transition towards hegemonic masculinities narrated in the music's symbolic world include the affirmation of one's own heterosexuality, 'status degradation ceremonies' (Garfinkel 1956) which are directed mainly towards women and less towards homosexual men, self-celebration attributable primarily to financial success, being emotionally detached (with only a few hegemonic men who permit themselves the luxury of talking about their pain and emotional presence), and finally displaying the will to do violence.

In the few songs written by a female songwriter or a group of male and female songwriters, we find tales of women who sit outside stereotypes (for example, those who play with their own desire), but who still fall into the rhetoric of 'mad or bad'.

Ladies' violence is a game, gentlemen's violence is deadly: The (ab)uses of gendered violence in advertising

Sveva Magaraggia

Advertising is 'central to the entire political economy of the media' (Gill 2007: 73) and also plays a pivotal role in our lives, as they 'sell values, images, and concepts of success and worth, love and sexuality, popularity and normalcy' (Kilbourne 1990: 2). Therefore, studying advertisements through a culturalist lens and a gender perspective is strategic to understanding, as Goffman (1976) teaches, what society considers banal and not noteworthy. In fact, through observing how advertisers use women's and men's positions and postures, we can understand 'something fundamental about relations between the sexes' (West 1996: 361).

The images of women and gender stereotypes shown in advertisements have been discussed extensively for five decades. There are numerous international studies (Borgerson and Schroeder 2002; Wolin 2003; Gill 2008; Rome et al. 2015; Grau & Zotos 2016; Huhmann & Limbu 2016; Bryła et al. 2018; McCartan & McMahon 2020; see Landreth Grau & Zotos 2016; Sandhu 2021 for a recent review) as well as Italian studies (Capecchi 1995, 2006; Buonanno 2005; Capozzi 2008; Capecchi & Ruspini 2009; Corradi 2012; Nadotti 2015; Bucchetti 2021) that have examined its contents and effects. It is now widely believed that advertisements are 'technologies of gender' (De Lauretis 1987), or further 'a locus of oppression, the carrier of images denigrating women by representing them as passive objects of the male "gaze"'(Stern 2003: 216) capable of defining our social existence. The social existence of women is still met today with advertising discourses that insist on proposing our own 'symbolic annihilation' (Tuchman 1978: 532), presenting women in stereotypical and demeaning ways (Reichert & Lambiase 2003; Gill 2007; Phillips & McQuarrie 2010; Carter 2011). The pervasiveness of graphic displays of sex in advertising is increasing (Reichert et al. 2007) despite the effectiveness of displaying attractive and sexualized women in adverts not being proven (Bower 2001; Davidson 2003; Bushman 2005; Lawrence 2021).

The explicit representation of male and female IPV in commercial advertisements has been studied less. Analysing advertisements with explicit violent references does not only mean contextualizing images in the sexualization process – made through the depiction of nudity and sexualized behaviour (Reichert 2003) – but also asking how visual and discursive effects of representations of violence serve to construct meanings about masculinity and femininity, and the relationships between them. Which little gendered stories do the adverts tell through the depiction of IPV?

Therefore, the cognitive questions that guide this case study are the following: does violence work differently according to gender or instead enjoy a universal representation? Does it maintain its role if a man or a woman does it? Which articulations of the gender order are deemphasized and which ones are accentuated?

From gender hyper-ritualization to pornification

To provide proof of the importance of analysing media, and advertising in particular, in order to understand the symbolic construction of the feminine and the masculine, we can recall a keystone text from second-wave feminism, namely *The Feminine Mystique*, written by Betty Friedan in 1963. Friedan's study gives ample space to the analysis of this sector of the cultural industry, as it 'shapes women's lives today and mirrors their dreams' (ibid., 62). Indeed, we know, from the numerous studies conducted, that the role of advertising is not only to show 'how men and women really behave, but how they should behave according to the conventional rituals approved by society: we witness a standardization, simplification and exaggeration (defined phenomenon of hyper-ritualization) of gender roles, which are not natural' (Capecchi 2006: 30).

It is women in particular who are subjected to a gendered gaze because, as Bourdieu explains,

> dependence on others (and not only men) tends to become constitutive of their being (...). Continuously under the gaze of others, women are condemned constantly to experience the discrepancy between the real body to which they are bound and the ideal body towards which they endlessly strive. Needing the gaze of others to constitute themselves, they are continuously oriented in their practice by the anticipated evaluation of the price that their bodily appearance, their way of bearing and presenting it, may receive.
>
> (2001: 66–7)

In his 1976 study of advertising images, Goffman registers a dominant presence in the 1960s and 1970s advertisements of female images that are subordinate and deferential towards men. Playing on the consonance between the attitudes towards children and women, the advertisements of the time convey a sense of weakness and need of protection of the latter. Women are often in subordinate positions (lying down or sitting, with their leg or torso bent), and this is designed to convey an idea of instability and vulnerability. Meanwhile, men are depicted in stable, solid positions, which signify they own the land on which they stand. Women's hands stroke, hold or caress (themselves or the objects they are advertising) while men's hands grab, grip or manipulate; the female's gaze is withdrawn, and the male typically looks directly at the audience.

The increase in women's liberty achieved through the political and cultural struggles of the 1960s and 1970s is echoed in 1980s advertisements (Bretl & Cantor 1988). Images of liberated women and career women sit side by side with housewives that were seen in the preceding years. Nevertheless, alongside 'female masculinization', there is an increase in women's eroticization. They are sexually objectified as if to compensate for the acquisition of more power and increased visibility in the public sphere: a dynamic observed at the end of Chapter 3, in relation to films and TV series of this same period. Advertising continues to focus on a language of subliminal seduction (Key 1973), even dressing women managers in short skirts and lace blouses (Capecchi 1995).

The erotic spectacularization of the female body in advertising has now become much more accentuated because part of the increasing sexualization of contemporary popular culture (Gill 2007; Evans et al. 2010) and because it has been welded to the phenomenon of culture pornification[64] (Power 2009) due to the growing influence of easily accessible and widespread online pornography on the imaginary of (young) men and women (Paasonen et al. 2007). The contemporary hypersexualization of girls and women, an apparent consequence of sexual liberation, has been read as potentially harmful and restricts rather than increases women's choices and empowerment. Indeed, Gill (2003) labels this process as sexual subjectification, stressing that women are complicit in their own objectification (Walter 2010; Magaraggia 2015). It is essential also to note that recently the male body has become an object of desire too. Thus there is an impact affecting men too who compare themselves to the images portrayed, and become more insecure in their self-perception (Gulas & McKeage 2000; Cross 2002; Rohlinger 2002; Schroeder & Zwick 2004; Gulas et al. 2010; Jung 2011).

Advertising and violence

A significant body of research has confirmed that different types of violence appear in the media. Violence is represented in the most diverse contexts and is shown with very different intensities (Wilson et al. 2002). Exposure to violence on television causes increased societal violence (Bushman & Huesmann 2001; Bushman & Anderson 2002;

Freedman 2002; Bushman 2005; Murray 2008). Men enjoy violent content more than women (Haridakis 2006; Reichert et al. 2007). Children exposed to physical dominance are encouraged to engage in aggressive thoughts and behaviours and are desensitized to violent acts (Ashworth et al. 2010; Brocato et al. 2010).

In-depth reviews conducted specifically on sexualized violence, echo that which has emerged from research on violence in general. Exposure to this gendered form of violence also reduces the criticism of men's sexual aggression against women (Bronstein 2008). Again, the financial benefit gained using these images is questionable, as violent and sexual content on television seems to inhibit memory formation and causes lower intentions to buy (Bushman 2005).

A subgroup of studies on the reception and impact of media violence, which focused mainly on television and press advertising (Scharrer et al. 2006; Jones & Cunningham 2008; Tamburro et al. 2004), demonstrated that sexualized violence in adverts has consequences on rape myth beliefs. Also, 'the narrative viewpoint of victim versus perpetrator, as well as the type of victim portrayed' (Leonard et al. 2012: 88) affect the public's judgment of the violence being represented, going so far as to justify it in some cases. Age and gender seem to influence responses to violent representations (Capella et al. 2010), showing that, similar to general violence, violence against women is more criticized by women than by men (Manceau & Tissier-Desbordes 2006) and more by an older audience than by young adults (Dahl et al. 2009).

A recent body of studies also analyses the reception of violence displayed in online and viral advertisements (Kim & Yoon 2014; Kay et al. 2015; Sabri 2017; Karpinska-Krakowiak 2020; Aramendia-Muneta et al. 2020; Manyiwa & Jin 2020), showed visible traces of an ongoing transformation. We can see a more equal representation of men and women in non-stereotypical activities and roles even if the main roles are still chiefly attributed to men, and decorative roles primarily to women.

A different group of researchers analyse the advertisement intentions (à la Griswold 1989) and look at the representations of violence in television adverts or in printed adverts. Analysing the intentions contained in the advertisements often translates into a content analysis. It first focused on television commercials, developing timely sampling and coding methodologies (Wilson et al. 2002; Huesmann et al. 2006; Rifon et al. 2010; Giomi 2015). For example, American Super Bowl advertising has been widely studied (McAllister 1999; Nail 2007; Alessandri 2009; Blackford et al. 2011), as it is the perfect sample for an in-depth qualitative analysis.

Significant attention has been paid to television advertisements targeted at children, which has shown that they also contain a significant amount of violence (Larson 2001, 2003; Shanahan et al. 2003; Ji & Laczniak 2007; Ashworth et al. 2010; Brocato et al. 2010).

Longitudinal research shows that sexually oriented images are widespread in magazine advertising and have become increasingly explicit over time (Soley & Kurzbard 1986; Benokraitis & Feagin 1995). Content analysis of the images used in printed advertisements uses a shared and solid methodology to study violence representations (Dahl et al. 2003; Andersson et al. 2004; Scharrer 2004; Scharrer et al. 2006; Phillips & McQuarrie 2010; Leonard 2012; Gurrieri et al. 2016), but according to Tim Jones, Peggy Cunningham and Katherine Gallagher, does not always manage to go 'beyond simple counts of violent advertisements or acts of violence' (2010: 17) and to offer a deep analysis.

His violence kills, hers arouses: The gender of violence

The study presented here is based on an in-depth qualitative microanalysis of printed advertisements. This special research situation, as Goffman masterfully teaches us, is 'something between cryptography and doing jigsaw puzzles' that makes sure 'that the pattern in question will be clear to the viewer' and will 'provide a sense of structure, a sense of a single organization underlying mere surface differences' (1976: 24–6).

The sample comprises forty-two international and Italian printed advertisements collected over the past nine years, explicitly depicting any type of IPV.[65] These advertisements contain both representations of male violence against women and women's violence against men and appear online or in printed magazines. Such purposive sampling, used to exemplify rather than to be representative, is common in qualitative studies and, although the images collected are not representative of gender behaviour in real life or of advertisements in general, they have a heuristic relevance because they appear 'normal' to us, because we do not perceive them as being peculiar or unnatural. The advertisements are for many different products, ranging from high fashion to clothes and household cleaning products. Here too, violent content, like 'the depiction of women in stereotypical contexts, continues to exist in advertisements for several product categories' (Capella et al. 2010: 37).

Two closely connected limitations of the proposed visual analysis are acknowledged: Firstly, the study is based on a relatively small number of advertisements. Secondly, the sampling is purposive, so the main goal is not to generalize research findings but rather to sketch a typology of the central representations of IPV committed by men and women so that they can be examined to understand if violence is gendered and what role it plays in the construction of masculinity and femininity.

The advertising images collected were first analysed in their manifest contents – their observable features – and then organized by their latent content – their themes – and explicit attention was paid to the type of violence represented and the person who committed it.

By organizing the image analysis by type of violence and by the aggressor's gender, a first incontrovertible characteristic emerges: femicide is recurrent and we do not find IPH where the murderer is a woman. Therefore, men are seen killing women because of their being women, but not women killing men because of their being men. This male over-representation as offenders and absence as victims differs from previous research (Gulas et al. 2010) that found that both offenders and victims of violence are more often men than women.

The predominant feature of all the images of femicides analysed is their systematic association with an idea of normality. As we have observed in other media forms (see Chapter 3), the murderous man's expression is usually smug, and above all, relaxed and unperturbed. It is not distorted at all by the violence just committed. The faces of the women victims, when they are seen, are not upset or disfigured, the scenes are 'clean', and we do not see signs of either a struggle or blood. This is true whether the violence takes place in a private or public space. It is that process of 'an-aestheticization' of removing pain,[66] which involves sanitizing and eroticizing lethal violence.

'Cadaverization' is typical of the contemporary media sphere. It is a process in which 'images and stories of dead women have both obsessive strength and a disciplinary function' (Clarke Dillman 2014: 1). These representations also have clear implications in terms of role models and gender relations: the highest expression of femininity is knowing how to accept violence, abuse and even death while remaining sexy and elegant. The advertisements representing a scene of femicide seem to result from that same necrophilic gaze detected in television series and music videos, a gaze that eroticizes murder by showing the corpses in lingerie and through the fetishization of passivity and (eternal) female silence (Borgerson & Schroeder 2002; Tait 2006; Clarke Dillman 2014). It plays with a 'grotesque' aesthetic (Phillips & McQuarrie 2010: 387) and makes violence sexy (Parikka 2015). A naked body is the fulfilment of patriarchal desire: an exanimate woman deprived of her agency who offers herself to the male gaze by enclosing Eros and Thanatos – love and death – in an exemplary synthesis, is the result of absolute domination (Bronfen 1992).

Therefore, these images are not limited to symbolizing male dominance over women and women's desire and masochistic pleasure in such extreme violence; instead, they promote a false idealization of female passivity and compliance (Bordo 1997; Minowa 2014).

Making violence against women glamorous is part of the process of normalizing this social fact. The multiple images of murdered women that we find in advertising daily seem to compose an infinite cautionary tale that reaffirms that femicide exists and is an integral part of women's experiences. Indeed, this realistic gaze has a reason to exist: femicide is widespread, as it is documented in every society and concerns many intimate relationships. Its diffusion is so widespread that, unfortunately, we are beginning to come to terms with it. It seems to have lost the power to upset and shake our sensibilities.

The image of women killing men because of their gender is a sporadic phenomenon and therefore less visible and marginal also in our common sense. It is not used in advertisements. One of the few adverts in Italy which shows the murder of a man by a woman is for a cleaning cloth by an Italian company. It was shown shortly after the original version, depicting a femicide,[67] received robust criticism.

Comparing the two images, which were constructed as equivalents, allows us to identify interesting gender stereotypes. When a woman carries out the murder, she is eroticized (dressed in a miniskirt, high heel and with her legs bent and knees together), while when the killer is a man, he is not represented as erotic (the only element that goes in this direction is the unbuttoned shirt). Instead he is shown as strong (his feet well planted on the ground, his forearm and muscular shoulder are in the foreground); the woman is eroticized even when she takes on the role of the victim (we see the bare legs of a helpless body lying on the bed and there is a clear reference to a recently consumed sexual act). Instead, the male victim is fully and elegantly clothed, and the context of his killing is devoid of erotic connotations (instead of a bed, he lies on the floor of an empty office), all focussed on the female assassin. These images slavishly refer to the hyper-ritualization of the feminine and the masculine found in advertising of the 1970s and 1980s and mentioned in the first part of this chapter.

The women in these adverts remain beautiful, feminine and seductive both when they are the victim and the perpetrator of the violence. This is obviously dependent on the persuasive and commercial purposes of advertising, which must provoke a narcissistic projection. However, concerning female-perpetrated violence, it is interesting to note the continuity between the contemporary advertising image and the representative tradition that originates with the femme fatale of the 1930s and 1940s, 'whose violence doesn't completely disrupt the traditional gender categories; on the contrary, it leaves much of femininity intact' (Neroni 2005: 26).

In addition to lethal violence, the world of advertising also stages a violence that humiliates and rapes, and the differences remain clear according to the gender of the perpetrators: men are rapists who act in violence without the consent of women, creating malaise and suffering, while women are dominatrixes, engaged in a sadomasochistic game, and therefore by definition consensual. The advertisements depicting the first type of violence have dark places as their backdrops, and the women's faces appear suffering and anguished. The men's faces are red, sweaty and contrite. The scenes depicting violence committed by women have light, neutral colours and contextualize it with serious, concentrated but satisfied facial expressions. As Yuko Minowa, Pauline Maclaran and Lorna Stevens (2014) found, in adverts where women exercise domination and humiliate men it is BDSM[68] play. The places where the different images are set, and the facial expressions, postures and contact between bodies unequivocally show these gendered differences.

This proposes a stereotypical view of sexuality, completely stripped of the emotional elements, and refers to articulations of gender relationships and violence also detected in other media forms: a female who is capable of acting violently does so only to satisfy the sexual fantasies of men and this is counterbalanced by an essentialist vision of male violence.

The same differences and same stereotyping are found if violence is committed by a group of men or of women. Men are built like predators and naturally violent (Katz 2003; Kellner 2008), they harm the women with whom they come into contact. Women are constructed as capable of acting violently only to excite the male gaze and relationships between the two genders are constructed as domination relationships, in which she appears as the 'conquered subject' (Gurrieri et al. 2016b: 1456) and he of the conqueror.

If, in other words, she can exercise violence, but it is only within the limits and purposes authorized by the male, he does not need to ask permission, because – it is the implicit assumption – violence is normal practice for him: precisely as happens in the news reports of IPV, which tend to omit motives and causes if the culprit is a man, but not if the culprit is a woman (see Chapter 3).

Female violence has a much stronger destabilizing force than male violence, and its discourse requires the simultaneous use of devices aimed at mitigating it. Female violence is sanitized and re-signified in an erotic game. Female violence undermines certainties our society defines about gender (Jack 2001), namely using aggression and violence to signal a paramount difference between males and females. Contextualizing female violence within the frame of an erotic game serves this end precisely – it normalizes it – and the effect is amplified not only by the advertising slogans and claims but also by the inclusion of erotic instruments in the scenes that belong to the sadomasochistic world. The visual vocabulary of fetishism appears in advertisements through a specific set of objects, such as high heels, black leather garments or whips (Schroeder & Borgerson 2003; Minowa 2014). The figure of the mistress or dominatrix, although imbued with power, aims to fulfil male fantasies, because it exists to satisfy them sexually.

The advertisements analysed do not use a playful interpretation and representation of male aggression, as found by Jonathan Schroeder and Janet Borgerson (1998). 'Mock assault' in which women do not show fear 'implying that male violence towards women is not only normal but also linked to masculine expressions of passion' (1998: 187) was not depicted in the contemporary advertisements analysed.

The advertisements examined clearly show how men's violence kills or humiliates, while women's violence excites. Even with this limit and the other limits already discussed, the contemporary advertising imagery seems to have definitively welcomed a representation of active female sexuality. However, at the same time, it also proposes the antidote to women's agency: the increasing sexualization of women's bodies. It is an ambivalence very similar to that observed in crime TV series, which compensate for the female detectives' violent agency with the eroticization of female corpses and the killing of women (see Chapter 7).

In today's advertising – we shall now observe it more closely – this compensation is increasingly entrusted to violent dehumanization and objectification (Morris & Goldenberg 2015): The female body is sliced up to expose it, or it is made it appear like pieces of butchered meat, as can be seen in many advertisements circulating online and in popular magazines. As Lauren Gurrieri, Jan Brace-Govan and Helene Cherrier (2016) state, the public is called to watch a glamourized representation of women as vulnerable beings, that 'combined with her zoomorphic construction as a slaughtered animal (...) is constructed as prey' (2016: 1456). In this extreme form of objectification, her personhood and human nature are denied, her agency and moral status erased (Nussbaum 1995; Loughnan et al. 2010), 'women-as-prey' are eaten and consumed (López Rodríguez 2009). As Hardy pinpoints, '[T]o be rendered as "animal" is, in the context of a deeply anthropocentric system, to be marginalized in the most fundamental of ways' (2014: 195).

Animalization in advertising uses the zoomorphic constructions of both men and women. However, it is no longer done just to mark women as creatures of emotion, nature, and desire (Ortner 1974), nor to stress their sexual and reproductive functions (Vaes et al. 2011; Morris & Goldenberg 2015), instead the advertisements we analysed show an interesting (thus worrying) gendered way of representation. If women are shown as slaughtered animals, dismembered – as a 'piece of meat' (Gurrieri et al. 2016: 1454) offered for public consumption, men remain active (Gulas et al. 2010; Tipler 2019) represented as a live bull, so to speak, ready to horn an eager blonde woman, dressed in red, waiting for him with open legs. This was the image chosen for a fashion advertising campaign made by Richardson, a photographer who in the past has worked with the most renowned names in fashion and whom the #MeToo movement removed from the scene.[69] If provoked by female desire, male animal strength responds with a dangerously violent sexuality, aimed at injuring and destroying. Active female desire, which excites men so much, must be punished.

Conclusion

Advertisements invite the public to participate and identify with the scenes that they propose. As we have already stated, they have a great deal of power to connote how our social relationships are represented and negotiated. They also provide meaning to them too by decreeing hierarchies and values (Sturken & Cartwright 2002; Capecchi 2006).

As this study shows, in addition to the known strategies of female subordination and male hegemony, the repertoire of contemporary advertising also incorporates other discourses, all of which are meant to sanitize and/or fetishize men's violence against women by depicting women as negligible objects: 'cadaverization' (Clarke Dillman 2014), 'dehumanization' (Volpato 2011) and 'animalization' (Vaes et al. 2011). By using violence, the advertisements outline a very specific gender order in which women are the object of male sexual desire, are represented as 'other', whose experiences include being killed or abused by a man, have to fear their home as it can become a place of death. They represent a masculinity that is pleased to kill a woman, and who, if provoked, no longer controls his own sexuality and legitimately transforms himself into a weapon of destruction. There is no grey area in this hierarchy, since even advertisements representing violent women re-domesticate them, placing them in well-defined roles and contextualizing them in sadomasochistic scenarios: violence does not break down nor mess up the gender order but strengthens it. Women's violence appears to be represented and therefore representable only if inscribed in the rhetorical frame of sadomasochism, consensual by definition. Female violence is fetishized rather than feared, which is the opposite of male violence.

Thus, depicting women's violence is legitimate only if in the service of male desire; the female desire, however marginal, when present is heinously repressed and narrated as guilty of causing men's loss of control.

Furthermore, by painting women as subjugated, animalized and dead, these adverts participate in the normalization of rape culture. The adverts analysed overwhelmingly portrayed white models, thus also erasing ethnic differences (similar to what emerged in Chapter 7).

The persistence of these stereotypical images of women and gender roles can be read as a resistance to change. Women's emancipation, the liberation of men from hegemonic masculinity, the redefinition of gender roles with a consequent breakdown of the dominant narrative regime is frightening, and all available cultural devices are used to reinforce the status quo. The glamourization of violence against women in advertising – which thus qualifies as an entire apparatus dedicated to the production of cautionary tales – seems to have the precise function of offering a warning, showing what happens to those who transgress the gender order.

The good news is that many groups that monitor advertising representations have recently emerged. In Italy, the Institute for Self-regulation of Advertising (IAP) has a category, 'women's image', that is the most used for the warnings of citizens. In the UK, the independent regulator, the Advertising Standards Authority (ASA) has, since 2019, promoted a ban on harmful gender stereotypes in adverts that covers both broadcast and non-broadcast media, including online and social media. The ASA argued for more robust regulation of adverts displaying stereotypical gender roles, following the publication of a report (2017) on *Depictions, Perceptions and Harm*. These institutions have translated empirical evidence from much policy research, research that has shown that gender stereotypes help limit young people's freedom of expression and limit their expressive potential.

The web is also populated by ethically alert women and men, not only, as Umberto Eco states, 'by imbeciles who previously spoke only at the bar after a glass of wine, without harming the community'. There are numerous pages on different social media active in monitoring and reporting offensive advertisements. This is a sign of increased gender sensitivity amoung social media users.

'Not real women' and 'real madmen': The double standard(s) of female and male-perpetrated IPV in factual entertainment

Elisa Giomi

Description of the case study

As we observed in Chapter 3, factual entertainment is one of the media genres where the representation of interpersonal violence is most often brought to the fore. Within the audiovisual realm, the subgenre of true crime documentary is currently the most popular: starting from the *Serial* podcast (2014–2016), the *Making a Murderer* (Netflix 2015) and *The Jinx* (HBO 2015) TV series, this subgenre has been renovated, adapting to narrative formulas, production standards and audience engagement modes typical of an on-demand mediascape. These, and many other similar audiovisual products released later, were analysed in relation to gender issues, including violence (see the illuminating book by Horek 2019). In particular, IPV also finds visibility in the spread of celebrity culture (McDonnell 2019), but the largest portion of the IPV narrative, especially that involving ordinary people, is still found in the hundreds of low-budget and globally circulating factual entertainment programmes that feed free-to-air TV and basic cable channels on a daily basis. The empirical case presented in this chapter permits the analysis of male- and female-perpetrated IPV, within this little explored, but decidedly relevant realm.

This case study is the documentary TV series *Who the (Bleep) Did I Marry? (WTBDIM?)*. It was broadcast for five seasons (2010–2015) on the US cable channel Investigation Discovery. Each episode lasted 22 minutes telling 'true stories in which some details have been altered'; they speak of 'lying spouses, criminals and thieves (…), of deep and dark secrets overlooked by unsuspecting wives'. Of a total of 83 total episodes, 68 have a woman as the protagonist/victim and a man in the role of antagonist/perpetrator (the 'who the bleep' in question). In the remaining fifteen cases, the roles are reversed. The stories are told through fictional techniques and materials (re-enactments by actors, with the word 'reconstruction' superimposed; storytelling techniques; musical accompaniment) and factual techniques and materials (archive materials; crime scene photos, police videos and videos from trials; and interviews with the protagonists, people close to them, the investigating authorities, lawyers and doctors). Like many other similar docuseries, the style of the programme is highly spectacular and sensationalized. Each episode is separated into three sections that follow the classic canons of storytelling: initial equilibrium, breakdown of the equilibrium, new equilibrium. The first phase tells the story of the protagonist and his/her partner and ends with a commercial break. The first warning signs suggesting the partner was not what they seemed, and which are normally underestimated by the protagonist, are also shown during this phase. Even when these signs are alarming enough to prompt the protagonists to distance themselves, the situation remains apparently ordinary. After the commercial break, the second phase begins. It shows the breakdown of the equilibrium. It is as long as the first phase, and in the cases we will examine, includes violence or more often culminates with it. This is where the 'true nature' of the partner emerges. The final phase is very brief and films the survivor in their current city of residence, telling the audience of their newfound balance, often in the form of a 'moral of the story'. Unlike the protagonist and the people close to him/her, the audience is omniscient thanks to the prologue of each episode and a preview of what is to come after the commercial break.

The type of violence staged and the concept of the program are of great interest when comparing the representation of male- and female-perpetrated IPH. The focus on (attempted) murder responds to the sensationalist logic illustrated in Chapters 1 and 3, at the expense of other and far more common offences. At the same time, the seriousness of the crime is likely to mobilize many of the representative strategies outlined in Chapter 3, providing an opportunity to observe these strategies 'in action'. The concept of the programme, which involves an 'obscure' and unsuspected side of the antagonist emerging, and which is predicated as his or her 'true identity', is part of the same sensationalist logic. In addition, this approach, which involves the stigmatization of the perpetrator, required the programme makers to exclude cases where there were mitigating factors for the violence. This produces a bias especially on the female front: it excludes violence exercised as self-defence or as a reaction to past abuses and intimate terrorism, which nonetheless are the most recurring motives underling female-perpetrated IPH.

In contrast, the construction of the perpetrator as 'evil' and the high degree of standardization of the narrative process leading to this construction allows background variables to be kept 'fixed'. Other fixed variables are represented by the type of crime and its motives, which we have selected so that we can compare female and male perpetrators.

Research questions, corpus and analysis methodology

The presence of fixed variables, that is, form (the dramaturgical mechanisms of the program) and content (similar stories), allows us to effectively explore our research questions: is the stigmatization process gender sensitive? Does the discursive order underling the demonization of the perpetrator's 'true' identity remain the same for males and females? Which figures, which narrative themes and which de-responsabilization/justification strategies (if any) are deployed in representing violence and its perpetrators? Lastly, we will analyse the features of the general discourse on IPV developed by *WTBDIM?* as well as the frames that are used and their implications.

We considered all of the episodes where the female antagonist was violent: nine out of fifteen cases (one case of murder, eight cases of attempted murder). The male antagonists were violent in twenty-nine out of sixty-eight cases, with attempted murder in fifteen of them. We selected five cases that presented exemplifying characteristics, and at the same time were comparable to female cases, both in terms of the charges and motives: revenge due to abandonment is at the base of four of the nine attempted murders committed by women and eleven of the fifteen committed by men; economic reasons and/or desire to 'get rid' of the partner appear in four cases out of nine and in four cases out of eleven, respectively. Child custody is a motive in only one female case. We chose to start with female violence and dedicate more space to this in order to compensate for its under-representation in the previous empirical chapters. Therefore, we will first analyse the episodes with a female antagonist, exploring how the stigmatization premised by the programme develops. We will then look at the episodes in which the violence is carried out by a man, focusing the comparison on the representation for the offender, the motive as well as the dynamics of the crime.

The methodology and analysis grid were inspired by the work of Lorenzo-Dus (2009), one of the first to focus on television discourse and, which has greater relevance to our analysis, on non-fictional American and British programmes (newscasts, documentaries, reality shows, etc.). This work falls within the tradition, which from the 1990s onwards, through the contributions of Scannell (1991), Fairclough (1995), Hutchby (2006), marks a returning interest in the spoken discourse of broadcasting. Following this approach, we transcribed the fourteen episodes into a four-column grid. In the first column we reported the names of those speaking and in the second a transcription of what they said, while the other two columns were used to account for the interaction between the verbal code and the iconic code. In particular, the third column contains the description of the images that accompany the 'discourse', their grammar (composition, framing, and angle) as well as syntax (camera movements, construction of sequences, editing solutions). In the last column, which is used to provide supporting information, we included screenshots of key images related to the most relevant elements for our analysis, mainly the antagonists and crime sequences.

In the following section, which is dedicated to female-perpetrated IPV, we conducted a detailed analysis of an episode-type, identifying general operating 'laws', which we then applied to the rest of the episodes. In so doing, we used the tools of socio-semiotics and, in particular, the methodology deployed by Venäläinen (2016) in the aforementioned study of Finnish tabloids (see Chapter 3, De-responsibilizing the perpetrator and minimizing violence). This study attempts to dissect how the identities of female suspects/perpetrators of violence are constructed. It therefore provides useful categories to analyse the discursive production of the 'true nature' of women and men charged with (attempted) murder. Applying the categories of Greimas's semiotics (1985), Venäläinen (2016: 265–7) believes it is possible to formulate a 'continuum of agency' on the basis of 'modalizations' (modalities) that appear to dominate in the narratives of violence: an (in)ability to avoid committing violence, linked to factors that appear to be beyond the control of the perpetrator (e.g. drinking, temporary or permanent states of impairment) and therefore implying a low level of agency; an (in)competence to avoid doing violence (due to the lack of skills and knowledge acquired through learning); a willingness to do violence, denoting stronger agency and often being associated with the competence to deceive. Neither inability nor incompetence in avoiding violence implies intentionality, therefore they do not result in the femininity of the subject who exercises the violence being brought into question. Vice versa, the willingness to do violence points towards the actor's internal desires, linking violent action most firmly to their identity, which therefore appears to be at odds with (a normative definition of) femininity.

Female-perpetrated IPV

This section is dedicated to the nine female antagonists who killed or attempted to kill their partner. A first consideration relates to their profile and the circumstances of the crime. With one exception none were unemployed or belonged to the most marginalized groups in society or suffered from substance abuse disorder. The attempted murder did not occur during an argument that escalated into lethal violence, nor did it happen after a night of drinking. These conditions are, for a large proportion of women's IPH, the individual and situational characteristics. However, due to their ordinariness, they attract no or little news coverage (see Chapter 3). These characteristics are also not compatible with *WTBDIM?*'s concept, which relies on staging sensational/atypical cases ('stories at the limit' is the programme's tagline). Indeed, immediately from the introduction, or during the narration, the women are marked as deviant as a result of past bad habits (Astrid, Tina, Lisa W.) or harassing behaviour against previous companions (Melissa, Jodi, Meri).

Each episode's prologue explains what will be unveiled during the programme, introducing the women with the standardized formula of 'something hidden behind something else'. In all nine cases we examined, the appearance is that of normative femininity, i.e. conforming to traditional gender roles and/or aesthetic ideals (Dorothy Luther is a 'shy sweetheart', Lee Ann Armanini a 'happy mother' and Tina Pomroy a 'perfect girl', Melissa Stredney, Andria Stanley, Meri Jane Woods, Jodi Arias, Astrid K. Tepatti and Lisa Whedbee are said to have a 'charming smile' or a 'beautiful face').[70] The dark side is even more unambiguously portrayed in the descriptions of wickedness: 'a diabolical woman' (Lisa, Dorothy), 'pure evil' (Andria), 'a diabolical plan' (Jodi, Astrid), 'a sinister plot' (Lee Ann), 'a dark secret' (Melissa). At best we find only 'demons' (Tina). In short, the programme's concept for the females is applied didactically: they truly are 'devils'. Nevertheless, as we will see in the following sections, the 'evil figure' the antagonists personify are diverse.

Evil manipulators and *femmes fatales*

As many as seven of the nine perpetrators analysed mobilize the figure of 'evil manipulator'. It applies above all to the woman acting in a couple (see Chapter 3, Exorcizing violence: Othering and pathologizing). In our sample this only happens in three cases (Astrid, Lisa W. and Lee Ann), but the emphasis on the antagonist's deception is strong and pervasive in the others as well. However, the object of the deception varies: five of the 'devils' (Melissa, Andria, Meri, Jodi and Astrid) have always been what they prove to be/have always intended to hurt, cleverly concealing both things; the other two women (Lisa W., Lee Ann) instead undergo a transformation which the viewer witnesses, and which ends with a conspiracy against their husbands.

In three of the episodes (Melissa, Meri and Andria) the programme's elementary structure and the Manichaean vision are slightly complicated. In the initial phase a particularly pronounced semiotic instability is presented. The warning signs presented here are in fact minimized or justified as factors relating to mental/emotional fragility, thus offering a taste of the rhetorical functioning of the stock 'mad' narrative used to frame the women's crimes. We will now examine a paradigmatic episode.

In this episode, the protagonist is Jamie Hart, a 27-year-old. The first image we are given of his partner Melissa, a young university assistant, is an old photo of her smiling with him. From this moment on, and for the entire duration of the first segment, Melissa's body and voice are those of an actress portraying her. The reconstruction starts from their first meeting, which is retraced from Jamie's point of view. From his perspective Melissa appears as a 'beautiful girl'. She is always smiling, although in some brief moments her image is distorted and curved, framed through a wide-angle lens with a 180-degree angle (fish-eye), as if we were observing her from the peephole in a door. This is a common stylistic solution in the programme, and clearly suggests the notion of suspicion regarding the partner's identity.

In this first phase of the programme (initial equilibrium), Melissa begins to show the first inexplicable and occasionally aggressive behaviours, even being physical, towards Jamie. The causes are presented as problems with anxiety, depression and especially instability which arose after a miscarriage of triplets. The violent female subject's reduced responsibility is not only produced through her pathologization (anxiety, depression), but more specifically by sexualizing such pathologization. This is the precise pattern that connects female deviance to 'dysfunctions' that are linked to the reproductive cycle. As we saw in Chapter 2, such a pattern has a history of over a century and a half. Nevertheless, the programme's concept, which is based on the demonization of the antagonist, requires that these initial mitigating factors are invalidated and the antagonist can be attributed full responsibility for his/her actions. The transition from the first to the second phase of the episode can, in fact, be interpreted as a passage from mad to bad or, to use the conceptual apparatus of Venäläinen, as a passage to a modalization of violence that implies stronger agency.

In the first phase, the violence is presented as the subject's inability to avoid committing it due to the intervention of external factors. In Melissa's case, her mood has been altered by depression and miscarriage. In the corpus of articles analysed by Venäläinen, the modalization of inability is more frequently found in the coverage of non-lethal forms of violence. *WTBDIM?* is no exception, as in the first phase, Melissa's attacks are limited to minor ones. Also, this modalization attributes a low degree of responsibility for the violence, therefore it never implies questioning the femininity of those carrying it out. In the preview preceding the commercial break, it is said that Jamie, who has thus far been inclined to justify his beloved, must come to realize 'that his unhappy girlfriend was not only depressed, but was also a monster'. We are shown the second documentary image of Melissa: a mug shot in which the girl appears abject and sinister. This serves to introduce the second phase, that of the equilibrium breaking down, in which the violence is presented as an explicit 'will to do harm' (in Venäläinen's terms), thus revealing Melissa's 'true identity'.

In this phase, it becomes clear that the specific figure of evil embodied by Melissa is not that of the monster but that of evil manipulator. We observe Jamie increasingly distance himself from Melissa and the woman beginning to persecute him in an increasingly insistent and aggressive manner until she stalks him, forcing him to get out of his car. Then she shoots him in the head in cold blood, causing him to lose an eye. Jamie reconsiders the past in the light of this gesture, which triggers the process of revealing 'Melissa's misleading nature'. The woman seems to have lied about every aspect of her identity, and the entire dissimulation process seems to be gendered. In the programme's reconstruction, Melissa's competence to deceive – which is strictly associated with the modalization of violence as a will to do harm – involves the capacity for imitating a traditional gender identity. In the 'initial equilibrium' phase, alongside the first displays of aggression, Melissa has faked an entire repertoire of traits and behaviours associated with normative femininity: emotional fragility, vulnerability, the need for male protection. More importantly, she simulated a pregnancy, which represents the very core of femininity from an essentialist point of view. This was all just a lie 'to keep him tied to her', Melissa's aunt suspects. Of course, as there had not been a pregnancy, Melissa feigned her miscarriage which, let us remember, was presented as an external factor responsible for Melissa's inability to avoid doing violence. In short, this modalization of violence, along with the demeanour of traditional femininity, turns out to be fake, while the true nature of the social actor has been clearly revealed: that of being a violent woman.

Venäläinen (2016: 267) notes that the violent woman's ability to deceive is presented by the tabloids as a tool both to impart the violence and to avoid being accused. Melissa first tries to conceal the evidence and then defends herself from the charge of attempted murder by exhibiting her medical history of being admitted to psychiatric institutions and a diagnosis of bipolar disorder. She 'exploits her mental illness to achieve her goals', that is, to 'ruin my life' Jamie reports. Put differently, Melissa continues to simulate being mad, while Jamie/the programme unmasks her as being bad. She passes from the (deceptive) identity of 'feminine woman' to (the true) identity of 'violent woman' (Venäläinen), from 'not criminal' to criminal, and therefore 'not woman' (Worral 1990: 31). All of the figures of bad, including the evil manipulator, work precisely to affirm that criminal/violent women are not 'real women' (see Chapter 2, Etiologies based on biological determinism and sexuality: How (and why) to exorcise female violence).

Two other cases use exactly the same format, in which the disclosure consists of the passage from (apparently) mad to (truly) bad, from zero responsibility to full attribution of guilt. Such a passage is based on the same discursive order implied in Melissa's case: that of reproduction. Both the mitigating factors initially suggested (which, again, are all versions of mad) and the manipulative arts (revealing the antagonist as bad) relate to the reproductive cycle. In the prologue, Andria is defined as a 'sick person'. She uses a first pregnancy (we are made to doubt the veracity of this, thus we believe it is also contrived in this case) in order to get married. The subsequent miscarriage and rape suffered in the past serve to simulate mental instability and above all feminine fragility. 'Crazy' Meri masks her outbursts behind hormonal problems related to childbirth, and then traps her husband, who has plans to leave her, with a second pregnancy. Andria's failed attempt to kill her husband and the serious injuries that Meri inflicts on hers reveal the true, lethal nature of the two. So they resort to manipulative arts, exploiting motherhood – a 'power available to women' according to the Public Prosecutor in Meri's case – for their retaliation. They fabricate repeated accusations of sexual abuse of their children by their husbands ('if children were involved, all she had to do was cry wolf and the judges ended up believing her', explains Andria's husband). In the first part of the programme, both Andria and Meri were also made to appear 'simply' mad; in the second part of the programme, Andria is explicitly attributed with 'true cruelty' and Meri a 'will to do evil'. From 'mad' to 'bad'.

The narrative trajectory of the other four evil manipulators – Jodi, Astrid, Lisa W. and Lee Ann – lack the mad phase, nonetheless reproduction and more generally sexuality, remain central to the discursive construction of the 'bad'. The four women, all described as beautiful, exploit their sexuality in different ways. One uses sex to trap a lover who abandoned her and then kills him (Jodi); one wins over her husband and traps him with a baby boy, only to then plan his murder and get money from it (Astrid). Whereas Lisa W. and Lee Ann are depicted as happy brides and mothers: they actually embody a traditional gender identity in the beginning. We witness their transformation and estrangement from their husbands, which after separation evolves into the aim of killing them for financial gain and/or child custody. And yet even these two women can be classified as evil manipulators: Lisa W.'s and Lee Ann's murderous plans rely on their ability to stage their previous identity of devoted brides and conceal their true, violent identity. The two women convince their husbands they want to save the marriage and lure them into murderous traps, in which seduction and red negligees play a central role. On the visual level, the eroticization of female violence is evident as is the analogy between evil manipulators and the stereotyped deadly dolls that dominated Hollywood cinema at the beginning of the 1990s (see Chapter 3, Exorcizing violence: Othering and pathologizing).

However, it is only Jodi who is represented as a *femme fatale*. There are similarities to the way Amanda Knox was represented. In Jodi's case too, beauty was combined with remarkable coldness and self-control that was shown at the trial ('whenever she cried it seemed to be a show for the cameras'). Jodi was assigned the harshest sentence: the death sentence for first degree murder. Of course, she is the only one that actually killed her partner, and moreover in a heinous way (twenty-seven stab wounds, a slit throat and a gunshot to the head), but we know that even 'the appropriateness and authenticity of the reaction to crime' count a great deal in how the judicial system responds to women accused of IPV (Frigon 2006: 11).

Monsters and bad mothers

Both Dorothy and Tina initially appear as women with a number of feminine virtues, but over time they become despotic and violent, to the point of hiring hitmen to murder their husbands after their separations. Their transformation also affects their physical aesthetic. The narrator and photos depict 'beautiful' young brides, while as the episode progresses they finish embodying two different monstrosities. Due to sudden weight loss during the trial and excessive cosmetic surgery, Dorothy passes from being a grotesque fat lady adorned in leopard-print clothes to a real witch. As for Tina, the archive images show a scruffy-looking woman with unkempt hair and a scowl: a hag. The re-enactment by an actress portraying her enhances this effect. Although distorted photos are also used in the case of Melissa, the insistence with which those of Dorothy and Tina are shown, the close-ups of denigratory details and the ferocity with which they are ridiculed have no equal. They are reminiscent of the 'status degradation ceremonies' (Garfinkel 1956) directed at women which we cited in Chapter 4 in relation to rap and hip-hop lyrics.

Such a commitment, on the part of the programme, to the 'ritual destruction' of Dorothy and Tina is interesting, especially because the violence they partake in is not as serious: they do not act in first person but hire others for the murders. However, their plans are foiled by investigators. The penalties are also lower (five years for Dorothy; 22 months for Tina) as is the extent of their deceitfulness: it does not concern their identity, as they do not pretend to be anything other than what they are, but they transform over the course of the narration, like Lisa W. and Lee Ann. Moreover, unlike the latter, they do not even attempt to conceal the transformation by restoring their old identity of devoted wives. More generally, Dorothy and Tina are the only ones who do not implement any kind of deception that uses their bodies as sexual tools.

Paradoxically, this becomes an aggravating circumstance: their wrongdoing is precisely the pronounced transgression from gender norms. Dorothy and Tina are two viragoes in body and spirit. The first plunders her husband's possessions because she is moved by 'control mania' according to her sister, as well as excessive greed, a characteristic that greatly conflicts with the feminine. Tina's masculinity is even more pronounced as she falls into her past habit of drug addiction, joins a band of motorcyclists and adopts a dissolute lifestyle and butch clothing.

Furthermore, while the evil manipulators are presented as young and beautiful, Dorothy and Tina are older women who age and physically 'degenerate' during the episode.

Lastly, five out of nine cases mobilize the figure of the bad mother. Tina is shown living with her children in a deteriorating state and her custody is revoked. Lee Ann, Astrid and Meri are guilty of seriously neglecting their children. Meri and Andria use them to falsely accuse their husbands while Lisa W. even goes so far as to abandon her daughter with Down syndrome and restart her life elsewhere. However, only Tina is represented as a 'monster', despite the neglect of her children being part of the more general loss of control over her life. Moreover, Tina is the only one out of the nine that corresponds to an identikit of female perpetrators of IPH which we discussed in Chapter 2: at the time she commissions the hit on her husband Tina is unemployed, belongs to a marginalized group, and suffers from a substance abuse disorder which she overcame in the past, but which now returns to afflict her. Evidently, to be ungainly and masculine constitutes an unforgivable crime in the moral universe of the programme, a fault capable of obscuring any other attenuation.

This permits us to delimit the difference between the evil figures analysed in this section. Both the 'monster' and the evil manipulator – the diabolical woman who goes against her 'natural' feminine orientation to do good by others – serve to negate that the woman could 'act as a woman'. But they imply a different degree of transgression of the feminine: greater in the first case, lesser in the second. As a confirmation to that, the subtle and indirect art of manipulation has always been the most common form of aggression practised by women, because for them it is more admissible than physical aggression (Gilbert 2002: 1279). Instead, the narrative of mythical monsters is triggered precisely 'by adhering to the ideological constructions of deviant femininity' (Jewkes 2004: 125).

Our analysis seems to offer proof on the functioning of the principle of *aut aut* (either or), which positions women as either victims or victimizers in relation to violence. The episodes with Andria and

Tina speak of 'demons' from which the two were never able to free themselves: in Andria's case this is rape, which the programme passes as proof of the woman's manipulative arts but which no one actually denies; in Tina's case the demon is a long and painful past as a heroin addict. These elements do not in any way mitigate the stigmatization of the antagonists. As we note in Chapter 3, Exorcizing violence: Othering and pathologizing, in the binary logic of popular culture (and not only) when the narrative of the victimizer prevails, the status of victim is denied, which instead would help make the behaviour of the offenders more understandable.

A final note: the deviance of all the antagonists, whether evil manipulators or 'monsters', is enhanced by the contrast with their partners, depicted as stable and loyal husbands and above all, model fathers. In fourteen episodes out of fifteen, that is, all those in which a couple with children is featured, end with images that celebrate the dedication of the male protagonists to their children or grandchildren. We see them pushing swings, helping with homework and at the stove, often struggling with the demands of parenting. Parenting requires sacrifices but has also become their main reason for living. As we shall see in the next section, the theme of paternity is also featured in the episodes where it is the men who impart violence.

Comparison of female and male IPV

Episodes with a male antagonist are distinguished by heinousness. This could contribute to the false belief that victims and perpetrators of IPH are different from 'normal' people. However, compared to the episodes with female antagonists, the motives in the stories selected by the programme are in line with those told in the statistics (see Chapters 1 and 2), which indicate revenge for having been abandoned as the most recurring motive underlining femicide. This is also the motive behind all of the attempted femicides staged by *WTBDIM?* with the exception of Billy Cox's case, whose motive was intolerance of his wife.

Another element of adherence to reality is that lethal violence is not represented as being 'out of the blue' but as the result of an escalation of abuse. This is functional to the production of increasing tension targeted by the program, but at least it prevents misrepresenting IPH as an unpredictable event. Similarly, the need for condemning the perpetrator leads to avoiding the pattern of conflict of the couple, which in news coverage of IPV is found to convey a sense of mutual combat and responsibility (Chapter 3, De-responsabilizing the perpetrator).

In *Scarred by Love* (2×21) the successful actor Shelley Malil stabbed his wife Kendra twenty times while she was with her new companion; in *Dangerous Consequences* (5×10) Darrell Wilson stalks his wife Rachel McFarland along with their children and her new companion, until he kills the latter and rapes Rachel (rescued at the last minute by the police before being killed). Audrey Mabrey *(Hearts Afire,* 3×3) was also subjected to sexual violence, which only led to even worse things in the end: Chris Hanney, whom she left after discovering his lies and gambling addiction, rapes her, beats her with a hammer and lastly sets her on fire. Cecil Torrence (*Torrence the Tyrant*, 3×17) is no exception: he beats his wife Lisa Jefferson for 30 minutes and finally shoots her several times while the woman begs him to spare her, for the sake of the children. Lastly, after 40 years of beating his wife Carolyn, Billy Cox *(Till Death Do Us Part*, 2×6), one day decides to torture her and tries to kill her with the exhaust gas of his car and finally commissions a person he met in prison to murder her.

This brief summary in no means conveys the true horror of the protagonists' acts, which are decidedly more heinous than their female counterparts (with the sole exception of Jodi). It is therefore surprising that many of the forms of stigmatization detected in the female group are lacking in this one.

Only two cases (those of Cecil and Darrell) are introduced in the prologue using the usual key of 'something hidden behind something else', but in the narrative development, the overturning from courteous, gallant, solid and devout men to obsessive, possessive, ferocious men, is not so much recounted as a revelation, as is common in the female cases, but as a transformation. Chris appears to be the only manipulator, a skill he uses to conceal his true identity and to try to avoid the consequences of violence (similar to the depiction of all the female devils).

In the initial segment, in line with the programme's format, the first warning signs are depicted, and the partner minimizes or justifies them. With the female antagonists, these signals, aggression included, were initially excused based on disturbances connected to the reproductive cycle. For the males, there are various mitigating circumstances, but the main one concerns work: having been fired is presented as a reason for the change and increasing aggressiveness of Darrell and Cecil, while Billy's wife sees his highly stressful career as a plausible reason for his 'temper tantrums'. The implications of such a narrative are evident in terms of the models of gender roles: the professional dimension is strengthened as a key feature of identity, an elective area of symbolic investment for men, to the point that what happens in this dimension can even justify offensive behaviours. None of the female devils were allowed similar mitigating circumstances. A double standard along gender lines is also found with regard to the second mitigating circumstance in the men's IPV: the consumption of alcohol is mentioned in four cases out of five, and Audrey will go as far as to forgive Chris's first attempted rape because it resulted from drinking. For female perpetrators of IPV, drinking is presented as an aggravating circumstance, as is the case with Tina.

The motives for attempted murder are also presented very differently for the males and females. For the men, use is made of some well-known forms for eliminating responsibility: in four cases out of five, it is said that they acted as 'real madmen', despite repeated references to the premeditated nature of their act. In three cases their behaviour is referred to as rash misconduct (Darrell and Cecil) and in one, a state of permanent emotional alteration (Billy's 'deep-rooted anger'). In the press, emotional stress is much more commonly attributed to female IPV than to male IPV (Carlyle et al. 2014: 10); instead, the women of our sample never benefit from this extenuating circumstance and are all depicted as authors of clearly woven plans.

Indeed, this is the most significant aspect: the narrative of the diabolical, which one would expect to prevail given the concept of the programme – and which in fact characterizes all the female cases – is weakly summoned here: 'there was something sinister in him' is the maximum demonization in the men's cases, even in that of Billy who tortures his wife and is called an a**hole by his own daughter. The only exception is Chris ('evil took hold of him'). Chris, Cecil and Darrell are called 'monsters', but only once in all three cases, and in the last one the same term is paired with the reference to jealousy ('jealous monster'): evoking the romantic frame. This term is likely to mitigate the perpetrator's culpability. Unlike the episodes featuring women as antagonists, those featuring men never resort to visual expedients aimed at altering (in the direction of monster or devil) the men's physicality, even when they do not meet the Western aesthetic canons of youth, thinness, or 'whiteness' (Billy is an elderly gentleman; Chris is a stout African American).

The figure of the devoted father not only contributes to praising the male victims of IPV but also the male perpetrators of IPV: Shelley is dedicated to Kendra's children, Darrell is loving with his own, Cecil is a 'perfect househusband', while Chris 'would do anything for his son'. Photos are shown depicting the protagonists in tender scenes with their children. On the other hand, the faults and defects of these same fathers are completely ignored, while the theme of the bad mother, as we have seen, was an integral part of the women's stigmatization: motherhood is a given and an obligation, to the point that being female coincides *tout court* with it; paternity, on the contrary, is a choice and an opportunity, and therefore being an 'unsatisfactory' father (Boyle 2005: 118) is not as serious.

One common theme in the discourse regarding both the male and female perpetrators of IPV derives from the peculiar ideology of the programme, which has its cornerstone in the American Dream: economic stability, social mobility and professional ambition are the qualities that seduced the unfortunate wives of Cecil and Billy. The wives are eager to 'pursue the American dream' with their husbands and 'earn everything through their own hard work'. Similarly, Jodi's role as a professional woman contributes to her charm (while Dorothy is criticized for being reluctant to 'let go of her husband's bank account'). Strength, independence and ambition are no longer valued negatively, as was true in the articles on the female victimizers and victims of IPV in the 1990s analysed by Wykes (2001: 157) when, as an effect of the backlash, career women were represented as unhappy or as materialistic bitches led astray by feminism. Over 20 years later and 'thanks' to neoliberalism, popular media culture appears to be feminist-friendly, 'appears' being the key word here.

The frames and discourse of *WTBDIM?* relating to domestic violence

The premise of the *WTBDIM?* discourse on IPV resides in the choice of extreme cases. This choice suggests that the protagonists are 'abnormal', far from average, and suggests both the reading and the solution have an individual key (that is, within an episodic frame, see Chapter 3, Deresponsibilizing the perpetrator). The violence of the programme's male and female antagonists is in fact presented as a result of aberration, but in very different forms. This leads us to the fundamental question of our analysis centred around the gender-sensitive nature of the process through which male and female 'devils' are discursively constructed.

Everything in the depiction of the female figures serves to mark their atypical nature, their abnormality as women, as indicated by the same figures of evil manipulator and mythical monster. Whereas, for the men, this aspect of evil is much less pronounced: despite the greater degree of brutality, they are allowed extenuating circumstances (rashness, folly, jealousy, alcoholism) that the women have been denied, even with the same motive and type of history. The 'monsterification', on the other hand, occurs in three cases out of five, but in softer forms than in the female counterparts. Above all, the monster figure works differently for males who commit IPV. They are seen as being an exception to the entire species, rather than an exception to their gender. We are told that men perpetrating IPV did not 'act as men' (human beings), but they still remain 'real men'. Whereas women perpetrating IPV are an exception to their gender and are portrayed as not 'real women'. The configuration of the nexus of gender and violence present in this programme highlights (and reproduces) the notion of male as the canon, the norm of mankind (see Chapter 2, The contribution of sociology and feminist criticism: The gender lens and the deconstruction of the male as the norm). However, this configuration presents ulterior elements worthy of note too. The woman-killers or aspiring woman-killers featuring in *WTBDIM?* are not stigmatized for having broken the taboos related to masculinity (on the contrary, they are praised for their paternal qualities). They are stigmatized, generally for having broken the law. That is, the only discursive context for male violence is crime, while for women it also includes that of conformity to gender roles and above all to normative sexuality, which in *WTBDIM?* becomes the dominant discursive order for female-perpetrated IPV. The coherence of the discursive patterns across the ages is striking, as the same double standard can also be found in the English press of the 1990s (Wykes 2001: 159). In doing so, the programme offers a paradigmatic demonstration of the gendering power of violence and its media representations. On the one hand, violence is dissociated from the female gender because it invalidates those being violent from belonging to it, thus having a disciplinary effect as a cautionary tale for women. On the other hand, by omitting any relationship between masculinity and violence, the legitimacy and normality of male violence are perpetuated: symbolic concealment always determines the reproduction and naturalization of that which is concealed.

In fact, the relationship between masculinity and violence is correctly addressed at the end of the episodes with female antagonists, when the survivors 'make their point'. Their declarations offer a confirmation that the gendered nature of the term 'victim' (see Chapter 1) and forms of hegemonic masculinities restrict the ways in which male victims of IPV are able to understand, experience and respond to it (see Chapter 2,

Women's IPV): 'It was difficult for me to admit to having been a victim of domestic violence: I was ashamed as a man and as a policeman' (Tina's husband John); 'I hope to demonstrate that even a strong man can be the victim of abuse' (Meri's husband Matt). However, these affirmations do not serve so much to explore male victimization in a gender key, but rather to demonstrate that female violence does exist, and in particular female IPV, despite the resistance of society to recognizing it. In turn, this contributes to constructing a precise frame. Violence, both that suffered by women (in four of the five episodes analysed) and that suffered by men (three episodes out of nine), is expressly labelled as 'domestic violence', through the words of the protagonist or a comment on the final screen. Thus, we are in the presence of a thematic frame, which all in all turns out to be that of gender symmetry. To sustain the mutuality of lethal violence contradicts the statistics, which in the United States show a gap between male and female IPH of over 40 percentage points (see Chapter 2, Women's IPV). The samples offered by the programme's five seasons are also in contradiction with the gender symmetry thesis (29 violent men versus nine violent women with incomparable degrees of brutality). An additional sub-frame, reinforcing that of gender symmetry, is inserted within the 'moral of the story' recounted by each survivor. Male and female victims complain that their dream of love was smashed by their evil partner. In the programme's moral universe, this dream is an integral part of another, the American Dream, which is also therefore compromised by the antagonists' behaviour. The implication is that violence imparted by women and men is equivalent, because it produces horrendous but identical effects on all levels.

Nonetheless, as we have shown, only the women are narrated as evil manipulators that deceive the victim, refuse to confess, dismiss the investigations, lie at the trial. The female figure therefore constitutes a danger not only to her partner but to all of society, because she is positioned as the antagonist in the personal story and the public one (Venäläinen 2016). She hinders the search for the truth pursued by the investigating authorities, the judicial authorities and the system as a whole. *WTBDIM?* also contributes to this belief. The women's manipulative ability also emerges in the many cases in which the 'devils' invent rapes, accuse their husband of domestic violence, or having sexually abused the children. This is confirmed by the ease with which social services and authorities 'believe the woman' (an aspect which *WTBDIM?* greatly emphasizes) and proceed against her husband. All this can only raise questions about the actual dimensions of male violence against women, and supports an accusation that patriarchal rhetoric has historically aimed at feminism, with the goal of invalidating its interpretation of domestic violence: male-bashing, i.e. spreading a denigrating image of men as bad and sexually threatening (Berns 2004: 114).

Thus *WTBDIM?* fully expresses the post-feminist quality of so much contemporary media culture: superficially feminist-friendly in its celebration of equal opportunities, female independence and commitment against gender violence, while deeply reactionary in the punitive attitude towards 'non-compliant' women and consistent with arguments held dear by the backlash.

'[If a] man of any size lays hands on me, he's going to bleed out in under a minute': The new politics of representation of gender and violence in transnational crime TV series

Elisa Giomi

Crime series are perhaps the area in which the current process of feminization of traditionally male-dominated media genres is most evident. In this case, it also arises from the need to diversify a genre that today sees an unprecedented increase in production and transnational circulation. This increase is part of the general trend in the massive drama resurgence favoured by contemporary television distribution spaces, which is dominated by VODs (video on demand) and SVODs (subscription video on demand). In this process, a fundamental role has been played by the global influence of Nordic Noir (see Hill & Turnbull 2016), which has helped reinvent a new breed of mini-series and series, adapting them to the production, aesthetic and narrative standards of the new television environment (Creeber 2015), and the on-demand engagement opportunities offered to consumers. The demand for distinctive programming created by OTT (over the top) services aimed at enticing subscribers boosted international sales of drama, first from Scandinavian countries and the UK (Steemers 2016: 748), and then from other European countries, were quality crime dramas started to be produced (Hansen 2020).

Following *Forbrydelsen/The Killing* (DR1, 2007–2012, DK), *Bron/ Broen-The Bridge* (SVT1/DR1, 2011–2018, SW/DK), and *Den som dræber/Those Who Kill* (TV2, 2011, DK), a small female 'army' has invaded the Euro Noirs as the new wave of European-produced crime series are called.[71] A recurring trope in these series is the close relationship between the female investigators and the female victims of crime (McCabe 2015). This relationship, however, is no guarantee of an innovative look at gender-based violence: as Dillman notes (2014: 7), in many media narratives, graphic deaths by sexual violence and the after-effects of this violence on the woman's body often visually nullify the agency gained by powerful women figures (police officers and other professionals). According to Coulthard et al. (2018), this paradox serves as part of this genre's transnational legibility: it is precisely the articulation of women's issues in crime series through a set of iterative features of content and form, which act as transnational currencies.

Our exploration of this subject began a few years ago (Giomi 2016, 2018) and moved from a similar hypothesis:

1. the belief that in contemporary crime series with the influence of Nordic Noir, a new politics of gender representation, paradigmatic of 'peak TV' series, was being defined (Lotz 2018);
2. the belief that violence is a privileged point of observation to understand similarities and differences between this politics of representation and that found in many popular culture products.

In this chapter, we present the results of this line of enquiry, comparing the representation of male violence against women and female violence against men.

Description of the corpus and methodology of analysis

Our corpus is made up of four series. One is produced in the United States, *True Detective 2* (HBO 2015), and written and conceived by Nick Pizzolatto, starring Antigone 'Ani' Bezzerides as main female character (she is the Criminal Investigation Division Sergeant at Ventura County Sheriff's Office). Three of the series are produced in Europe: *Forbrydelsen* as mentioned above, written and conceived by Søren Sveistrup, whose leading character is Detective Inspector Sarah Lund; *The Fall* (RTÉ One/ BBC Two 2013–2016), written, conceived and directed by Allan Cubitt, with Detective Superintendent Stella Gibson as the main character; *Unité 42/Unit 42* (La Une, 2017–present), written by Julie Bertrand, Annie Carels and Charlotte Joulia, whose central female character is police officer and former hacker Billie Webber, who partners detective Sam Leroy.

The four series were chosen because they were produced in the same years, all had transnational circulation and all contain both male violence against women and female violence against men. In three out of four cases, the latter is committed by the leading police officer and in contexts/for reasons unrelated to their work. The European series are considered as Nordic Noir (*Forbrydelsen*), or as Euro Noirs (*The Fall* and *Unit 42*). Whereas *True Detective 2* is an example of an American series similarly moulded to the aesthetic and narrative principles of the Nordic Noir subgenre (Creeber 2015), as revealed, for instance, by the presence of the double storytelling (Redvall 2013: 210): the exploration of ethical and political themes starting from a single murder case. All the series have enjoyed great public and critical success and have won numerous awards, except *Unit 42* which is still in production. This one is thought-provoking because it explores the role of technology in crime and its prosecution. In our analysis, we will pay attention to the type of violence shown, to the construction of the victims and the perpetrators, detecting the presence of the configurations highlighted in the first part of this book. For the depiction of female violence, we will also consider the construction of female leads, which constitute 'transgressive' characters for the sole reason of being female police officers. They do not transgress the law, on the contrary they actually enforce it, but they are nonetheless seen to challenge the symbolic order and pose a problem to the representational system: like criminals, female police officers wield a weapon, which makes them 'phallic' and therefore threatening; in addition, they work in a traditionally male profession (moreover, in some of the corpus' series, they occupy a top position), requiring skills, behaviours and psychological traits that were once culturally coded as masculine.

Male violence against women

The actors and causes of violence

In *Forbrydelsen*, in terms of the relationship between the victim and perpetrator, the cases closely mirror the statistics, which indicate that the majority of femicides originate in the private sphere. In the first season, Sarah Lund investigates the murder of the young Nanna Birk Larsen, which turns out to be the work of a close family friend. In the third season too, the perpetrator is known to the victims: Niels Reinhardt, the elderly assistant to Robert Zeuthen, president of the main Danish shipping and oil company (Zeeland), tortured, raped and killed Louise and other young girls who lived in an orphanage, taking advantage of their social marginality and his position of power.

According to Colbran (2014: 199), *Forbrydelsen* is the first procedural series to break with the genre's conventions, putting the victim at the centre of the story through the exploration of the consequences to family members by the disappearance of Nanna Birk Larsen and the obsessive repetition, at the beginning of each episode, of the frames of the chase as she escapes her tormentor. Even in the third season, with Louise's storyline, Lund is committed to giving a name to the little girl, initially claimed by no-one, to reconstruct the story. In line with Stieg Larsson's *Millennium* literary trilogy (O'Neill & Seal 2012: 60), *Forbrydelsen* shows a thematic concern recurring in Nordic Noir: the difference in economic and social status between authors and victims/survivors (Reinhardt and the girls of the orphanage) and between victims themselves: abuse, death or disappearance of some gets the attention of the media, politics and investigators (it happens with Emilie, the daughter of Zeuthen, who is kidnapped); others are soon forgotten (the young orphans). However, among the variables that may lead to a disadvantaged status, race does not feature. The victims are all white and as is the case in most of the European-produced crime series, including those in our corpus. As mentioned in Chapter 3, Spectacularizing violence: Eroticizing and an-aesthetizing, according to Klinger (2018: 522), the white female victim acts as a 'gateway body': an apparatus of capture, evincing formal, generic, and cultural proximities that are translatable.

In *The Fall*, the viewer immediately learns the perpetrator is a serial killer, namely, psychologist Paul Spector. The choice is a source of bias, given that, compared to murders committed by a known person, femicides by strangers are statistically irrelevant (see Chapter 1). In addition, we find many of the mystifications typical of serial-killer narratives here (see Chapter 3, Male violence in the media): Gender-based violence is otherized as the product of a stranger (the 'stranger-danger' trope), who identifies their victims on the internet and 'grabs' them in clubs, parks, workplaces. Cyberspace and the public sphere are made to appear unsafe places for women. The strength of this cautionary tale is amplified by the typifying of the victims each of whom is identified by a precise socio-demographic profile: 30-year-old, professional, white, beautiful and sexually free. This contravenes the evidence that rape affects women from very varied backgrounds and with different characteristics (as effectively shown by *Unbelievable*, despite its focusing on a serial killer, too). The explanation of the serial killer Paul Spector's actions lies in past traumas (the abandonment of his mother and abuse). *The Fall*, therefore, risks feeding the false belief that those who act and suffer gender violence are 'atypical' individuals. The commitment to make Spector appear a normal man (handsome, esteemed psychologist, devoted husband, and a nurturing father to young children), on the one hand prevents 'othering', but on the other, sends the message that anyone can be a serial killer. If we add to this the absence of positive male characters, there is a real risk that *The Fall* will normalize gender-based violence, representing it as an inevitable and structural fact of social reality and male nature.

In fact, in many other respects, the series pays close attention to debunking the false belief of the perpetrator's atypicality: Spector is not a monster, explains Detective Superintendent Stella Gibson to her boss and former lover Jim Burns, but 'just a man', and not too different from Burns himself, who the day before tried to kiss Gibson without her consent. The 'narrative complexity' characteristic of contemporary TV series (Mittell 2015) and the intertwining of the main plots and secondary storylines allow *The Fall* to establish thematic connections between different types of abuse (Berridge 2013): the lethal violence of the stranger; violence in the workplace; the IPV of which the wife of the paramilitary Jim Taylor is a victim; the violence of businessmen who beat and humiliate prostitutes or sex workers. In so doing, *The Fall* counteracts the main plot's episodic frame – which could suggest a reading of violence in an individual aberration key – with a thematic frame, which brings violence back to the order of gender relations ('it's just misogyny', Gibson tells Spector in 1x5). What is more, the exercise of violence is conceptualized in remarkably similar forms to those we have conceived in this book, namely as a 'gendering' practice, one which is constitutive of gender and gender difference. This quotation of Margaret Atwood by Gibson is very telling: 'Men feel threatened by women because they are afraid that women might laugh at them; whereas women feel threatened by men as they are afraid that they might kill them' (1x7). This self-conscious engagement with feminist discourse is a staple of contemporary crime series (Horeck 2018) and in *The Fall* it even acquires a meta-textual taste, touching upon the issue of media representation and victim-blaming. Winking at Benedict's text (1992), Gibson declares that 'dividing victims between virgins and vamps' (3×1) is the cornerstone of the cautionary tale's function in newspaper articles.

In *True Detective 2*, the violence is mostly sexual and is closely related to the protagonists: the wife of co-lead detective Ray Velcoro has been raped; the Ventura County detective Antigone 'Ani' Bezzerides was sexually abused as a child. The issue, however, is explored mostly concerning exploitation and prostitution. Bezzerides and colleagues will discover that representatives of the city establishment, including the late city manager, local entrepreneurs, the Russian Mafia and even top police, are involved in a network of corruption. They regularly hold private parties in elegant villas where they participate in orgies with young prostitutes/sex workers. One of the leads, career criminal Francis 'Frank' Semyon, owns many lap dance venues, where girls can be paid for 'extra' services. Pornography and the conditions of its production are also dealt with by the series, through the inclusion of Bezzerides's sister, Athena, as a 'cam-girl' in a porn studio. The result is that fetishized, young female bodies, practically act as wallpaper for each episode: a denunciation of the hyper-sexualization of women in the contemporary imagery. On this, the series has a clear position, which it immediately communicates to the viewer: 'It is not right. It's not healthy', Bezzerides tells her sister when talking about her profession (1×1). In the following episode, one more step is taken: through Velcoro's words, the series qualifies the questioning of the exploitation of the female image as 'feminist' ('Well, just so you know, I support feminism. Mostly by having body image issues').

Men who exploit or consume prostitution share a demeaning, objectifying conception of women. The night club girls are subjected to 'degradation rituals' (see Chapter 5), with the men who 'feel them up' every time they pass by as if it were an automatic reflex. The prostitutes/sex workers on the jet set's clandestine 'parties' are forced to take drugs before orgies and are beaten if they refuse to have sex. It is precisely when Bezzerides infiltrates one of the parties that we discover her trauma. Altered by drugs, exposed to the horror of young bodies being preyed on by elderly men, the memory of sexual abuse she suffered as a child at the hands of a grown man, a friend of her parents, resurfaces in her. The connection between various abuses built throughout the series now comes to include the last and most serious parallelism: that of prostitution and sexual violence. In doing so, the series denounces the contiguity between the individual story and broader forms of exploitation, between material and representative practices. If combating gender-based violence means questioning 'the connections between structural, cultural, symbolic and interpersonal violence' (see Chapter 1), *True Detective 2* undoubtedly offers a very advanced reading. As a confirmation of this, the concept of violence as a gendering practice also characterizes this series: 'The difference between the two sexes', says Bezzerides, 'is that one can kill the other with his bare hands' (2×2). Violence is therefore presented as a typically male conduct, which 'makes a difference' in the sense that it is an effect, and at the same time, a means of reproducing gender inequality. Unlike *The Fall*, however, the male characters are more complex and multifaceted and there are (anti)heroes such as Velcoro and Woodrugh. A bias remains: all the characters who implement some form of violence against women are also negative and all negative characters also implement some form of violence against women. This is a tautological construction on which popular culture often 'stumbles' (see Chapter 3).

On the victims' side, in line with *The Fall* and especially with *Forbrydelsen*, *True Detective 2* plays close attention to the difference in status between victims and 'executioners', clients and prostitutes/sex workers, exploiters and exploited: the first rich, mature/elderly, white and powerful, the second poor, non-white, young. This is consistent with US data, where non-Latina Black women have the highest rate of IPH victimization, and Latinas, in turn, have a higher rate than non-Latina White women (see Chapter 1). This thematic concern emerges from the very first scenes of *True Detective 2*, with the raid of a dilapidated pornographic studio by Bezzerides and the team. The girls appear to be predominantly Black or Latinas and Bezzerides suspects they are clandestine. All turn out to have regular IDs, but the message is that the cam-girl profession seems to be practised by those with limited choices or troubled girls like Athena. However, the series manages to articulate the complexity of the knots surrounding pornography and prostitution, still unresolved in feminist thinking and politics: Vera Machiado, a Latina girl of humble condition whom Bezzerides believes she saved from the private party scene, does not deny the violence suffered by those who initially forced her into sex work, but claims it as a free choice, a preferable choice to the alternatives available to her.

One of the strengths of *Unit 42* is the ability to emphasize the contiguity of two seemingly distant phenomena such as violence perpetrated through digital technologies and violence in the offline world. In relation to the first, episode 8 presents child pornography. A victim, Diane, who has grown into an adult, executes those who bought the video of her abuse as a child, which is still circulating on the deep web. The story represents the incessant reproduction of the trauma with great effectiveness, the infinite renewal of the violence inflicted on the victims through the network ('I couldn't bear anyone to watch that video anymore', Diane says, 'and going … through it again'). If in this case we are dealing with real-world violence that 'mutates genetically', amplifying its viral load when it arrives online, other episodes show how hatred via social media produces effects in the physical world instead. In episode 3, a young, female hacker is killed by her father's associate. Her boyfriend, a technology teacher who uses an avatar with which he incites 'misogynistic hatred', is initially suspected. Episode 4 is about Anna, a schoolteacher and sadomasochistic film actress killed by her son's foster mother. The initial suspect is a student infatuated with Anna, who has previously committed revenge porn against her by posting images of Anna on her profile, dressed as a porn actress and animated GIFs in which she is beaten and has her throat slit: 'a virtual lynching', as detective Sam, the central male character, calls it. Not only are these technologically facilitated forms of violence (Henry & Powell 2016) called by their name, making it clear that symbolic violence is in all respects violence, but the very fact that the perpetrators of such violence are also suspected of being the perpetrators of femicides sends the important message that symbolic violence nourishes material violence.

As in *The Fall*, in *Unit 42* gender-based violence is conceived as a 'continuum' of more serious manifestations (rape, lethal violence) and more common forms of coercion (Kelly 1988). When Leroy interrogates the student, he continues to obsessively call Anna a 'whore' and Emmy, his schoolmate and Leroy's daughter, a 'slut'. Leroy, like the viewer, knows about the winking photos Emmy posted on social media, which gave rise to persecution and suffering. Although the abuses suffered by the two women are of very different severity, combining them serves to underline their common matrix. If gender-based violence is as a continuum, it is also because of the normalization of rape culture. This is clearly pointed out in *Unit 42*. In the fourth episode, it is Leroy who re-victimizes Anna, echoing the division between 'virgin and vamps': '[W]hat is a teacher doing in a sadomasochist's cage?' he wonders irritatedly. The central female character, Billie Webber, distances herself from the binary logic and dichotomous oppositions in which women have always been divided, pointing out that she became a police officer after first being a hacker. Later, talking to the school principal, Leroy allusively calls Anna's clothing 'sexy'. The principal does not bite and sends the accusation back to the sender: 'I don't care what she does in her private life: she's a good teacher'. It is certainly a progressive message in a society that still tends to discredit victims of violence on the basis of their sexual conduct and in which revenge porn can cost the victim their job (this happened in Italy as we wrote this book, to a teacher who was then reinstated). Moreover, *Unit 42* avoids the apocalyptic vision of *The Fall* (where there are no positive male characters) and the dichotomy of *True Detective* (only negative male characters commit violence). Here there are positive male characters, such as Leroy, who nevertheless shares myths on gender violence, and this functions to show how widespread these are. The figures of the perpetrators are also realistic. They are all known to the victim except the serial killer in the first episode. Instead, a weakness lies in the representation of the victims, who are strongly typified here too: white, young and beautiful. In addition, the only power/status differential between perpetrators and victims concerns technological competence, which is often the condition that causes the abuse to occur. Moreover, the central issue of cyber-security assumes the facet of sexual vulnerability only in the case of women: this double standard along the gender line, as we have seen, is one of the forms through which female victimization is normalized in popular culture.

The violence visibility regime: Beyond eroticizing, before erasing

In two of the series of our corpus, there is a striking disconnect between the narrative level and the visual level. In *The Fall*, a largely correct discursive construction of gender-based violence is accompanied by an iconography that appears highly exploitative, particularly in the first season. The violence is even 'glamorized' here: after sadistically killing the victims, Spector washes them, dries them, applies their nail polish and lipstick, poses them for photographs and later masturbates in front of their images. The corpse thus becomes the object of fetish pleasure, which invites a necrophilic look (Jermyn 2016: 11). We find the phenomenon of anaesthetizing described in Chapter 3, and in Chapter 4, whereby violence is sanitized, young bodies remain beautiful and sexually palatable even after death, and there is not a single frame that serves to recognize them for what they are: dead women, killed. Also, on the visual level we find the same sensationalism, that which on the narrative level is expressed in the choice of an uncommon type of violence, perpetrators and victims.

In *Unit 42*, the disconnect between the narrative and the visual level becomes even more contrasted. The series does not seek sensationalism, it is realistic, it is aware of the issue of image-based violence against women in the digital environment. Yet *Unit 42* reproduces the same imagery of rape culture that it would like to counter. Here, too, the first episode begins with a 'gateway body': a beautiful white, naked, and lifeless female body, lying on the ground; breasts exposed, sexy underwear scattered around the room. What happens next is surreal: the team surveys the scene and draws hypotheses, they talk to each other, there is even a veil of comedy, underlined as such by the musical commentary. The victim is not worthy of a glance – if not in the sarcastic comments of the police chief – and is repeatedly bypassed as if she were something in the way. In the overall economy of the scene, it assumes the role of an object with an ornamental function, which is not spared other rapid, fetishizing shots: dehumanization at its fullest (see Chapter 3, Normalization of female victimization). The same voyeuristic aesthetic characterizes all the femicides of this episode (the work of a serial killer who hacked victims' webcams so that he could spy on them and record them whilst he killed them). The fourth episode also begins with the discovery of a beautiful female corpse, that of Anna, who died inside a cage on the set of a sadomasochistic video, with the camera lingering on the scabrous particulars. The striking contrast between the horror of death and the conviviality of the living becomes a fixed formula, which is repeated at every autopsy. The focus is on the comedy and growing flirtatious interactions between Leroy and the pathologist or on the teasing between team members. The naked bodies of young women, who even in this series never look like corpses and remain appealing, lie on the metal table like wallpaper. This also happens with male corpses, although in a less pronounced way. The intention is in fact to communicate the inevitable 'habituation' to death and corpses of those who do this work, but the effect is grotesque. What is naturalized is above all the 'cadaverization' of contemporary visual imagery or the associated idea of female passivity. Unsurprisingly the distressing tope of the 'dead-but-not-gone' also appears in this series, another recurring strategy of deprivation of female agency in popular culture. Leroy's wife, who died of cancer, continues to appear as a ghostly, contrite, mute, powerless witness to the scenes of greatest difficulty and despondency of the man who is now struggling with the three children.[72]

Due to the superfetation of scenes of violence against women and female corpses in contemporary visual imagery, the very act of showing them can be problematic. However, recalling the considerations made in Chapter 3, Exorcizing violence: Othering and erasing, the tradition of 'gaping elision' is equally problematic because it confines gender-based violence to invisibility. The series in our corpus present interesting solutions. In *Forbrydelsen*, scenes of brutalization are removed, but not the effects it has on the body of female victims. We never see them 'in real life', but only through quick shots of forensic photos, and the gaze through which these are shown plays a key role. There are two types of gaze, that of the victims' relatives and the gaze of the female detective. As for the first, in *Forbrydelsen* season 1, the clinical photomontage showing the bound, injured body of Nanna Birk Larsens is glimpsed by her parents through a door left open by mistake. This confers a pathemic charge to the neutral, 'aseptic' aesthetic of this medical report, making it painful, shocking and capable of conveying the entire horror of violence while at the same time discouraging voyeurism.[73] The device of looking at a girl's dead body through the desperate eyes of her parents has a 'moralizing role' (Greimas & Fonatanille 1991), which shows us how to react, being a powerful antidote to the normalization of cadaverization in visual culture.

The gaze of the female detective is a slightly different device but has the same effect: in *Forbrydelsen* season 3, we look at the corpse or at the forensic photos through the empathetic gaze of Sarah Lund. The meaning of the female detective's look at female corpses was highlighted by Jermyn in her analysis of *Prime Suspect* (ITV 1991–2006). It is the look of recognizing women, which means identifying women and acknowledging them: re-humanizing them. This is confirmed by the findings from research we are conducting on the functions of the look in female and male-led in productions from the same countries and period (in some cases, also by the same broadcasters).[74] *The Fall* and *Unit 42* stage a 'technologically upgraded' version of the female detective's gaze. There are numerous scenes in which Stella Gibson, distressed, observes the violence committed by Spector through computer screens and monitors. As noted by Horeck, the 'privileging of Gibson's face, and the emotions it expresses, is revealing of how the series wants its digital remediation of images of gendered violence to be understood and responded to' (2018: 577). In *Unit 42*, Webber finds herself witnessing: the serial killer's attempt to kill a girl through the hacked webcam, the video of Anna's abuse as a child, and photos from many crime scenes. The scenes are not shown to us, but their horror is effectively expressed through Webber's facial mimicry.

In *True Detective 2*, the female detective's viewpoint is combined to the use of out-of-focus images. This applies to any scene showing the exploitation of women, including female bodies on escort websites and scenes from the orgy involving prostitutes/sex workers and their clients. In this latter case, Bezzerides' view is altered as she was drugged, and the sight of the naked female body is only partially revealed to us: a means to denounce rape culture without reproducing its disturbing imagery. When the exploitation is 'lighter', such as with Frank and colleagues 'touching up' the pole dancers in his club, a close-up of Bezzerides' troubled face prompts us to share her disgust. It is important to highlight that, in *True Detective 1* featuring two male detectives as central characters, the numerous bodies of young women killed are shown using the typical fetishizing aesthetic.

Female violence against men

The actors and causes of violence

As for the violence by women, in three series this is acted by the female lead and in one, *Unit 42*, by a secondary character. In *Forbrydelsen* this is the last season finale: Lund coldly shot a man, before fleeing abroad as a criminal, forced to give up her loved ones. It was certainly not that self-defencing violence that legal and media discourse often dismisses as 'not a real crime'; nor does Lund enjoy the excuse of a moment of raptus, because she acted calmly and lucidly. The victim is Reinhardt, who tortured, raped and killed Louise and other little girls at the orphanage. Lund found out that the minister of justice and part of the Zeeland's board covered up Reinhardt's work. 'If she had evidence against him, why shoot him?' asks Mathias Borch, a colleague and companion. The viewers know why. The sequence in which Lund is persuaded of Reinhardt's guilt runs parallel to those in which the President of Zeeland and the Prime Minister do the same. Both would like to bring the man to justice, but their entourages dissuade them. The viewer's frustration grows at the emergence of details of Louise's torture, at the materialization of the network of silence around her executioner, at the realization that 'good people at the top' can do nothing if the system is corrupt. Frustration turns to anger when Reinhardt reminds Lund that the evidence against him is invalid, and sarcastically adds: 'But I admire your tenacity, your commitment and your precision in the work you do. I will see if I can learn from your lesson for the future', words that suggest that there will be other young victims, equally destined for oblivion. Words Lund reacts to by shooting him in the head. It is a true reversal that we are seeing in this scene. Throughout the series, Lund has been portrayed as a talented police officer but not immune to professional errors and severely lacking in the private sphere, with an existence characterized by the big and petty problems of ordinary people. A 'low-mimetic' heroine who, in short, becomes a 'high-mimetic' (Frye 1957) heroine in the finale. She sacrifices herself to avenge the oppressed men and indeed women and redeem us all – in line with the moral message of the Nordic Noirs (Creeber 2015: 27). As with rape-revenge, which genders the narrative device of revenge, here too the area in which Lund's avenging action unfolds is male violence against women. It is difficult to establish its value: is it reductive because it morally authorizes female violence only for 'gender issues'? Or, on the contrary, is it empowering precisely because the emphasis is not only on female victimization but also on female strength? And finally, taking up one of the issues mentioned for Lisbeth Salander from Stieg Larsson's *Millennium* trilogy (see Chapter 3), is Lund's violence an expression of physical feminism or, as violence, is it a denial of feminist principles?

These questions will be easier to answer after analysing the next cases. Unlike Lund, Bezzerides from *True Detective* is more than used to 'extra-curricular' violence: her only pastime is going to pubs, getting drunk, gambling and brawls. In addition to the service gun, she carries a knife tucked into her boot, and it is when her colleague Velcoro asks her why her nails are so sharp that Bezzerides sets out her vision of the difference between the sexes: 'one of them can kill the other with their bare hands'. 'Yet', she continues, 'man of any size lays hands on me, he's going to bleed out in under a minute (*sic*)'. Despite the risks of her job, Bezzerides' vulnerability is articulated predominantly in terms of sexual violability, because she explains that she would keep her nails so long even if she were not a police officer 'No man could walk around like that without going nuts' (2 × 2). The message is that despite Bezzerides being a police officer, she still belongs to a weak gender exposed to men 'going nuts'. But claiming the male prerogative to inflict death with her bare hands, she reverses this message and the whole order of gender relations that underpins it. Hers is not just a statement of principle: four episodes later, having infiltrated the private party, Bezzerides knocks down a client who demands a sexual act. Soon after, she kills another, who had tried to strangle her. She then flees carrying Vera Machiado, one of the girls involved in the 'high-end' prostitution ring. The whole sequence also has a liberating effect because the audience share Bezzerides' disgust at the prostitutes/sex workers' young naked bodies being 'molested' by aged and wealthy clients, and her apprehension about the infiltration operation ('f**k or flee', her sister warns her). Not only that: the amphetamine administered to her brings about her first memory of the man who abused her as a child, and he appears to her with a dirty smile. Her suffering, amplified by drugs, is psychic and physical together: the montage alternates her memories with the orgiastic images she is witnessing now, producing a climax that culminates with the overlapping of the image of her abuser to that of one of the clients, intent on masturbating in front of the sex scenes. The sequence has the effect, described in the previous pages, of establishing a parallel between the violence suffered by the child and the commodification of the adult body, denouncing both as forms of oppression of one gender over the other.

In killing the customers, Bezzerides not only defends herself but rebels against an entire system:[75] in one fell swoop she punishes the executioners, frees the 'victim' and avenges the child she was. As with the scene in which Lisbeth Salander takes revenge on the heinous violence of her guardian, the viewer/spectator feels pleasure for the reversal of the experience of oppression, for the transformation of the body from a source of vulnerability and sexualization in a place of control, a weapon against sexism and rape culture (De Welde 2012: 471). However, the series takes care to present violence as an extreme resource, emphasizing its consequences also on those who exercise it: 'I think I killed a man', Bezzerides says, and barely holds back her anger and pain. It is rare for male police officers in TV dramas to do the same.

The female members of the task force led by Gibson in *The Fall* also feel discomfort at the use of lethal violence. In 3×2, police officer Danielle Ferrington is baffled that she had to kill a man. However, Gibson reassures her, it was self-defence and an expression of a 'combative instinct that not in all women is strong enough'. In fact, Gibson is the only one of the four leads analysed here who refrains from violence: she practises with a gun at the firing range of course and, in the presence of a threat, her statuesque posture turns into the agile one of the experienced police officer; but it is always and only potential violence. On only one occasion does it become a reality: here too, as with Bezzerides, violence is exercised with bare hands and aimed at rejecting an advance. In episode 2×3, Gibson's boss and former lover Jim Burns shows up in her hotel room drunk and shaken: he fears for his career, which would be put at risk if it turns out he is corrupt; his pride is wounded (a colleague called him weak, and he has started drinking again). He decides that the only way to compensate for so many assaults on his ego, is to have sex with Gibson: 'Please', he whimpers 'I have to forget all the crap I've seen'. The calmer and firmer she appears in her denial, the more harassing and pathetic he becomes, until the moment he grabs the nape of her neck and violently pulls her to him. In response, Gibson breaks his nose: another liberating moment. It is subsequent developments that show us how we should interpret this gesture: 'Why are women emotionally and spiritually so much stronger than men?' asks Burns immediately afterwards, while Gibson medicates his nose. Leaving aside that Gibson has just shown herself to be physically, if not a superior, at least a worthy rival to a man, Burns' observation ratifies important psychological and professional differences: he reacts to the 'crap' with which his job puts him in daily contact, with the attitude of a lost child in need of refuge within a female body; instead Gibson, who saw the same horrors that day, never lost control and lucidity. She is aware of this: 'Because the basic human form is female', she calmly replies, 'maleness is a kind of birth defect'. It is difficult to imagine a sharper reversal of Genesis and all the other narratives that conceive maleness as the human canon, and femaleness its imperfect derivation.

The most interesting case of female violence in *Unit 42* is in episode 8 and mobilizes the trope of the victim-turned-avenger. It is told with a sequence characterized by a pressing and complex visual syntax, and by the wise use of the iconic code: proof that *Unit 42* is perhaps marked by oscillations between good and bad practices in representation even more so than *The Fall*. The lead character in the episode is Diane, who was abused when she was nine years old. As an adult she begins a vendetta to track down, torture and kill the men who bought the video of her abuse on the deep web. At the end of the episode, Diane, having arrived at the home of one of these men, stuns him and is about to begin her revenge. This scene cuts between two other scenes, both showing flashbacks to different times in the recent past. One shows Diane executing her previous victims, where she beats her prisoner and burns out his eyes. The other shows Diane sitting in front of a screen, crying, watching the video of her abuse as a child. At this point the recent past collapses into the distant past and images of the abuse are seen from the perspective of the abuser, who is also the filmmaker. The video camera first frames nine-year-old Diane's disturbed face, then pans down the girl's legs and underwear.

At the end of this long, articulated and disturbing sequence, we suddenly cut back to the present: Diane tells the man who she is going to kill that buying a video of child abuse makes him directly responsible for that abuse. 'Know what's like to be raped for years and for no one to do a thing?!', she yells at him. She answers her own question when Leroy, the head of the cybersecurity unit, arrives and tries to prevent her from killing the man by pointing a gun to her: 'I died 20 years ago', Diane says. The concept is emphasized by the following montage. Diane shoots the man and then collapses crying (again, this does not often happen to male 'lonely avengers'). Her face as a child is framed again, with the frightened gaze reflected in the gaze of the Diane in the present, surrendered and emptied: an icastic representation of the effects of sexual abuse on minors. As in *Forbrydelsen* with Lund, the narrative's message is clear: it is impossible to erase violence, repair its damage, or prevent others through formal justice ('When he gets out of jail he'll start over', Diane tells Leroy, referring to the man she is going to kill). The entire sequence is constructed in such a way that the audience empathizes with Diane and justifies the violence she has committed. The moral of the story is then stated by Webber, a female heroine who, unlike her colleagues, does not use physical violence but fully endorses the revenge of others: 'I was shocked to see the video of the abuse, but she even *experienced* it, and if I were in her place … ' (implying 'I would have done the same').

Standardization, justification and punishment of heroine

Several strategies are used to motivate, compensate, or exorcise the destabilizing potential of these heroines who occupy the male domains of police work and high tech but moreover, who exert violence. Sexuality, as we saw in Chapter 3, Female violence: De-responsabilizing the perpetrator and minimizing violence, plays a very ambivalent role. In one moment, it amplifies the transgressive effect of violent women, and in another contains it. Gibson's character is sexually active and liberated. Having arrived at the crime scene, the first thing she does is eye a young police officer, James Olson, and entice him back to her hotel room for a sexual encounter (in which he merits neither a smile nor conversation). Bezzerides is also introduced to us by means of her sexuality. In the first scene of the first episode, her partner Steve Mercier is disoriented and embarrassed by a request that he evidently was unable to satisfy: 'I didn't think women liked that'. Gibson and Bezzerides' non-normative sexuality opens a space for great freedom. At the same time, by putting it in the foreground from the beginning, non-normative sexuality is used to mark these female leaders in a male, homo-social world, as exceptions to the rule ('not real women', one would imagine). However, *The Fall* is very complex and offers other interpretations around the value of Gibson's sexuality. In 2×3, she exchanges an impassioned kiss with the pathologist Tanya Reed Smith, whom she invites to her hotel room, but when the woman declines, she desists gracefully. The violation of (hetero)sexual norms is associated with conduct that is respectful of female self-determination, and this contrasts sharply with the following scene in which Burns attempts to kiss Gibson against her will. She breaks his nose, and the gesture is presented as legitimate and liberating: another expression of female 'strength'.

The series has built a chain that unites, and positively rewrites the meaning of female conduct that the patriarchy calls 'deviant' (bisexuality and violence). The critique of the male norm (which as we saw in Chapter 2, is the main contribution of the Difference feminism), is based precisely on the fundamental theoretical and political gesture of re-signifying female deviance as a practice of freedom. Gibson's statement about femaleness being the 'basic human form' and maleness being like a 'birth defect' could not find a more suitable place than at the end of this chain.

Finally, sexuality is central not only in the discursive production of transgression but also in the processes of normalization. This is borne out by the intimate scenes between Lund and her colleague Borch, between Bezzerides and Velcoro, and Webber and her boyfriend (in the second season). Although they are just alluded to – there is no nudity or voyeurism – they serve to reassure us about the leading characters' gender conformity, femininity being also and above all affirmed through sexual contacts with male subjects (and vice versa). Sexuality, in other words, acts as a gendering device. How and with whom people 'make' love – an emblematic expression of the performative view of sexuality at play in our culture and society – determines what kind of femininity or masculinity we enact. Moreover, the heteronormative ideology, which feeds on a 'binary and dimorphic logic of sex/gender' (Shepherd 2013: 28), is thus strengthened.

Finally, we find one of the *Excusatio* strategies seen in Chapter 3, namely the heroine's relationship with her father. It is central in the cases of Bezzerides and Gibson, where sexuality is explored more. In the 'tomboy' figure, to which Bezzerides conforms not only in terms of her look but also in terms of general unruliness (brawls, gambling, etc.), this relationship becomes an explanatory framework of the masculine and active nature of the heroine. She can try to replace her father, to meet or, as in our case, contradict his expectations (Tasker 1998: 81–82). In 2×1, it is Bezzerides' father himself, Eliot, who suggests that his daughter's entire life responds to her need to get back at him ('your entire personality is an extended criticism of my values'). To this need he also attributes his daughter's failures with the other sex ('You're angry at the entire world. And men in particular'), and even her choice to join the police ('Do you even like what you do? Or is it just a reflexive urge toward authority out of defiance?'). In the construction of this unruly female police officer, the trope of the heroine in search of 'reconciliation with authority' is applied in full – she is called 'Ani' from Antigone – despite the roles being apparently reversed. At the text's denotative level, Bezzerides embodies the Law (she is a law enforcement officer) and her father embodies anti-authoritarianism and 'free-will' values. In 2x7 a sort of reconciliation with Eliot happens, when he concedes that his daughter did not have an easy life and defines her as 'the most innocent person he has ever known'. This can be seen to initiate the Oedipal trajectory towards resolution. In the next episode, the series finale, we discover that the 'transgressive and perverse' heroine (Tasker 1993: 169–70), who in the meantime has fallen in love with colleague Velcoro, has had a son with him. Her sexuality is fully recovered within the patriarchal order, of which Bezzerides has become guarantor. Having fled to Venezuela, she is ready to risk her life to uncover the truth behind the network of corruption involving the Vinci city jet set, which cost Velcoro his life. 'I owe it to him and his children', she explains to a journalist with her child in her arms and a knife in her boot. Again, she is armed, but again in the name of the Father (and this time, it is worth saying, also of the Son: the 'maternal heroine' is the figure being mobilized here).

Gibson's father died when she was a teenager, but their relationship remains a dominant motif even in this heroine's journey. Gibson wakes up in the middle of the night to write down dreams in which her father appears. On more than occasion, she is unable to hold back tears in front of the tender interaction between the serial killer Spector and his daughter. It is Spector who suggests that Gibson suffers from an Electra complex and thus explains her 'dysfunctionality' ('sweet little Stella, who misses her dad so much […] Stella angry at the world of men', 2x3).

In line with the 'broken body/inquiring mind' trope, the female police officers in our corpus pay for their leadership role and their independence with emotional isolation (Gibson) and loss: Lund, in the first season, is abandoned by her partner due to her excessive devotion to work, the romantic partners of Bezzerides and Webber die. Finally, it is striking how the post-feminist theme of 'failed motherhood' (Bradshaw 2013) involves Lund herself, a more genuinely counter-current figure in the group and a prototype of a whole new generation of investigators.

Conclusion: Crime series and feminism

Despite some contradictions produced on the visual or narrative level, or, more often, by a misalignment of the two, the series in our corpus testify to the new politics of representation of the gender and violence nexus that has become typical of post-Nordic Noir crime series. In many popular culture products, especially television series, the essentialist view of violence (sexual and non-sexual) as being inherent and intrinsic to the masculine ('a blood matter', Chapter 3, Minimizing and normalizing violence) is still widespread. This view is matched by the representation of women's violence as a product of the emancipationist logic of liberal feminism: men's rights – including the right to violence – are extended to women, and, in so doing, women are homologated to men. According to Shepherd (2013: 23), Cordelia's character from the *Angel* series is paradigmatic towards this vision. When remarks on her masculine attitude are made by Billy ('So you can dress like a man, talk like a man, does that make you feel superior?'), Cordelia does not refute the accusation that it is precisely this attitude that empowers her, 'in keeping with a liberal notion of the gendered subject that sees the masculine as the neutral or universal'.

In the series of our corpus, violence is made to appear as typically masculine. In *True Detective 2* and *The Fall* it is explicitly cited as being constitutive of the masculine with respect to the feminine (a gendering practice) but is not traced back to a principle of nature. The matrix of differences is not biological: or rather, in the universe of these series, violence, if defensive, translates to a survival instinct and as such is common to the whole species. However, violence is correctly depicted as a culturally authorized performance in men and repressed in women. The figures examined engage in violence to defend their right to self-determination and the sexual safety of themselves and other women (Bezzerides and Gibson) or as a form of private justice to repair past abuse and prevent abuse in the future (Lund and Diane). In so doing, all of these female leads rebel against an entire system of power that finds foundation and expression in sexuality. In two cases (Bezzerides and Gibson), violence is explicitly invested with a female empowerment value, but in none of the four cases does the exercise of violence, lethal or not, appear a mere emulation of male logic. On the contrary, there is a strong contrast between the ordinariness, the structurality of men's violence (against women, but also against other men) and a resistance of women to normalize its exercise, even when it takes place in self-defence and during the performance of their duties. There is no doubt that analysis of Coulthard et al. (2018: 510) applies here. Self-conscious feminist tropes in contemporary crime series enable their transnational circulation, and these tropes reflect second-wave feminism concerns. However, it seems to us that the feminism underlying the series in our corpus is partly different from the liberal one that has, until now, dominated popular television culture. Valuing female specificities and female deviance as means to deconstruct the patriarchal social and moral order, these series exhibit, consciously or not, elements of the Difference feminism. Although the enhancement of the bonds between women is almost exclusively focused on those between the detective and victim (with the sole exception of *The Fall*), it still supersedes the post-feminist paradigm of 'individual choice', which envisages individual solutions to social problems such as gender-based violence. On the other hand, the choice of heroines and victims invariably white (with the sole exception of *True Detective*) is to be read in the key of post-feminism (or second-wave feminism). There is a growing focus on the power disparity between perpetrators and victims, but the effects of the intersecting factors of race, class, ethnicity, sexuality and ability remain largely underrepresented.

Conclusion

Sveva Magaraggia

This book came from a desire to place gender at the centre of the analysis of the relationship between violence and media representations and to conceptualize it fully, so as a relationship between males and females and not simply as a synonym of women. Therefore, not only have we chosen to study GBV in the form of male violence against known women, but also as violence committed by women. Two phenomena that have very different connotations, the first being weaved into our culture, the second being an exception, and yet once put into tension and examined closely, capable of illuminating the many faces of the prism 'gender and violence'.

Our hypothesis is that media representations of both phenomena obey common logics. We conceptualize gender and violence as 'performances' and as being mutually constitutive, capable of having normative and productive effects on our imaginary and social worlds. Therefore, we have asked ourselves which models of femininity, masculinity and gender relations do the media representations of the two forms of violence draw on and simultaneously reproduce? We found significant lines of continuity alongside signs of change that are beginning to emerge. Let us look at the main characteristics of media representations, analysing them by gender.

Violence committed by men

The increased visibility of male violence against known women is, as we have seen, accompanied by a quantitative persistence of the phenomenon in the real world and by a dangerous recurring narrative in its media representation. The arguments used to represent and explain male violence against women are always the same. It is a monolith that shows how unwavering and limited common understanding around this issue is.

The first configuration in which representations of male violence against known women appears, in many diverse contexts such as news media, pop music, TV series and advertising, is the passionate or patemic type. Violence is interpreted as a typical reaction to conflict between couples, as an acceptable practice. Moreover, violence is normalized also through the view that a loving relationship oscillates between opposite extremes ('ups and downs'). This discourse presents violence as a measure of passion.

Jealousy becomes a legitimate motive for killing one's female companion and, because she provoked her partner, she is considered jointly responsible. These rhetorical devices build a romantic vision of IPV, which is dominant and is capable of increasing the culture of impunity.

The normalization of violence also takes place by means of naturalizing masculinity, in which gender and violence are co-constituted: a man is violent because he is male, and he is a man precisely because he is violent. The essentialist reference to a supposed biological matrix serves as justification.

The link between masculinity and violence in the media's discursive order is unwavering, precisely in terms of gender naturalization. Unlike female violence, male violence does not require explanation or authorization because it is a normal conduct of the male gender. Man is legitimized and sometimes forced to resort to violence because his partner does not conform to his wishes or gender expectations. The act of correcting and regulating his partner is his opportunity to reaffirm his hegemonic masculinity.

The romanticization and naturalization of IPV are functional strategies used to protect the contemporary gender order. It is precisely for this reason that violence continues to be represented as an irrational act and not as an exasperated expression of the gender order. It is narrated as the result of madness, the momentary loss of control and most definitely not a behaviour that is firmly rooted in our culture.

Finally, the polarization of men contributes to the protection of the gender order. A clear line is drawn between good men (normal) and bad men (violent). It proposes the monsterification, by far the most recurrent strategy to exorcise violence, which dismisses it as an individual aberration and de-genderizes how it is read. This discursive set-up is entirely in line with other orientations widely found in other studies as well as in our empirical analyses: a predilection for the episodic frame over the thematic one. This set-up makes cases appear as isolated events rather than an expression of a broader phenomenon, and the selection of extreme examples suggests that the protagonist is abnormal.

Violence suffered by men

A completely different image of masculinity emerges from the representation of men who themselves suffer violence. They are constructed as ideal victims, celebrated for their role as solid, caring husbands, and above all, loving fathers. This celebration, in turn, is produced through a discursive device of particular importance to our analysis: the juxtaposition of masculinity with care.

To understand its implications, it is necessary to consider the centrality of care in defining the gendered subject. The separation of the public and the private sphere is still 'one of the main tests of the manhood of man, and an important indicator, if not component, of his social success' (Markus 1987: 103). Given the centrality of the care work in defining the subject, it is evident that the subject also changes if the relationship with care changes. Therefore, the transformation of gender role models is significant: in many of the factual and fictional products analysed, men who are victims of violence are associated with caring fatherhood, characterized by dedication and self-denial in everyday life. It can, in extreme situations, also become a renunciation of one's life, according to the traditional narrative of 'heroic fatherhood', in which the father saves his child. We believe that the novelty is radical: heroic fatherhood has taken on a sacrificial element, historically a monopoly of motherhood.

Finally, the media representations analysed show relationships between the different masculinities that are no longer marked by mockery and violence (of hegemonic men towards those who are subordinate). Specifically, in the songs analysed, the transition to hegemonic masculinity does not go through the humiliation – and therefore the distinction – of homosexual men, once considered subordinate *par excellence*.

Violence committed by women

The rhetorical construction of women perpetrators and women victims is hinged on very similar elements, partly based on the patriarchal symbolic order. This is evident in the centrality that, despite the apparent dichotomy of the phenomena under analysis, they acquire two intertwined aspects: agency and sexuality.

Many of the forms of rationalization of female violence, elaborated by different discursive orders (scientific, legal, media), are more often aimed at disowning rather than illuminating it. They are in fact attempts to invalidate the perpetrator's agency: denying the criminal nature of their conduct or denying that they acted like a woman. The biological functions of the sexed body are cardinal in both cases. On the one hand, the pathologization of the female sex cycle (the 'dysfunctions' produced by premenstrual syndrome, pregnancy, childbirth, menopause, etc.) is used to state that it is not a 'real crime'. On the other hand, a sexuality presented as deviant (because it is excessive, non-monogamous, non-heteronormative, active and desirable) serves to postulate that the women perpetrators are not 'real women'. While male violence against women is still all too often ungendered, represented in forms that prevent its analysis through the lens of power and gender order, on the contrary a gendered understanding is imposed on female violence. Biological determinism has the opposite function with women's violence than when it is used to justify male violence. Violent women are bad mothers who contravene the very essence of femininity, or manipulative devils who use seduction to commit violence, in a dangerous ambiguity in which the ability to give life becomes instrumental to that of giving death. As Gentry and Sjoberg argued, if violent men are 'bad' men, violent women are not only bad women; they are also bad 'as women' (2015: 3).

In fiction, for female police officers and combatants, the devices used to mitigate the impact of their violent (albeit legitimate) agency are gendered. Once again, this passes through sexuality and reproduction: the motive of rape revenge justifies transgression; pregnant bodies, motherhood and fetishization compensate for her violence; the lack of children, or the trope of punishing the bad mother. Conversely, transgression is amplified through 'excessive', 'non-conforming' sexuality, often appearing as a copy of stereotypical male behaviour.

In media fiction, this process runs parallel to the feminization of men and once again results in feeding a binary and complementary construction of genres. The gender configuration (re)produced by violence is such as to preserve the function of gender as an authorizing principle, a 'stable signifier' (Shepherd 2012: 798) around which everything else can become relative.

Exceptions to this pattern are still rare and all concentrated in the fictional domain, where occasionally female violence appears for what it is: a performance, not a biological destiny. Of course, contemporary heroines are primarily white, in line with the dominant aesthetic canons, and of medium-high extraction. One of the positive aspects of the visual representation of violent women is that we can begin to 'allow ourselves to imagine the possibilities of fighting violence with violence' (Halberstam 1993: 191).

Violence suffered by women

Women's agency is perhaps the most latent value in representing male violence against known women, but it is called into question the most systematically. Coverage of sexual and/or fatal assaults is ascribed in the rhetoric of a cautionary tale. Those we have examined can also have the side effect of regulating women's conduct, censoring their wishes, restricting their autonomy and freedom; in a nutshell taming their self-determination.

We also find similar implications in not punitive but hagiographic narratives, such as music that celebrates the spirit of female denial, renouncing herself in the name of romantic love. The ideology of romantic love continues to carry with it a violation of individuality accompanied by a potential for destructiveness. Therefore, violence seems to be a sign of his passion, a measure of the intensity of his attachment, and specularly accepting violence becomes a testimony to her devotion.

There is also the persistent reading of the sexual history of the women who have suffered violence as a central criterion of their culpability or de-responsibility. It divides victims between those who were 'asking for it' from those who were 'innocent'. If the male gender is polarized between good men and bad men, the female gender is divided between virgins and whores (Bernau 2007). A dichotomy that traps women's agency, ascribes their desire with sinful and perverse imagery, and makes sexual objectification and moral and physical debasement legitimate.

We are also witnessing the fetishization of dead women. Cadaverization, initiated by TV series, is now being used in commercial advertising, and is the most hyperbolic expression of that glamourization of male violence against known women that we have found in all the media forms analysed. A woman, deprived of her agency is offered to the male gaze, unable to return it. This is the final result of absolute domination.

The aestheticization of violence also has repercussions on gender relations. Knowing how to take a punch or even be killed and yet remain sexy and beautiful becomes synonymous with full femininity, just as being devoted to men becomes a value that increases one's social desirability.

The bodies of these women, immobile and lifeless, are the counterpoint to the active and mobile bodies of women who, since the 1970s, have acquired increasing visibility and protagonism. Cadaverization is a form of symbolic destruction of feminist conquests: at least in the domain of representation, women are silenced (forever). The opposite phenomenon, namely the proliferation of women in different violent, often lethal ways, is also to be considered a response to the tensions generated by the redefinition of the gender order: warning signs and catharsis at the same time.

A redefinition that is at the core of contemporary feminisms, interested by a new desire to reinvent genders radically. Tired of binary definitions and eager for libertarian, positive signifiers, protagonists of fourth-wave feminisms (Magaraggia 2015) are turning into political practice that which has been affirmed theoretically in academia: men are also victims of the patriarchal order, masculinity has also to be re-signified. This awareness urges a strategic alliance between genders to jointly plan the construction of a new symbolic order, which will be capable of enhancing, not fearing, the relationship with otherness.

Notes

Introduction

1   By 'male' and 'female' we refer to both cis and transgender subjects, as well as to non-binary people.

Chapter 1

2   The most recent definition comes from the Istanbul Convention of 2011 on Preventing and Combating Violence against Women and Domestic Violence: '[T]he expression gender-based violence means any violence directed against a woman as such, or that disproportionately affects women (…) It is intended to designate a violation of human rights and a form of discrimination against women, including all acts of gender-based violence which cause or are likely to cause physical, sexual, psychological or economic damage or suffering, including threats to carry out such acts, coercion or arbitrary deprivation of liberty, whether in public life or in private life' (Istanbul Convention 2011: 5).

3   According to Jennifer Lawson, 'this term was chosen as the best option to maintain objectivity and avoid implicit agreement with any particular theoretical framework; it avoids openly endorsing a feminist perspective, but it also focuses the discussion on the male/female partner relationship as the specific unit of analysis warranting attention apart from the larger concept of family violence' (Lawson 2012: 574).

4   It is estimated that 73 per cent of women globally are victims of online abuse, of which eighteen per cent or nine million women, have reported serious consequences (UN Broadband Commission for Digital Development 2015).

Chapter 2

5   Eighty per cent of the world population of prostitutes/sex workers are female and 90 per cent of all prostitutes/sex workers are dependent on a pimp (ProCon.org 2018).

6   This tradition is explained following the reconstruction provided by Verdolini in the volume edited by A. Simone, I. Boiano and A. Condello, titled *Femminismo Giuridico*, soon to be published by Routledge.

7   According to Pitch (1989: 52), it is necessary to speak not of crime but of a 'criminal question': this makes it possible to consider crime in relation to the processes themselves that define it, to the instruments that are used for its management and in relation to the political dimension.

8   Each one implies a different motivation: intimate terrorism (or coercive controlling violence); situational couple violence; violent resistance and mutual violent control.

9   *Source:* our elaboration of Eurostat 'Intentional homicide victims by victim-offender relationship and sex' https://appsso.eurostat.ec.europa.eu /nui/show.do?dataset=crim_hom _vrel&lang=en

Chapter 3

10   Love the Way You Lie by Rihanna and Eminem © 2010 Universal Music Publishing Group.

11   In the film *Elle* (Verhoeven 2016), the protagonist's violence is also related to that of her father, the author of a massacre of children she witnessed as a child. Although this episode is presented as a real 'imprinting' for Elle, the frame is not that of naturalization: her violence is not the result of a genetically transmitted inclination, but rather appears to be a response to a trauma, but unlike in *Natural Born Killers*, here, it is not pathologized.

12   Love the Way You Lie by Rihanna and Eminem © 2010 Universal Music Publishing Group.

Chapter 4

13   This same stereotypical representations in the lyrics of popular music have been traced from the 1980s, when studies 'have found women to be described as (a) pretty; (b) heavenly or angels; (c) possessions of men; (d) submissive; (c) causing injury to men; and (f) lacking in fidelity' (Cooper 1985: 500).

14   Before the titles of the songs is the year, month and day, as well as the position it occupies in the hit parade.

15   'Testa coda, sto con la mia tipa su una Tesla/Chiappe sode (...)/A
      centottanta mettendo la sesta/Lei mi dice rallenta (skrt, skrt)' (2018 04
      28#1 Tesla, Capo Plaza feat. Sfera Ebbasta & DrefGold, © Soundreef Ltd.)

16   'Fallo lentamente/Ti ho messo il reggaeton così mi spegni quel corpo/
      Fallo fino alla fine, quel movimento è difficile' (2019 01 19# 3 Calma
      (remix), Pedro Capó ft. Farruko, © Sony/ATV Music Publishing LLC,
      Warner Chappell Music, Inc)

17   Perfect by Ed Sheeran © 2017 Emi April Music Inc., Bmg Platinum Songs
      Us, Virginia Beach Music, Prescription Songs, Holy Cannoli Music, Mo
      Zella Mo Music, Music Of Big Deal, The Family Songbook, Bob Erotik
      Music, Ppm Music, Aidenjulius Music, Ppm Music Ltd.

18   'Bitch ogni giorno non mi lasciano libero (no)/Le ordino da casa come
      su Deliveroo' (2019 02 02 #2 TVTB, Fedez & Dark Polo Gang, © Ultra
      Music Publishing Europe Ag, Asian Fake Srls, Two Fingerz Srl, Triplosette
      Enterteinment Srls).

19   'Pussy rosa, pink shocking/La tua lei con me a fare shopping/G-U-E, sai che
      lo tengo pucciato/La riempio come il suo marsupio gucciato' (2018 09 22 #1
      Borsello, Guè Pequeno, © Universal Music Italia Srl., We Publish Music
      Gmbh & Co Kg).

20   'Frate', poi piscio in testa a chi ci contesta/Queste tipe perfette sono la
      ricompensa' (2019 06 15 #1 Poison 7, Gemitaiz, MadMan, © Universal
      Music Italia & Tanta Roba).

21   'Questa città è come una bella donna/Che aspetta solo che qualcuno se la
      faccia' (2019 07 13 #2 YOSHI, – prod. Massacre, © Epic release).

22   'Mi sa lo sai il resto (ye)/Che ti scrivo pure oggi/Mi chiedo dove ti appoggi/
      Che fai dopo, esci con me? /(…) E vienimi a prendere/In mezzo alla
      polvere/Ricordi? non c'erano soldi, c'eravamo io e te' (2018 04 28#3 Davide,
      Gemitaiz ft. Coez, ©TantaRobaLabel).

23   'Il mio frero non lo cambio, siamo separati al parto' (2019 10 12#3 Gigolò,
      Lazza, © Ultra Tunes, Warner Chappell Music, Inc).

24   'È già scaduto il tuo tempo/Sei passato di moda come il tuo borsello, damn'
      (2018 09 22#1 Borsello, Guè Pequeno © Universal Music Italia Srl., We
      Publish Music Gmbh & Co Kg).

25   'La tua b-b-b, dice, "Sì, sì, sì"/Ma chissà com'è, quando sta con te dice, "No,
      no, no"' 2020 11 28#2 Tik Tok RMX, Sfera Ebbasta (ft. Marracash, Guè
      Pequeno, © 2021 Universal Music Italia Srl).

26 'Oh, sì, metto pellicce come una pussy (Oh yes)/Uzi, io e la gang abbiam
    gli stessi gusti' (2020 05 16#2 Pussy, Dark Polo Gang ft. Lazza e Salmo, ©
    Universal Music Italia).

27 'Marlena, vinci la sera/Spogliati nera, prendi tutto quello che fa comodo
    e sincera/Apri la vela, dai viaggia leggera' (2018 03 31#2 Morirò da re,
    Maneskin, © Måneskin).

28 'Odio queste cicatrici perché mi fanno sentire diverso/Posso nasconderle da
    tutti, ma non da me stesso/(...)/Ogni ferita è un passaggio che porta al lato
    migliore di noi/Perché attraverso loro puoi guardarmi dentro/Sentire cosa
    provo, capire cosa' (2020 04 04#3 Fiori di Chernobyl, Mr. Rain, © Warner
    Chappell Music, Inc).

29 'No, non avere paura/Quando vai a dormire sola /Se la stanza sembra
    vuota/(...)Mi prenderò cura, io di te' (2019 10 05#2 Non avere paura,
    Tommaso Paradiso, © Emi Music Publishing Italia Srl, Universal Music
    Italia Srl., The Sold Out Music Srl).

30 'Ora il mio nome lo sa l'Italia intera/Voglio un Panamera/Ora a mia
    madre pago la crociera/Ora ogni giorno c'ho le scarpe nuove/E una tipa
    diversa da ieri' (2018 09 15#2 Trap Phone, Guè Pequeno, © Universal
    Music Italia Srl).

31 'Penso ancora senza il rap, su una moto in tre/Come quando mi guardavan
    se giravo nei blocchi/Ma ero in studio per portare i miei fuori dai blocchi'
    (2020 02 01#2 Calmo, Shiva ft tha supreme, © Warner Chappell
    Music, Inc).

32 'Non sai cosa ho passato, l'ho visto pure io il baratro/(…)/Noi siamo
    giovani, ma cresciuti presto, yah, yah' (2020 06 13#3 Polvere (ft. Capo
    Plaza) – Tedua feat, © Ultra Tunes, Warner Chappell Music, Inc).

33 'Queste strade sono fredde ma/Ho una nuova giacca di Vuitton, ah/
    Quanto costa essere libero tu non lo sai/Molto più di queste macchine, di
    questo ice' (2019 10 12#3 Gigolò, Lazza, © Ultra Tunes, Warner Chappell
    Music, Inc).

34 'Non è facile essere famoso/Perché quando ce la fai li hai tutti contro' (2020
    22 28#3 Hollywood, Sfera Ebbasta, © Kobalt Music Publishing Ltd.,
    Peermusic Publishing, Thaurus Publishing).

35 'Sono una rockstar, rockstar/A uccidermi no, non sarà una stronza, ehi/Il
    mio cuore è freddo (...)/E se provi a scaldarlo rischi che si sciolga' (2018 02
    27#2 Rockstar, Sfera Ebbasta, © Soundreef Ltd., Thaurus Publishing).

36 God's Plan by Drake – God's Plan by Drake © 2018 CONSALAD CO., Ltd, Kobalt Music Publishing Ltd., PFIVE Entertainment Mexico, Sony/ATV Music Publishing LLC, Universal Music Publishing Group.

37 *'Chiedono del nostro amore, (…) Ho perso la ragione, la ragione sei tu/ Che mi fai andare fuori'* (2018 11 24#2 Il cielo nella stanza, Salmo feat. Nstasia, © Emi April Music Inc).

38 *'Ci ho pianto troppo, però tutte le lacrime che ho/Ti ho dato tutto, te no, eri Crudelia De Mon'* (2019 11 09 #3 Crudelia- I nervi, Marracash, © Universal Music Italia srl)

39 *'Gli occhi rosso ciliegia/dal tetto Milano mi pare Las Vegas'* (2020 04 04 #3 le feste di Pablo, Cara ft Fedez, ©Universal Music Italia Srl).

40 *'Fai una canna, che così ci passa/Questa incazzatura non ci fa parlare (no, no)'* (2020 06 20#3 M' Manc Shablo, Geolier, Sfera Ebbasta, © Universal Music Italia Srl).

41 *'A scuola avevo la lean nel backpack, lean/Curavo l'incertezza e l'imbarazzo/Io mi imbarazzo quando penso a te'* (2019 11 09#2 Supreme – L'ego, Marracash, © 2020 Universal Music Italia Srl).

42 *'Fumo questo missile che riuscirebbe a bucare il marmo/È il mio segreto per stare calmo (babe)'* (2018 04 28#3 Davide, Gemitaiz feat. Coez, © TantaRobaLabel).

43 *'Metto dieci bombe girate dentro la sua borsa di Hermes e poi/Ay, sei già fatto e comunque aspiri/L'ansia mi mangiava, ora no (ora no) /Faccio due o tre tiri, fra' che dici'* (2019 09 28#2 Fuori e Dentro, Gemitaiz e Madman, © TantaRobaLabel).

44 *'Mamma guarda senza mani, sono una rockstar/Mamma sai che a parte te non amo nessun'altra'* (2018 02 27#2 Rockstar, Sfera Ebbasta, © Soundreef Ltd., Thaurus Publishing).

45 *'Il testo è vero, sai che mamma è fiera'* (2020 04 04#2 Blue Car, Shiva feat Eiffel 65 Prod. Adam11, © Sony Music Entertainment Italy S.P.A.).

46 Shallow by Lady Gaga and Bradley Cooper © 2018 Sony/atv Songs Llc, Downtown Dmp Songs, Downtown Dlj Songs, Songs Of Zelig, White Bull Music Group, Stephaniesays Music, Warner Olive Music Llc., Warner-barham Music Llc., Concord Copyrights, Sg Songs Worldwide.

47 *'Una lacrima salata bagna la mia guancia mentre/Lei con la mano mi accarezza in viso dolcemente'* (2018 10 06#1 Torna a casa, Maneskin, © Sony/ATV Music Publishing LLC).

48 'E il dolore profondo/Guarda come ha travolto la mia vita/Schioccherò le dita e ancora mi ritroverò/A parlarti con il cuore in mano' (2019 09 07#3 Chiasso, Random, © Random).

49 The 'will to do violence' is also present in depictions of female violence in factual entertainment but, unlike depictions of male violence, it is considered a 'modalisation' of the violence that attributes strong agency to the female subjects who carrying it out, and it is therefore associated with their stigmatization. See Chapter 6.

50 'Entro in un cinepanettone, mhh/Con un fucile a pallettoni/Sono sotto l'albero della tua tipa, le do il cazzo col fiocco' (2019 12 14#3 Charles Manson (Buon Natale 2), Salmo, © Sugarmusic s.p.a.).

51 'Cinepanettone' is a contraction of Cinema and Panettone, an Italian Christmas cake, and it indicates a comical Italian farce film for Christmas.

52 'Cattivo vampiro con il canino lo affilo/Vedi un puntino sei a tiro/Ti uccido perché ti miro/Mi fotte un cazzo, sono pazzo' (2019 06 15#1 Veleno 7, Gemitaiz, MadMan, © Universal Music Italia & Tanta Roba).

53 'Nuoto tra gli squali per la ricompensa/Fuori trovi gratis solo armi e violenza/Niente che ti parli della conseguenza' (2019 12 07#3 Soldi in Nero, Shiva e Sfera Ebbasta, © Soundreef Ltd., Warner Chappell Music, Inc).

54 'Nella mia testa c'è una tempesta/E non è temporaneo, questo temporale/Sbaglio a chiamare, sbaglio chi amare/(…)E forse ti sembrerò un'idiota totale/Quando ti manderò questa nota vocale/Tanto non mi rispondi mai' (2018 01 06#3 Irraggiungibile, Shade feat. Federica, © 2017 Warner Music Italy).

55 'E non è colpa tua/Se tutti questi destri, destri, destri, al muro non ci fanno ritornare lì/A quei momenti lì/A quando andava tutto a gonfie vele' (2020 10 24#2 Destri, Gazzelle, © Maciste Dischi / Artist First).

56 'E riempirei di mazzate quel tuo vecchio ragazzo/ (…) E riempirei di mazzate quel tipo che ci prova/(...)E c'è una parte di te che è una parte di me' (2020 09 19#3 Superclassico, Ernia, © Universal Music Italia Srl).

57 A scuola nascondeva i lividi/A volte [suo padre] la picchiava e le gridava soddisfatta/Linda sentiva i brividi quando quel verme entrava in casa sbronzo/E si toglieva come prima cosa solo la cravatta' (2019 02 16#3 La ragazza con il cuore di latta, Irama, © Warner Music Italy).

58 'Resto solo, fotte proprio niente dei tuoi scazzi live/quella volta ti presentai ai parenti come mia lei/Se non fosse che sei un po' fake/Troppo fake, troppo flame' (2019 11 16#2 blun7 a swishland, tha Supreme, © Sony Music Italy).

59 Blinding Lights by The Weeknd © 2019 Universal Music Corp., Sal And Co Lp, Songs Of Wolf Cousins.

60 Bad Guy by Billy Eilish © 2019 Kobalt Music Publishing Ltd., Universal Music Publishing Group.

61 '*E provo a raccontarlo in ogni canzone/Ma la gente pensa sempre "parli di altre persone"/Ma come tu così carina/Con la faccia da bambina/Ma la bambina è cresciuta troppo in fretta/Tra i muri di una cameretta in cui ha iniziato a stare stretta*' (2018 12 01#3 Cherofobia, Martina Attili, © Sony Music Italy).

62 '*Hola papito, no hablo español/Quanto sei figo capisci che dico/Sarai un tattoo di cui mi pentirò*' (2018 07 07#2 Da zero a cento, Baby K, © Sony Music Entertainment).

63 '*Quando penso a te io sorrido/E dopo non m'importa di niente/Se il vestito mi scende tu ti perdi completamente*' (2020 07 25#3 A Un Passo dalla Luna, RoccoHunt e Ana Mena © Sony Music Entertainment).

Chapter 5

64 As Susanna Paasonen, Kaarina Nikunen and Laura Saarenmaa stress, 'This phenomenon has been discussed and diagnosed as the mainstreaming of pornography, pornographication (McNair 1996; Driver 2004), pornification (Paul 2005; Aucoin 2006), normalisation of porn (Poynor 2006), porno chic (McNair 2002; Duits and van Zoonen 2006)' (2007: 1).

65 Due to copyright, it has been not possible to include the images of the advertisements analysed.

66 In advertisements, it leads to an excess of the aestheticizing tendency that is inherent in photographs. Susan Sontag explains how the photographs are a 'medium which conveys distress' but 'ends by neutralising it' (2004: 85), and that 'cameras implement an aesthetic view of reality' (ibid., 138).

67 In 2013, the year in which a new law on femicide was passed in Italy, a company that produces household cleaning cloths embarked on a national advertising campaign in which, against the background claim 'delete all traces', the theme of the adverts were the murder of a woman by a man and – released shortly after this first one – the murder of a man by a woman. Both killings had just been committed. Complaints were made to IAP

the Institute for Self-regulation of Advertising (IAP), which published an injunction (no. 45/2013) stating that '[a] great many reports have been received by the Institute, testifying that the public's decoding of the message – even though it was beyond the advertiser's intentions – is likely to have offended widely shared sensibilities, and also have led to trivializing a dramatic and widely debated social problem, that of violence against women' The company apologized, but not before the images had gone viral.

68 BDSM stands for Bondage and Discipline or Dominance (BD), Sadism or Submission and Masochism (SM).

69 In 2017 the photographer Richardson was banned from working with many major magazines due to the sexual harassment and assault allegations against him by many women, thanks to the #MeToo movement.

Chapter 6

70 From this point on, in line with how they are addressed in *WTBDIM?*, we will also identify the protagonists by their first name. Dorothy appears in *You Get What You Pay For*, 3×7; Lee Ann in *An Exercise in Murder*, 2×12; Tina in *Addicted to Love*, 2×15; Melissa in *Blinded by Love*, 3×20; Andria in *Witt's End*, 5×2; Meri in *Evil Beauty*, 5×12; Jodi in *Perfect Stranger*, 3×16; Astrid in *A Dangerous Affair*, 5×4; Lisa W. in *Lisa Outlaw*, 4×2.

Chapter 7

71 To name but a few: in Swedish we find *Modus* (TV4 2015–2017), and *Sthlm Rekviem/Stockholm Requiem* (C More 2018); in Norway we find *Monster* (NRK 2017) and *Wisting* (Viaplay/TV3 Viasat 2019); in Finland *Cover story* (Yland TV1 2017–2018), and *Karppi/Deadwind* (Areena/Yle TV2 2018); in Iceland *Brot/Wallhalla Murders* (RÚV 2019). In the UK, the most popular female leads of the 'Celtic Noir' are found in *Vera* (ITV 2011–present), *Broadchurch* (ITV 2013–2017); *The Fall* (RTÉ One/ BBC Two 2013–2016), *Happy Valley* (BBC 1 2014–present); *Marcella* (ITV 2016–present); in French-speaking countries, among the most recent, *The Forêt/ The Forest* (Netflix 2017), *Zone Blanche/Black Spot* (France 2 2017–present), *Le Mystère*

du lac/Vanished by the Lake (TF1, 2015); for Italy and Spain, where a 'Mediterranean Noir' is taking hold, we can mention *Non uccidere/Don't kill* (RAI2/RAI3 2015–2016), and *O Sabor das Margaridas/Bitter Daisies* (CTV 2018–2020).

72 In the second season, which is not analysed here, Webber also often evokes the memory of her dead boyfriend, but, significantly, these scenes communicate only sadness and there is no sense of helplessness.

73 Klinger's analysis of a 'gothic striptease' based on intermittent visual hints (Klinger 2018, 528) implies a spectator who is sexually aroused by such hints. Instead, they are framed by an aesthetics that is far from inviting.

74 For example, *Glacé/The Frozen Dead* (Netflix 2017) vs. *The Forest*; *Sorjonen/Bordertown* (Yle TV1 2016,) vs. *Deadwind*; *Wallander* (DR, SF, TV4 2005–2013) vs. *Modus*; *Ófærð/Trapped* (RÚV 2015-) vs. *Vallhalla Murders*.

75 The movie character archetype of the sex worker who kills a client and, in so doing, symbolically rebels against an entire system of oppression is clearly represented by the protagonist of the movie *Jeanne Dielman, 23, quai du Commerce, 1080 Brussels* (Akerman 1975).

Bibliography

Abramsky, T., Watts, C. H. & Garcia-Moreno, C. et al. (2011), 'What factors are associated with recent intimate partner violence? Findings from the WHO multi-country study on women's health and domestic violence', *BMC Public Health*, 11(109): 1–17.

Abrisketa, J. et al. (2015), 'Human rights priorities in the European Union's external and internal policies: An assessment of consistency with a special focus on vulnerable groups', *FRAME Deliverable 12.2*. Available online: http://www.fp7-frame.eu/wp-content/uploads/2016/08/24-Deliverable-12.2.pdf (accessed 04 March 2021).

Adams, T. & Fuller, D. (2006), 'The words have changed but the ideology remains the same: Misogynistic lyrics in rap music', *Journal of Black Studies*, 36(6): 938–57.

Adler, F. S. (1975), *Sisters in Crime: The Rise of the New Female Criminal*, New York: McGraw-Hill.

Adorno, T. W. (1941), *Sulla musica popular*, trans. it. Rome: Armando, 2004.

Adorno, T. W. (1945), 'Una critica sociale della musica radiofonica', trans. it. *Studi Culturale*, 1(1): 109–22.

Adorno, T. W. (1962), *Introduzione alla sociologia della musica*, trad. it. Turin: Einaudi, 1971.

Agbo-Quaye, S. & Robertson, T. (2010), 'The motorway to adulthood: Music preference as the sex and relationships roadmap', *Sex Education*, 10: 359–71.

Åhäll, L. (2015), *Sexing War/Policing Gender: Motherhood, Myth and Women's Political Violence*, New York: Routledge.

Alberoni, F. (2008), *Lezioni d'amore*, Milan: Rizzoli.

Alessandri, S. W. (2009), 'Promoting the network brand: An exploration of network and local affiliate on-air promotion during the super bowl, 2001–2006', *Journal of Promotion Management*, 15(1/2): 150–64.

Alexander, S. (1999), 'The gender role paradox in youth culture: An analysis of women in music videos', *Michigan Sociological Review*, 13: 46–64.

Alt, B. & Wells, S. (2000), *Wicked Women: Black Widows, Child Killers and Other Women in Crime*, Boulder: Paladin Press.

Anderson, C. A. & Bushman, B. J. (2001), 'Effects of violent video games on aggressive behavior, aggressive cognition, aggressive affect, physiological arousal, and prosocial behavior: A meta-analytic re-view of the scientific literature', *Psychological Science*, 12: 353–9.

Anderson, C.A. & Bushman, B.J. (2002), 'The effects of media violence on society', *Science*, 295: 2377–8.

Anderson, E. & McCormack, M. (2018), 'Inclusive masculinity theory: Overview, reflection and refinement', *Journal of Gender Studies*, 275: 547–61.

Andersson, S. Hedelin, A. Nilsson, A. & Welander, C. (2004), 'Violent advertising in fashion marketing', *Journal of Fashion Marketing and Management*, 8(1): 96–112.

Andsager, J. & Roe, K. (1999), 'Country music video in the country's Year of the Woman', *Journal of Communication*, 49: 69–82.

Andsager, J. & Roe, K. (2003), '"What's your definition of dirty baby?" Sex in music video', *Sexuality and Culture*, 7: 79–97.

Aramendia-Muneta, M. E., C. Olarte-Pascual & L. Hatzithomas (2020), 'Gender stereotypes in original digital video advertising', *Journal of Gender Studies*, 29(4): 403–19.

Arcidiacono, C. & Di Napoli, I. eds (2012), *Sono caduta dalle scale. I luoghi e gli attori della violenza di genere*, Milan: FrancoAngeli.

Armstrong, E.G. (2001), 'Gangsta misogyny: A content analysis of the portrayals of violence against women in rap music', *Journal of Criminal Justice and Popular Culture*, 8: 96–126.

Arnett, J. (2002), 'The sounds of sex: Sex in teens' music and music videos', in J. D. Brown, J. R. Steele& K. Walsh-Childers (eds), *Sexual Teens, Sexual Media: Investigating Media's Influence on Adolescent Sexuality*, 253–64, Mahwah: Erlbaum.

Arnett, J. J. ed (2007), *Encyclopedia of Children, Adolescents, and the Media: Two-volume Set*, Thousand Oaks: Sage Publications.

ASA (2017), *Depictions, Perceptions and Harm. A Report on Gender Stereotypes in Advertising*, UK: Author.

Ashworth, L. Pyle, M. & Pancer, E. (2010), 'The role of dominance in the appeal of violent media depictions', *Journal of Advertising*, 39(4): 121–34.

Åström, B., Gregersdotter, K. & Horeck, T. eds (2013), *Rape in Stieg Larsson's «Millennium Trilogy» and beyond*, New York: Palgrave Macmillan.

Aubrey, J. S. & Frisby, C. M. (2011), 'Sexual objectification in music videos: A content analysis comparing gender and genre', *Mass Communication and Society*, 14: 475–501.

Aubrey, J. Hopper, K. & Mbure, W. G. (2011), 'Check that body! The effects of sexually objectifying music videos on college men's sexual beliefs', *Journal of Broadcasting & Electronic Media*, 55(3): 360–79.

Ayre, J., Lum On, M., Webster, K., Gourley, M. & Moon, L. (2016), *Examination of the Burden of Disease of Intimate Partner Violence against Women in 2011: Final Report*, Sydney: ANROWS.

Bahun, S. & Rajan, V. J. (2016), *Violence and Gender in the Globalized World: The Intimate and the Extimate*, New York: Routledge.

Bal, J. (2020), 'Toxic masculinity and the construction of Punjabi women in music videos', *Gender Issues*, 1–10.

Ballinger, A. (2000), *Dead Woman Walking: Executed Women in England and Wales 1900–1965*, Aldershot: Ashgate Publishing.

Barak, G., Leighton, P. & Flavin, J. (2010), *Class, Race, Gender, and Crime: The Social Realities of Justice in America*, 3rd edn, Lanham: Rowman & Littlefield.

Barberet, R. (2014), *Women, Crime and Criminal Justice: A Global Enquiry*, Routledge: New York.

Bartholini, I. (2015), *Violenza di genere e percorsi mediterranei*, Milan: FrancoAngeli.

Bates, E. A. & Weare, S. (2020), 'Sexual violence as a form of abuse in men's experiences of female-perpetrated intimate partner violence', *Journal of Contemporary Criminal Justice*, 36(4): 582–95.

Belknap, J. (2020), *The Invisible Woman: Gender, Crime, and Justice*, Thousand Oaks: Sage Publications.

Belluati, M. & Tirocchi, S. (2020), 'Tra tensioni e convergenze. Il prisma del discorso pubblico sul femminicidio e le pratiche dell'informazione e della politica', in P. Lalli (ed), *L'amore non uccide. Femminicidio e discorso pubblico: cronaca, tribunali, politiche*, 241–74, Bologna: Il Mulino.

Benedict, H. (1992), *Virgin or Vamps: How the Press Covers Sex Crimes*, New York: Oxford University Press.

Bennett, A. & Rogers, I. (2016), *Popular Music Scenes and Cultural Memory*, London: Palgrave Macmillan.

Benokraitis, N. & Feagin, J. (1995), *Modern Sexism: Blatant, Subtle, and Covert Discrimination*, 2nd edn, Englewood Cliffs: Prentice Hall.

Ben-Ze'ev, A., Goussinsky, R. (2008), *In the Name of Love: Romantic Ideology and its Victims*, Oxford: Oxford University Press.

Berberick, S. (2010), 'The objectification of women in mass media: Female self-image in misogynist culture', *The New York Sociologist*, 5: 1–15.

Bergman, K. Sarkar, P. O'Connor, T.g. Modi, N. & Glover, V. (2007), 'Maternal stress during pregnancy predicts cognitive ability and fearfulness in infancy', *Journal of the American Academy of Child & Adolescent Psychiatry*, 46(11): 1454–63.

Bernardi, D.A. & Steyn, F. (2019), 'A model for female-perpetrated domestic violence', *Victims & Offenders*, 14(4): 441–61.

Bernat, F. P. & Kelly Frailing, K. (2019), *The Encyclopedia of Women and Crime*, Oxford: Wiley-Blackwell.

Bernau, A. (2007), *Virgins: A Cultural History*, London: Granta.

Berns, N. (2004), *Framing the Victim: Domestic Violence, Media, and Social Problem*, New York: Aldine Transaction.

Berridge, S. (2013), 'Teen heroine Tv: Narrative complexity and sexual violence in female-fronted teen drama series', *New Review of Film and Television Studies*, 11(4): 477–96.

Berrington, E. & Honkatukia, P. (2002), 'An evil monster and a poor thing: Female violence in the media', *Journal of Scandinavian Studies in Criminology and Crime Prevention*, 3(1): 50–72.

Bettio, F. & Ticci, E. (2017), 'Violence and economic independence, Luxembourg', *Publications Office of the European Union*, Available online: https://op.europa.eu/en/publication-detail/-/publication/1643f084-92b0-11e7-b92d-01aa75ed71a1 (accessed 31 August 2020).

Bettio, F., Ticci, E. & Betti, G. (2020), 'L'eguaglianza di genere riduce la violenza sulle donne?', *Rassegna Italiana di Sociologia*, 1: 29–57.

Binder, A. (1993), 'Constructing racial rhetoric: Media depictions of harm in heavy metal and rap music', *American Sociological Review*, 58(7): 53–67.

Birch, H. ed (1993), *Moving Targets: Women, Murder and Representation*, London: Virago.

Bjørnholt, M. & Hjemdal, O. L. (2018), 'Measuring violence, mainstreaming gender: Does adding harm make a difference?', *Journal of Gender-Based Violence*, 2(3): 465–79.

Blackford, B. J. Gentry, J. Harrison, R. L. & Carlson, L. (2011), 'The prevalence and influence of the combination of humor and violence in super bowl commercials', *Journal of Advertising*, 40(4): 123–34.

Bloom, S. S. (2008), *Violence against Women and Girls: A Compendium of Monitoring and Evaluation Indicators*, Chapel Hill: Carolina Population.

Boddewyn, J.J. & Loubradou, E. (2011), 'The control of "sex in advertising" in France', *Journal of Public Policy & Marketing*, 30(2): 220–5.

Bordo, S. (1997), *Twilight Zones: The Hidden Life of Cultural Images from Plato to O. J.*, Berkeley: University of California Press.

Borgerson, J. L. & Schroeder, J. E. (2002), 'Ethical issues of global marketing: Avoiding bad faith in visual representation', *European Journal of Marketing*, 36(5/6): 570–94.

Bourdieu, P. (1998), *Masculine Domination*, Stanford, CA: Stanford University Press.

Bourdieu, P. (2001), *Masculine Domination*, Palo Alto: Stanford University Press.

Bourdieu, P. (2004), 'Gender and symbolic violence', in N. Scheper-Hughes & P. Bourgeois (eds), *Violence in War and Peace: An Anthology*, 339–42, Maiden: Blackwell.

Boutang, A. (2020), 'Girls against women: Contrasting female violence in contemporary young adult dystopias', in C. Maury & D. Roche (eds), *Women Who Kill: Gender and Sexuality in Films and Series of the Post-feminist Era*, 134–53, London: Bloomsbury Publishing.

Bower, A. (2001), 'Highly attractive models in advertising and the women who loathe them: The implementations of negative affect for spokesperson effectiveness', *Journal of Advertising*, 30(3): 51–63.

Bowleg, L. (2012), 'The problem with the phrase women and minorities: Intersectionality-an important theoretical framework for public health', *American Journal of Public Health*, 102(7),1267–73.

Boxall, H., Dowling, C. & Morgan, A. (2020), 'Female perpetrated domestic violence: Prevalence of self-defensive and retaliatory violence', *Trends and Issues in Crime and Criminal Justice*, 584: 1–17

Boyle, K. (2005), *Media and Violence: Gendering the Debates*, Sage: London.

Boyle, K. (2019a), '*#MeToo, Weinstein and Feminism*, Cham: Palgrave Pivot.

Boyle, K. (2019b), 'The sex of sexual violence', in L. Sheperd (ed), *Handbook on Gender and Violence*, Cheltenham: Edward Elgar Publishing.

Boyle, A., Jones, P. & Lloyd, S. (2006), 'The association between domestic violence and self harm in emergency medicine patients', *Emergency Medicine Journal*, 23(8): 604–7.

Bradbury-Jones, C. Clark, M. Paavilaainen, E. & Appleton, J. (2019), 'A profile of gender-based violence research in Europe: Findings from a focused mapping review and synthesis', *Trauma, Violence and Abuse*, 20(4): 470–83.

Bradshaw, L. (2013), 'Showtime's «female problem»: Cancer, quality and motherhood', *Journal of Consumer Culture*, 13(2): 160–77.

Brennan, P. & Vandenberg, A. (2016), 'Depictions of female offenders in front-page newspaper stories: The importance of race/ethnicity', *International Journal of Social Inquiry*, 2(2): 141–75.

Bretl, D. J. & Cantor, J. (1988), 'The portrayal of men and women in U.S. television commercials: A recent content analysis and trends over 15 years', *Sex Roles*, 18(9/10): 595–609.

Bretthauer, B. Zimmerman, T. & Banning, J. (2007), 'A feminist analysis of popular music', *Journal of Feminist Family Therapy*, 18(4): 29–51.

Britton, D. M. (2011), *The Gender of Crime*, Lanham: Rowman & Littlefield.

Brocato, E. D. Gentile, D. A. Laczniak, R. N., Maier, J. A. & Ji-Song, M. (2010), 'Television commercial violence: Potential effects on children', *Journal of Advertising*, 39(4): 95–107.

Bronfen, E. (1992), *Over Her Dead Body: Death, Femininity and the Aesthetic*, London: Routledge.

Bronstein, Carolyn (2008), 'No more black and blue: Women against violence against women and the warner communications boycott', *Violence against Women*, 14 (4): 418–36.

Brown, J. A. (2014), 'Torture, rape, action heroes and «The girl with the dragon tattoo»', in N. Jones, M. Bajac-Carter (eds), *Heroines of Film and Television: Portrayal in Popular Culture*, Lanham: Rowman & Littlefield.

Brown, J. A. (2015), *Beyond Bombshells. The New Action Heroine in Popular Culture*, Jackson: University Press of Mississippi.

Brown, W. (1995), *States of Injury: Power and Freedom in Late Modernity*, Princeton: Princeton University Press.

Bryła, P. & Gruczyńska, A. (2018), 'The perception of sexually provocative advertisements of American apparel by generation Y in Poland', *Polish Sociological Review*, 201(1): 109–25.

Bucchetti, V. (2021), *Cattive immagini. Design della comunicazione, grammatiche e parità di genere*, Milan: FrancoAngeli.

Buonanno, M. (2005), *Visibilità senza potere: le sorti progressive ma non magnifiche delle donne giornaliste italiane*, Naples: Liguori.

Buonanno, M. ed (2017), *Television Antiheroines: Women Behaving Badly in Crime and Prison Drama*, Bristol: Intellect Books.

Burawoy, M. (2005), 'For public sociology', *American Sociological Review*, 70(1): 4–28.

Burfoot, A. & Lord, S. eds (2006), *Killing Women: The Visual Culture of Gender and Violence*, Waterloo: Wilfrid Laurier University Press.

Burgazzi, R. (2021), *Il maschilismo orecchiabile. Mezzo secolo di sessismo nella musica leggera italiana*, Milan: Prospero editore.

Burgess, M. C. R. & Burpo, S. (2012), 'The effect of music videos on college students' perceptions of rape', *College Student Journal*, 46(4): 748–63.

Bushman, B. (2005), 'Violence and sex in television programs do not sell products in advertisements', *Psychological Science*, 16(9): 702–8.

Bushman, B. J. & Anderson, C. A. (2001), 'Media violence and the American public: Scientific facts versus media misinformation', *American Psychologist*, 56(6–7): 477–89.

Bushman, B. J. & Huesmann, L. R. (2001), 'Effects of televised violence on aggression', in D. G. Singer & J. L. Singer (eds), *Handbook of Children and the Media*, 223–54, Newbury Park: Sage.

Bushman, B. J. & Phillips, C. M. (2001), 'If the television program bleeds, memory for the advertisement recedes', *Current Directions in Psychological Science*, 10(2): 43–7.

Butcher, K. F., Park, K. H. & Piehl, A. M. (2017), 'Comparing apples to oranges: Differences in women's and men's incarceration and sentencing outcomes', *Journal of Labor Economics*, 35(1): 201–34.

Butler, J. (2017), *L'alleanza dei corpi*, Rome: Nottetempo.

Cain, M. & Howe, A. eds (2008), *Women, Crime and Social Harm: Towards a Criminology for the Global Age*, London: Bloomsbury Publishing.

Caman, S. Howner, K. Kristiansson, M. & Sturup, J. (2016), 'Differentiating male and female intimate partner homicide perpetrators: A study of social, criminological and clinical factors', *International Journal of Forensic Mental Health*, 15(1), 26–34.

Campbell, R. (1998), 'The community response to rape: Victims' experiences with the legal, medical and mental health systems', *American Journal of Community Psychology*, 25: 355–79.

Campus, L. (2015), *Non solo canzonette. L'Italia della ricostruzione e del miracolo attraverso il Festival di Sanremo*, Florence: Le Monnier.

Capecchi, S. (1995), 'Immagini di uomini e donne nella stampa periodica', *Problemi dell'informazione*, 1: 93–115.

Capecchi, S. (2006), *Identità di genere e media*, Milan: Carocci.

Capecchi, S. & Ruspini, E. (2009), 'Dal corpo vestito ai corpi "osceni". Ovvero: dall'erotismo alla pornografia online', in S. Capecchi & E. Ruspini (eds), *Media. Corpi, Sessualità. Dai corpi esibiti al cybersex*, 7–16, Milan: FrancoAngeli.

Capella, M. L., R. P. Hill, J. M. Rapp & J. Kees (2010), 'The impact of violence against women in advertisements', *Journal of Advertising*, 39(4): 37–52.

Capozzi, M. R. (2008), *La comunicazione pubblicitaria, Aspetti linguistici, sociali e culturali*, Milan: FrancoAngeli.

Carah, N. & Louw, E. (2015), *Media and Society: Production, Content and Participation*, Los Angeles: Sage.

Carlyle, K. E., Scarduzio, J. A. & Slater, M. D. (2014), 'Media portrayals of female perpetrators of intimate partner violence', *Journal of Interpersonal Violence*, 29(13): 2394–417.

Carlyle, K. E., Slater, M. D. & Chakroff, J. L. (2008), 'Newspaper coverage of intimate partner violence: Skewing representations of risk', *Journal of Communication*, 58: 168–86.

Caroline N. Tipler & Janet B. Ruscher (2019), 'Dehumanizing representations of women: The shaping of hostile sexist attitudes through animalistic metaphors', *Journal of Gender Studies*, 28(1): 109–18.

Carozzi, I. (2019), *L'età della tigre*, Milan: Il Saggiatore.

Carter, C. (1988), 'When the extraordinary becomes ordinary: Everyday news of sexual violence', in C. Carter, G. Branston & Allan (eds), *News, Gender and Power*, 219–32, London and New York: Routledge.

Carter, C. (2011), 'Sex/gender and the media: From sex roles to social construction and beyond', in K. Ross (ed), *The Handbook of Gender, Sex and Media*, 365–82, Oxford: Wiley-Blackwell.

Chesney-Lind, M. & Jones, N. (2010), *Fighting for Girls: New Perspectives on Gender and Violence*, New York: State University of New York.

Chesney-Lind, M. & Pasko, L. (2013), *The Female Offender: Girls, Women, and Crime*, Thousand Oaks: Sage.

Chodorow, N. (1978), *Reproducing Mothering*, Berkeley: University of California Press.

Ciccone, S. (2009), *Essere maschi tra potere e libertà*, Turin: Rosenberg & Sellier.

Clarke Dillman, J. (2014), *Women and Death in Film, Television, and News: Dead but Not Gone*, New York: Palgrave Macmillan.

Clover, C. J. (1992), *Men, Women, and Chain Saws: Gender in the Modern Horror Film*, London: BFI.

Cobb, M. D. & Boettcher, W. A. (2007), 'Ambivalent sexism and misogynistic rap music: Does exposure to Eminem increase sexism?', *Journal of Applied Social Psychology*, 37(12): 3025–42.

Coffey-Glover, L. & Handforth, R. (2019), 'Discourses of (hetero)sexism in popular music. The legacy of blurred lines', *Journal of Language and Sexuality*, 8(2): 139–65.

Collins, P. H. (2000), *Black Feminist Thought*, 2nd edn, New York: Routledge.

Collins, V. E. (2017), *State Crime, Women and Gender*, New York: Routledge.

Comas-d'Argemir, D. (2015), 'News of partner femicides: The shift from private issue to public concern', *European Journal of Communication*, 30(2): 131–6.

Connell, R. W. (1987), *Gender and Power*, Palo Alto: Stanford University Press.

Connell, R. W. (1995), *Masculinities*, Berkeley: University of California Press.

Connell, R. W. (2005), 'Globalization, imperialism, and masculinitie', in M. S. Kimmel, J. Hearn & R. W. Connell (eds), *Handbook of Studies on Men & Masculinities*, Thousand Oaks: Sage.

Cook, E.A. & Walklate, S. (2020), 'Gendered objects and gendered spaces: The invisibilities of "knife" crime', *Current Sociology*, 1–16.

Cooper, V. (1985), 'Women in popular music: A quantitative analysis of feminine images over time', *Sex Roles*, 13(9/10): 499–506.

Corradi, L. (2012), *Specchio delle sue brame, Analisi socio-politica delle pubblicità: genere, classe, razza, età ed eterosessismo*, Rome: Ediesse.

Costanzo, S. (2015), 'Omicidi passionali al femminile', in A. M. Casale, P. De Pasquali, A. Esposito, M. S. Lembo (eds), *Donne e reato. Aspetti giuridici, antropologici, medico-legali, criminologici, psicologici e psichiatrico forensi*, 263–77, Ravenna: Maggioli.

Coulthard, L., Horeck, T., Klinger, B. & McHugh, K. (2018), 'Broken bodies/ inquiring minds: Women in contemporary transnational TV crime drama', *Television & New Media*, 19(6): 507–14.

Council of Europe (2016), 'Preventing and combating violence against women', *Council of Europe*. Available online: https://www.coe.int/en/web/genderequality/violence-against-women#{%2216800160%22:[0]} (accessed July 2020).

Cowie, J., Cowie, V. & Slater, E. (1968), *Delinquency in Girls*, London: Heinemann.

Creeber, G. (2015), 'Killing us softly: Investigating the aesthetics, philosophy and influence of Nordic Noir Television', *Journal of Popular Television*, 3(1): 21–35.

Creed, B. (1986), 'Horror and the monstrous feminine: An imaginary abjection', in S. Thornham (ed), *Feminist Film Theory: A Reader*, 251–66, New York: New York University Press.

Crenshaw, K. (1991), 'Mapping the margins: Intersectionality, identity politics, and violence against women of color', *Stanford Law Review*, 43(6): 1241–99.

Crosby, S. (2004), 'The cruelest season: Female heroes snapped into sacrificial heroines', in S. A. Inness (ed), *Action Chicks: New Images of Tough Women in Popular Culture*, 153–78, New York: Palgrave Mcmillan.

Cross, G. (2002), 'Valves of desire: A historian's perspective on parents, children, and marketing', *Journal of Consumer Research*, 29(3): 441–7.

Cuklanz, L. (1995), 'News coverage of ethnic and gender issues in the big dan's rape case' in A. N. Valdivia (ed), *Feminism, Multiculturalism, and the Media*, 145–62, London: Sage.

Cummins, R. (2007), 'Selling music with sex: The content and effects of sex in music videos on viewer enjoyment', *Journal of Promotion Management*, 13: 95–109.

Cuzzocrea, V., Benasso, S. (2020), ' «Fatti strada e fatti furbo»: generazione Z, musica trap e influencer', *Studi culturali, Rivista quadrimestrale*, 3: 335–56.

Dahl, D. W. Frankenberger, K. D. & Manchanda, R. V. (2003), 'Does it pay to shock? Reactions to shocking and nonshocking advertising content among university students', *Journal of Advertising Research*, 43(3): 268–80.

Dal Lago, A. (1981), *La produzione della devianza*, Milan: Feltrinelli.

Daly, K. & Chesney-Lind, M. (1988), 'Feminism and criminology', *Justice Quarterly*, 5(4): 497–538.

Dardot, P. & Laval, C. (2013), *La nuova ragione del mondo. Critica della razionalità neoliberista*, Rome: Derive Approdi.

Davidson, K. (2003), *Selling Sin: The Marketing of Socially Unacceptable Products*, Westport: Praeger.

Davies, P. (2011), *Gender, Crime and Victimisation*, London: Sage.

Davoine, L. & Jarrett, E. (2018), *Uncovering Possible Causes of Violence against Women to Explain Country Differences across the EU, Manuscript*, Brussels: European Commission.

De Lauretis, T. (1987), *Technologies of Gender: Essays on Theory, Film and Fiction*, Bloomington: University of Indiana Press.

De Martino, E. (1959), *Sud e magia*, Milan: Feltrinelli.

DeNora, T. (2000), *Music in Everyday Life*, Cambridge: Cambridge University Press.

DeNora, T. (2003), *After Adorno: Rethinking Music Sociology*, Cambridge: Cambridge University Press.

Deriu, F. (2016), 'Violenza di genere, capacitazione, resilienza ed empowerment: Verso un nuovo framework interpretativo', *Autonomie locali e servizi sociali*, 39(2): 201–10.

DeTardo Bora, K. A. (2009), 'Criminal justice «Hollywood style»: How women in criminal justice professions are depicted on prime-time crime dramas', *Women and Criminal Justice*, 19(2): 153–68.

De Welde, K. (2012), 'Kick-Ass feminism: Violence, resistance, and feminist avengers in Larsson's trilogy', in D. King & C. Smith (eds), *Men Who Hate Women and Women Who Kick Their Asses: Stieg Larsson's Millennium Trilogy in Feminist Perspective*, 376–564, Nashville: Vanderbilt University Press (kindle edition).

Diaz-Aguardo, M. J. & Martinez, R. (2015), 'Types of adolescent male dating violence against women, self-esteem, and justification of dominance and aggression', *Journal of Interpersonal Violence*, 30(15): 2636–58.

Dietz, T. L. & Jasinski, J. L. (2003), 'Female-perpetrated partner violence and aggression: Their relationship to gender identity', *Women & Criminal Justice*, 15(1): 81–99.

Dillman, J. C. (2014), *Women and Death in Film, Television, and News: Dead but Not Gone*, New York: Palgrave Macmillan.

Dim, E. E. (2020), 'Experiences of physical and psychological violence against male victims in Canada: A qualitative study', *International Journal of Offender Therapy and Comparative Criminology*, 65(9): 1029–54.

Dobash, R. E. & R. P. Dobash. (1979), *Violence against Wives*, New York: The Free Press.

Dobash, R. E. & Dobash, R. P. eds (1998), *Rethinking Violence against Women*, Thousand Oaks: Sage.

Dobash, R. E. & Dobash, R. P. (2004), 'Women's violence to men in intimate relationships: Working on a puzzle', *British Journal of Criminology*, 44: 324–49.

Dobash, R. P., Dobash, R. E., Cavanagh, K. & Lewis, R. (1998), 'Separate and intersecting realities: A comparison of men's and women's accounts of violence against women', *Violence against Women*, 4(4): 382–414.

Dragotto, F., Giomi, E. & Melchiorre, S. M. (2020), 'Putting women back in their place. Reflections on slut-shaming, the case Asia Argento and Twitter in Italy', *International Review of Sociology*, 30(1): 46–70.

Durham, M. G. (2012), 'Blood, lust and love', *Journal of Children and Media*, 6(3): 281–99.

Early, F. & Kennedy, K. eds (2003), *Athena's Daughters: Television's New Women Warriors*, New York: Syracuse University Press.

Easteal, P., Bartels, L., Nelson, N. & Holland, K. (2015), 'How are women who kill portrayed in newspaper media? Connections with social values and the legal system', *Women's Studies International Forum*, 51: 31–41.

Easteal, P., Holland, K. & Judd, K. (2015), 'Enduring themes and silences in media portrayals of violence against women', *Women's Studies International Forum*, 48: 103–13.

Edwards, E. (2020), *Graphic Violence- Illustrated Theories About Violence, Popular Media, and Our Social Lives*, New York: Routledge.

Elmquist, J. et al. (2014), 'Motivations for intimate partner violence in men and women arrested for domestic violence and court referred to batterer intervention programs', *Partner Abuse*, 5(4): 359–74.

Enander, V. (2011), 'Violent women? The challenge of women's violence in intimate heterosexual relationships to feminist analyses of partner violence', *NORA – Nordic Journal of Feminist and Gender Research*, 19(2): 105–23.

European Commission (2018), *Report on Equality between Women and Men in the European Union*, EU.

European Commission (2020), *Gender Balance in Decision-making*, EU.

European Institute for Gender Equality (2020), *Gender Equality Index 2020 Report*, EIGE.

European Parliament (2019), *Women in Politics: A Global Perspective*, European Parliamentary Research Service.

Eurostat (2020), *Gender Pay Gap Statistics*, Author.

Evans, A. Riley, S. & Shankar, A. (2010), 'Technologies of sexiness: Theorizing women's engagement in the sexualization of culture', *Feminism & Psychology*, 20(1): 114–31.

Evans, M. (2003), *Love: An Unromantic Discussion*, Cambridge: Polity Press.

Fairclough, N. (1995), *Media Discourse*, London: Edward Arnold.

Faith, K. (1993), *Unruly Women: The Politics of Confinement and Resistance*, Vancouver: Press Gang.

Faludi, S. (1991), *Backlash: The Undeclared War against Women*, London: Chatto & Windus

Fanci, G. (2011), 'La vittimizzazione secondaria: ambiti di ricerca, teorizzazioni e scenari', *Rivista di Criminologia, Vittimologia e Sicurezza*, 5(3): 53–66.

Fariello, S. (2012), 'Madri assassine. La costruzione degli ordini discorsivi sul figlicidio', in A. Simone (ed), *Sessismo democratico. L'uso strumentale dei corpi delle donne nel neoliberismo*, 19–30, Milan: Mimesis.

Farrell, A. L., Keppel, R. D. & Titterington, V. B. (2011), 'Lethal ladies: Revisiting what we know about female serial murderers', *Homicide Studies*, 15(3): 228–52.

Fearing, A. Konkle, T. R. Laitsch, J. Pierce, H. Rater, C. Reece, K. Stoecker, R. & Varelis, T. (2018), 'Is hip-hop violent? Analyzing the relationship between live music performances and violence', *Journal of Black Studies*, 49(3): 235–55.

Ferber, A. (2012), 'Always ambivalent: Why media is never just entertainment', in D. King & C. Smith (eds), *Men Who Hate Women and Women Who Kick Their Asses: Stieg Larsson's Millennium Trilogy in Feminist Perspective*, 172–371, Nashville: Vanderbilt University Press.

Fernández De Vega A., Lombardo, E. & Rolandsen Agustin, L. (2016), 'Report analysing intersectionality in gender equality policies for the EU', *Politics*, 36(4): 364–73.

Ferraro, K. (2015), *Neither Angels nor Demons: Women, Crime, and Victimization*, Boston: Northeastern University Press.

Finley, L. (2016), *Domestic Abuse and Sexual Assault in Popular Culture*, Santa Barbara: ABC-CLIO.

Finley, L. ed (2018), *Violence in Popular Culture: American and Global Perspectives*. Westport, CT: Greenwood.

Fitz-Gibbon, K. & Walklate, S. (2018), *Gender, Crime and Criminal Justice*, New York: Routledge.

Flood, M. (2019), *Engaging Men and Boys in Violence Prevention*, Palgrave Macmillan: New York.

Flynn, M., Craig, C. Anderson, C. & Holody, K. (2016), 'Objectification in popular music lyrics: An examination of gender and genre differences', *Sex Roles*, 75: 164–76.

FRA – European Union Agency for Fundamental Rights (2014), *Violence Against Women: An EU-Wide Survey. Main Results*, Luxembourg: Publications Office of the European Union.

Franiuk, R. & Scherr, S. (2013), 'The lion fell in love with the lamb', *Feminist Media Studies*, 13(1): 14–28.

Fraser, N. (2009), 'Feminism and the cunning of history', *New Left Review*, 56: 97–117.

Fredrickson, B. L. & Roberts, T. A. (1997), 'Objectification theory: Toward understanding women's lived experiences and mental health risks', *Psychology of Women Quarterly*, 21: 173–206.

Freedman, J. L. (2002), *Media Violence and Its Effect on Aggression: Assessing the Scientific Evidence*. Toronto: University of Toronto Press.

Fridel, E. E. (2019), 'Leniency for lethal ladies: Using the actor–partner interdependence model to examine gender-based sentencing disparities', *Homicide studies*, 23(4): 319–43.

Fridel, E. E. & Fox, J. A. (2019), 'Gender differences in patterns and trends in US homicide, 1976-2017', *Violence and Gender*, 6(1): 27–36.

Friedan, B. (1963), *The Feminine Mystique*, New York: Norton.

Frigon, S. (2006), 'Mapping scripts and narratives of women who kill their husbands in Canada, 1866–1954: Inscribing the everyday', in A. Burfoot & S. Lord (eds), *Killing Women: The Visual Culture of Gender and Violence*, 3–20, Waterloo: Wilfrid Laurier University Press.

Frith, S. (1978), *The Sociology of Rock*, London: Constable.

Frith, S. (1987), 'Towards an aesthetic of popular music', in R. Leppert & S. McClary (eds), *Music and Society: The Politics of Composition, Performance and Reception*, 133–50, Cambridge: Cambridge University Press.

Frye, N. (1957), *Anatomy of Criticism: Four Essays*, Princeton: Princeton University Press.

Fulu, E. Warner, X. Miedema, S. Jewkes, R. Roselli, T. & Lang, J. (2013), *Why Do Some Men Use Violence against Women and How Can We Prevent It? Quantitative Findings from the United Nations Multi-Country Study on Men and Violence in Asia and the Pacific*, Bangkok: Partners for Prevention, UNDP, UNFPA, UN Women and UNV.

Garcia-Moreno, C. Heise, L. Jansen, Ha. F. M., Ellsberg, M. & Watts, C. (2005), 'Violence against Women', *Science*, 25: 1282–83.

García-Moreno, C., Zimmerman, C., Morris-Gehring, A., Heise, L. L., Amin, A., Abrahams, N. & Watts, C. (2005), 'Addressing violence against women: a call to action', *Lancet*, 385: 1685–1695.

Garfinkel, H. (1956), 'Conditions of successful degradation ceremonies', *American Journal of Sociology*, 61(5): 420–4.

Garland, T. S., Branch, K. A. & Grimes, M. (2016), 'Blurring the lines: Reinforcing rape myths in comic books', *Feminist Criminology*, 11(1): 48–68.

Gartland, D., H. Woolhouse, F. Mensah, K. Hegarty, H. Hiscock & S. Brown (2014), 'The case for early intervention to reduce the impact of intimate partner abuse on child outcomes: Results of an Australian cohort of first-time mothers', *Birth*, 41(4): 374–83.

Gartner, R. & Jung, M. (2014), 'Sex, gender, and homicide: Contemporary trends and patterns', in R. Gartner & B. McCarthy (eds), *The Oxford Handbook of Gender, Sex, and Crime*, 424–47, Oxford: Oxford University Press.

Gartner, R. & McCharty, B. eds (2014), *The Oxford Handbook of Gender, Sex, and Crime*, Oxford: Oxford University Press.

Gelles, R. J. & Straus, M. A. (1979), 'Determinants of violence in the family: Toward a theoretical integration', in W. Burr et al. (eds), *Contemporary Theories about the Family*, 550–81 New York: Free Press.

Gentry, C. (2020), *Disordered Violence. How Gender, Race and Heteronormativity Structure Terrorism*, Edinburgh: Edinburgh University Press.

Gentry, C. & Sjoberg, L. (2015), *Beyond Mothers, Monsters, Whores: Thinking About Women's Violence in Global Politics*, London: Zed Books.

Gerbner, G. & Gross, L. (1976), 'Living with television: The violence profile', *Journal of Communication*, 26: 172–94.

Gilbert, P. R. (2002), 'Discourses of female violence and societal gender stereotypes' *Violence against Women*, 8(11): 1271–300.

Gilchrist, K. R. (2020), 'Dysfunction, deviancy, and sexual autonomy: The single female detective in primetime TV', *Television & New Media*.

Gill, A. K. & Day, A. S. (2020), 'Moral panic in the media: Scapegoating South Asian men in cases of sexual exploitation and grooming', in S. Ramon, M. Lloyd & B. Penhale (eds), *Gendered Domestic Violence and Abuse in Popular Culture (Emerald Studies in Popular Culture and Gender)*, 171–97, Bingley: Emerald Publishing Limited.

Gill, R. (2003), 'From sexual objectification to sexual subjectification: The resexualization of women's bodies in the media', *Feminist Media Studies*, 3(1): 100–6.

Gill, R. (2007), *Gender and the Media*, Polity Press: Cambridge.

Gill, R. (2008), 'Empowerment/sexism: Figuring female sexual agency in contemporary advertising', *Feminism & Psychology*, 18(1): 35–60.

Gillespie, L. K., Richards, T. N., Givens, E. M. & Smith, M. D. (2013), 'Framing deadly domestic violence: Why the media's spin matters in newspaper coverage of femicide', *Violence against Women*, 19(2): 222–45.

Giomi, E. (2013), 'Il femminicidio nelle relazioni intime: analisi quantitativa del fenomeno e della sua rappresentazione nei TG italiani', in S.

Magaraggia, D. Cherubini (eds), *Uomini contro le donne? Le radici della violenza maschile*, 131–49, Turin: Utet.

Giomi, E. (2015), 'Tag femminicidio. La violenza letale contro le donne nella stampa italiana', *Problemi dell'informazione*, 40(3): 549–74.

Giomi, E. (2015a), *Quaderno di appunti di Gender e Media*, Rome: Pigreco

Giomi, E. (2015b), 'Tag femminicidio. La violenza letale contro le donne nella stampa italiana', *Problemi dell'informazione*, 40(3): 549–74.

Giomi, E. (2016), *Gender, Sexuality, and Violence in Contemporary TV Series. A Comparison between the U.S. and Europe*, [Paper presentation] Leicester, UK: International Association for Media and Communication Research (IAMCR) Conference, 27–31 July 2016.

Giomi, E. (2017), '"Really good at it": The viral charge of Weeds' Nancy Botwin (and popular culture's anticorps)' in M. Buonanno (ed), *Television Antiheroines. Women Behaving Badly in Crime and Prison Drama*, 105–24, Bristol: Intellect Books.

Giomi, E. (2018), *Man of Any Size Lays Hands on Me, He's Gonna bleed Out in under a Minute*, [Paper presentation], Oxford: 'Pleasures of Violence' International Conference, 7 e 8 March 2019.

Giomi, E. (2019), 'La rappresentazione delle violenze maschili contro le donne nei media. Frame, cause e soluzioni del problema nei programmi RAI', *Studi sulla questione criminale*, 1–2: 223–48.

Giomi, E. & Magaraggia, S. (2017), *Relazioni brutali: Genere e violenza nella cultura mediale*. Turin: Il Mulino.

Giomi, E. & Tonello, F. (2013), 'Moral panic: The issue of women and crime in Italian evening news', *Sociologica*, 3: 3–29.

Gius, C. & Lalli, P. (2014), 'I loved her so much, but I killed her»: Romantic love as a representational frame for intimate partner femicide in three Italian newspapers', *ESSACHESS. Journal for Communication Studies*, 7(2): 53–75.

Glueck, S. & Glueck, E. L. (1934), *Five Hundred Delinquent Women*, New York: Alfred A. Knopf.

Goffman, E. (1976), *Gender Advertisements*, New York: Harper.

Goffman, E. (1977), 'The arrangement between the sexes', *Theory and Society*, 4(3): 301–31.

Goffman, E. (1979), *Gender Advertisements*, Cambridge: Harvard University Press.

Gordon, M. K. (2008), '"Media contribution to African American girls" Focus on beauty and appearance: Exploring the consequences of sexual objectification', *Psychology of Women Quarterly*, 32(3): 245–56.

Gracia, E. & Merlo, J. (2016),'Intimate partner violence against women and the Nordic paradox', *Social Science & Medicine (1982)*, 157: 27–30.

Graham, L. M., Macy, R. J., Rizo, C. F. & Martin, S. L. (2020), 'Explanatory theories of intimate partner homicide perpetration: A systematic review', *Trauma, Violence & Abuse*, 22(1): 18–40.

Grau, S. L. & Zotos, Y. C. (2016), 'Gender stereotypes in advertising: A review of current research', *International Journal of Advertising*, 35(5): 761–70.

Greer, C. (2003), 'Sex crime and the media: Press representations in Northern Ireland', in P. Mason, Cullompton, W. (eds), *Criminal Visions: Media Representations of Crime and Justice*, 90–116, Devon: Willan Publishing.

Greimas, A. J. & Fontanille, J. (1991), *Sémiotique des passions. Des états de choses aux états d'âme*, trans. (1993), [The semiotics of passions: From states of affairs to states of feeling], Minneapolis: University of Minnesota Press.

Gribaldo, A. (2020), *Unexpected Subjects: Intimate Partner Violence, Testimony, and the Law*, Chicago: University of Chicago Press.

Grönevik, K. (2013), 'The depiction of women in rap and pop lyrics' Doc. Diss., Linnaeus University.

Guevara, N. (1996), 'Women writin' rappin' breakin'', *Droppin' Science*, 49–62, Philadelphia, PA: Temple UP.

Gulas, C. S. & McKeage, K. K. (2000), 'Extending social comparison: An examination of the unintended consequences of idealized advertising imagery', *Journal of Advertising*, 29(2): 17–28.

Gulas, C. S., McKeage, K. K. & Weinberger, M. G. (2010), 'It's just a joke: Violence against males in humorous advertising', *Journal of Advertising*, 39(4): 109–20.

Gurrieri, L., Brace-Govan, J. & Cherrier, H. (2016), 'Controversial advertising: Transgressing the taboo of gender-based violence', *European Journal of Marketing*, 50(7/8): 1448–69.

Hagan, J., Simpson, J. & Gillis, R. (1987), 'Class in the household: A Power-Control Theory of gender and delinquency', *American Journal of Sociology*, 92(4): 788–816.

Halberstam, J. (1993), 'Imagined violence/queer violence: Representation, rage, and resistance', *Social Text*, 37: 187–201.

Hall, C. P., West, J. H. & Hill, S. (2012), 'Sexualization in lyrics of popular music from 1959 to 2009: Implications for sexuality educators', *Sexuality and Culture*, 16: 103–17.

Hall, S. (1980), 'Recent developments in theories of language and ideology:
A. Critical Note', in S. Hall, D. Hobson, A. Lowe & P. Willis (eds), *Culture,
Media, Language: Working Papers in Cultural* Studies *1972–79*, 157–62,
London: Hutchinson.

Hall, S. (1986), 'On postmodernism and articulation: An interview with Stuart
Hall', *Journal of Communication Inquiry*, 10(2):45–60.

Hall, S. (1997), *Representation: Cultural Representations and Signifying
Practices*. London: Sage/The Open University.

Hansen, C. H. & Hansen, R. D. (1990), 'Rock music videos and antisocial
behavior', *Basic and Applied Social Psychology*, 11(4): 357–69.

Hansen, C. H. (2007), 'Music videos, effects of', in J. J. Arnett (ed), *Encyclopedia
of Children, Adolescents, and the Media*, 602–3, Thousand Oaks: Sage.

Hansen, K. T. (2020), 'From Nordic Noir to Euro Noir: Nordic Noir
influencing European serial SVoD drama', in L. Badley, A. Nestingen, J.
Seppälä (eds), *Nordic Noir, Adaptation, Appropriation*, 275–94, Cham:
Palgrave Macmillan.

Hardy, K. A. (2014), 'Cows, pigs, whales: Nonhuman animals, antifat bias, and
exceptionalist logics', in R. Chastain (ed), *The Politics of Size: Perspectives
from the Fat Acceptance Movement*, 187–206, Santa Barbara: Praeger.

Haridakis, P.M. (2006), 'Men, women, and televised violence: predicting
viewer aggression in male and female television viewers', *Communication
Quarterly*, 54(2): 227–255.

Harper, S. B. (2017), 'No way out: Severely abused Latina women, patriarchal
terrorism, and self-help homicide', *Feminist Criminology*, 12(3): 224–47.

Hart, L. (1994), *Fatal Women: Lesbian Sexuality and the Mark of Aggression*,
Princeton: Princeton University Press.

Haugen, J. (2003), '"Unladylike divas": Language, gender, and female gangsta
rappers', *Popular Music and Society*, 26(4): 429–44.

Haynes, J. (2009), 'Exposing domestic violence in country music videos', in
L. M. Cuklanz & S. Moorti (eds), *Local Violence, Global Media: Feminist
Analyses of Gendered Representations*, 201–21, New York: Peter Lang
Publishing.

Hearn, J. (1998), *The Violences of Men*, London: Sage.

Hearn, J. (2012), 'A multi-faceted power analysis of men's violence to known
women: From hegemonic masculinity to the hegemony of men', *The
Sociological Review*, 60(4), 589–610.

Hearn, J. Strid, S. Husu, L. & Verloo, M. (2016), 'Interrogating violence
against women and state violence policy: Gendered intersectionalities and

the quality of policy in The Netherlands, Sweden and the UK', *Current Sociology*, 64(4): 551–67.

Hegarty, K., Fracgp, Bush, R. & Sheehan, M. (2005), 'The composite abuse scale: Further development and assessment of reliability and validity of a multidimensional partner abuse measure in clinical settings', *Violence and victims*, 20(5), 529–47.

Heidensohn, F. (2006), 'New perspectives and established views', *Gender and Justice*, 34(2): 304–6.

Heidensohn, F. & Silvestri, M. (2012), 'Gender and crime', in M. Maguire, R. Morgan, R. Reiner (eds), *The Oxford Handbook of Criminology*, 336–69, Oxford: Oxford University Press.

Heimer, K. & Kruttschnitt, C. (2005), *Gender and Crime: Patterns in Victimization and Offending*, New York: New York University Press.

Henry, N. & Powell, A. (2016), 'Technology-facilitated sexual violence: A literature review of empirical research', *Trauma, Violence, & Abuse*, 19(2): 195–208.

Herd, D. (2009), 'Changing images of violence in rap music lyrics: 1979–1997', *Journal of Public Health Policy*, 30(4): 395–406.

Héritier, F. (1996), *De la violence*, Paris: Jacob

Higgins, L. & Silver, B. A. eds (1991), *Rape and Representation*, New York: Columbia University Press.

Hill, A., Turnbull, S. et al. (2016), 'Nordic Noir', in *Oxford Research Encyclopedia of Criminology*, 1: 1–21, Oxford: Oxford University Press.

Hill, M. L. (2009), *Beats, Rhymes, and Classroom Life: Hip-Hop Pedagogy and the Politics of Identity*, New York: Teachers College Press.

Hird, M. J. (2002), *Engendering Violence: Heterosexual Interpersonal Violence from Childhood to Adulthood*, New York: Routledge.

Hoffman, B. Ware, J. & Shapiro, E. (2020), 'Assessing the threat of incel violence', *Studies in Conflict & Terrorism*, 43(7): 565–87.

Hollander, J. A. (2001), 'Vulnerability and dangerousness: The construction of gender through conversation about violence', *Gender & Society*, 15: 1–8.

Hollander, J. A. (2014), 'Does self-defense training prevent sexual violence against women?' *Violence against Women*, 20(3): 252–69.

Holmlund, C. (1993), 'A decade of Deadly Dolls: Hollywood and the woman killer', in H. Birch (ed), *Moving Targets: Women, Murder and Representation*, 127–15, London: Virago.

Holt, S., Buckley, H. & Whelan, S. (2008), 'The impact of exposure to domestic violence on children and young people: A review of the literature', *Child Abuse and Neglect*, 32(8): 797–810.

hooks, B. (1994), 'Sexism and misogyny: Who takes the rap? Misogyny, gangsta rap, and the piano', *ZMagazine*, February

Horeck, T. (2013), *Public Rape: Representing Violation in Fiction and Film*, London: Routledge.

Horeck, T. (2018), 'Screening affect: Rape culture and the digital interface in the fall and top of the Lake', *Television & New Media*, 19(6): 569–87.

Horeck, T. (2019), *Justice on Demand: True Crime in the Digital Streaming Era*, Detroit: Wayne State University Press.

Huesmann, L. R. & Taylor, L. D. (2006), 'The role of media violence in violent behavior', *Annual Review of Public Health*, 27(1): 393–415.

Huhmann, B. A. & Limbu, Y. B. (2016), 'Influence of gender stereotypes on advertising offensiveness and attitude toward advertising in general', *International Journal of Advertising: The Review of Marketing Communications*, 35(5): 846–63.

Humphries, D. ed (2009), *Women, violence and the media*, Lebanon: Northeastern University Press.

Hutchby, I. (2006), *Media talk: Conversation Analysis and the Study of Broadcasting*, Maidenhead: Open University Press.

Illouz, E. (2013), *Why Love Hurts: A Sociological Explanation*, New York: Polity.

Illouz, E. (2021), *Why Love Hurts: A Sociological Explanation*, London: Polity Press.

Inness, S. A. (1999), *Tough Girls: Women, Warriors and Wonder Women in Popular Culture*, Philadelphia: University of Pennsylvania Press.

Istanbul Convention (2011), Council of Europe Convention on preventing and combating violence against women and domestic violence.

Istat (2021), *Autori e vittime di omicidio, Anni 2018–2019*, Rome: Author.

Iyengar, S. (1991), *Is Anyone Responsible?: How Television Frames Political Issues*, Chicago: University of Chicago Press.

Jack, D. C. (2001), *Behind the Mask. Destruction and Creativity in Women's Aggression*, Cambridge: Harvard University Press.

Jack, S. P., Petrosky, E., Lyons, B. H., Blair, J. M., Ertl, A. M., Sheats, K. J. & Betz, C. J. (2018), 'Surveillance for violent deaths – national violent death reporting system, 27 states, 2015', *MMWR Surveillance Summaries*, 67(11): 1–32.

Jasinski, J. L. (2004), 'Pregnancy and domestic violence: A review of the literature', *Trauma, Violence, and Abuse*, 5(1):47–64.

Jasinski, J. L. (2004), 'Pregnancy and domestic violence: A review of the literature', *Trauma, Violence & Abuse*, 5(1): 47–64.

Jermyn, D. (2016), 'Silk blouses and fedoras: The female detective, contemporary TV crime drama and the predicaments of postfeminism', *Crime, Media, Culture*, 13(3): 259–76.

Jernej, K. (2018), 'Reality of trap: Trap music and its emancipatory potential', *IAFOR Journal of Media, Communication & Film*, 5(2): 23–41.

Jewkes, Y. (2015), *Media and Crime: Key Approaches to Criminology*, London: Sage Publications.

Ji, Mindy R, & Russell N. Laczniak (2007), "Advertisers' implementation of CARU guidelines for advertising targeted at children', *Journal of Current Issues and Research in Advertising*, 29: 27–38.

Johnson, M. P. (1995), 'Patriarchal terrorism and common couple violence: Two forms of violence against women', *Journal of Marriage and the Family*, 57: 283–94.

Johnson, M. P. (2006), 'Conflict and control: Gender symmetry and asymmetry in domestic violence', *Violence against Women*, 12(11): 1003–8.

Johnson, M. P. & Ferraro, K. J. (2000), 'Research on domestic violence in the 1990s: Making distinctions', *Journal of Marriage and Family*, 62(4): 948–63.

Johnson, M. P. & Leone, J. M. (2005), 'The differential effects of intimate terrorism and situational couple violence: Findings from the national violence against women survey', *Journal of family issues*, 26(3): 322–349.

Johnson, J., Jackson, L. & Gatto, L. (1995), 'Violent attitudes and deferred academic aspirations: Deleterious effects of exposure to rap music', *Basic and Applied Social Psychology*, 16: 27–41.

Jones, N., Bajac-Carter, M. & Batchelor, B. eds (2014), *Heroines of Film and Television: Portrayal in Popular Culture*, Lanham: Rowman & Littlefield.

Jones, T. P. Cunningham, H. & Gallagher, K. (2010), 'Violence in advertising: A multilayered content analysis', *Journal of Advertising*, 39(4): 11–36.

Jouriles, E. N. Mueller, V. Rosenfield, D. McDonald, R. & Dodson, M. C. (2012), 'Teens experiences of harsh parenting and exposure to severe intimate partner violence: Adding insult to injury in predicting teen dating violence', *Psychology of Violence*, 2(2): 125–38.

Jung, J. (2011), 'Advertising images of men: Body size and muscularity of men depicted' men's health magazine', *Journal of Global Fashion Marketing*, 2(4): 181–7.

Karaian, L. (2014), 'Policing "sexting": Responsibilization, respectability and sexual subjectivity in child protection/crime prevention responses to teenagers' digital sexual expression', *Theoretical Criminology*, 18(3): 282–99.

Karpinska-Krakowiak, M. (2020), 'Gotcha! Realism of comedic violence and its impact on brand responses', *Journal of Advertising Research*, 60(1): 38–53.

Karsay, K. Knoll, J. & Matthes, J. (2018), 'Sexualizing media use and self-objectification. A meta-analysis', *Psychology of Women Quarterly*, 42: 9–28.

Karsay, K. Matthes, J. Buchsteiner, L. & Grosser, V. (2019), 'Increasingly sexy? Sexuality and sexual objectification in popular music videos, 1995–2016', *Psychology of Popular Media Culture*, 8(4): 346–57.

Katz, J. (2003), 'Advertising and the construction of violent white masculinity: From Eminem to "Clinique for Men"', in G. Dines, J. M. Humez (eds), *Gender, Race, Class and the Media*, 349–58, Thousand Oaks: Sage

Katz, J. & Earp, J. (1999), *Tough Guise: Violence, Media & the Crisis in Masculinity*, North Hampton: Media Education Foundation.

Kaufman, M. (1999), 'The seven P's of men's violence', www.michaelkaufman.com (august 1999).

Kay, M., Matuszek, C. & Munson, S. A. (2015), 'Unequal representation and gender stereotypes in image search results for occupations', in B. Begole & J. Kim (eds), *CHI 2015. Proceedings of the 33rd Annual ACM Conference on Human Factors in Computing Systems*, 3819–28.

Kellner, D. (2008), *Guys and Guns Amok: Domestic Terrorism and School Shootings from the Oklahoma City Bombings to the Virginia Tech Massacre*, Boulder: Paradigm.

Kelly, L. (1988), *Surviving Sexual Violence*, Minneapolis: University of Minnesota Press.

Key, W. B. (1973), *Subliminal Seduction: Ad Media's Manipulation of a not so Innocent America*, New York: Signet.

Keyes, C. (2002), *Rap Music and Street Consciousness*, Urbana: University of Illinois Press

Khan, U. (2017), 'Fetishizing music as rape culture', *Studies in Gender and Sexuality*, 18(1): 19–30.

Kilbourne, J. (1990), 'Beauty…and the beast of advertising', *Gender in the Media*, 49(2): 1–5.

Kim, Y. & Yoon, H. (2014), 'What makes people "like" comedic-violence advertisements? A model for predicting attitude and sharing intention', *Journal of Advertising Research*, 54(2): 217–32.

Kimmel, M. (2000), *The Gendered Society*, Oxford: Oxford University Press.

Kimmel, M. (2002a), '«Gender Symmetry» in domestic violence: A substantive and methodological research review', *Violence against women*, 8(11): 1332–63.

Kimmel, M. (2002b), 'Maschilità e omofobia. Paura, vergogna e silenzio nella costruzione dell'identità di genere', in C. Leccardi (ed), *Tra i generi. Rileggendo le differenze di genere, di generazione di orientamento sessuale*, 171–94, Milan: Guerini.

Kimmel, M. (2005), *The Gender of Desire*, Albany: State University of New York Press.

Kimmel, M. (2013), «Che cosa c'entra l'amore? Stupro, violenza domestica e la costruzione dell'uomo», in Magaraggia e Cherubini, *Uomini contro le donne?*, 20–34, Torino: Utet.

King, D. & Lee Smith, C. eds (2012), 'Men who hate women and women who kick their asses', *Stieg Larsson's Millennium Trilogy in Feminist Perspective*, Nashville: Vanderbilt University.

Kistler, M. & Lee, M. (2009), 'Does exposure to sexual hip-hop music videos influence the sexual attitudes of college students?', *Mass Communication and Society*, 13: 67–86.

Kitwana, B. (1994), *The Rap on Gangsta Rap*, Chicago: Third World Press.

Kivivuori, J. & Lehti, M. (2012), 'Social correlates of intimate partner homicide in Finland: Distinct or shared with other homicide types?', *Homicide Studies*, 16(1): 60–77.

Klinger, B. (2018), 'Gateway bodies: Serial form, genre, and white femininity in imported crime TV', *Television & New Media*, 19(6): 515–34.

Konradi, A. (1996), 'Preparing to testify: Rape survivors negotiating the criminal justice process', *Gender & Society*, 10(4): 404–32.

Krause, A. E. & North, A. C. (2019), 'Pop music lyrics are related to the proportion of female recording artists: Analysis of the united kingdom weekly top five song lyrics, 1960–2015', *Psychology of Popular Media Culture*, 8(3): 233–42.

Krug, E. G. L. Dahlberg, J. A. Mercy, A. B. Zwi & R. Lozano eds (2002), *World Report on Violence and Health*, Geneva: World Health Organization.

Kruttschnitt, C., Gartner, R. & Hussemann, J. (2008), 'Female violent offenders: Moral panics or more serious offenders?', *The Australian and New Zealand Journal of Criminology*, 41(1): 9–35.

Kubrin, C. E. (2005), 'Gangstas, thugs, and hustlas: Identity and the code of the street in rap music', *Social Problems*, 52: 360–78.

Laing, L. (2017), 'Secondary victimization: Domestic violence survivors navigating the family law system', *Violence against Women*, 23(11): 1314–35.

Lalli, P. (2020), *L'amore non uccide. Femminicidio e discorso pubblico: cronaca, tribunali, politiche*, Bologna: Il Mulino.

Lalli, P. (2021), *L'amore Non Uccide. Femminicidio e discorso pubblico: cronaca, tribunali, politiche*, Bologna: Il Mulino.

Lamb, S. (1999), 'Constructing the victim: Popular images and lasting labels', in S. Lamb (ed), *New Visions of Victims: Feminists Struggle with the Concept*, 108–38, New York: University Press.

Landreth Grau, S. & Zotos, Y. C. (2016), 'Gender stereotypes in advertising: A review of current research', *International Journal of Advertising*, 35(5): 761–770.

Langhinrichsen-Rohling, J., Misra, T. A., Selwyn, C. & Rohling, M. L. (2012), 'Rates of bidirectional versus unidirectional intimate partner violence across samples, sexual orientations, and race/ethnicities: A comprehensive review', *Partner Abuse*, 3(2): 199–230.

Larsen, M. (2016), *Health Inequities Related to Intimate Partner Violence against Women. The Role of Social Policy in the United States, Germany, and Norway*, Cham: Springer.

Larson, M. S. (2001), 'Interactions, activities and gender in children's television commercials: A content analysis', *Journal of Broadcasting and Electronic Media*, 45(1): 41–56.

Larson, M. S. (2003), 'Gender, race, and aggression in television commercials that feature children', *Sex Roles*, 48(1/2): 67–75.

Latino, A. (2019), 'Manifestazioni e considerazioni della violenza nei confronti delle donne alla luce della Convenzione di Istanbul', *Studi sulla questione criminale*, 1–2: 165–86.

Laviosa, F. (2011), 'Women's drama, men's business sexual violence against women in Italian cinema and media', in F. Brizio-Skov (ed), *Popular Italian Cinema: Culture and Politics in a Postwar Society*, 229–55, London: Bloomsbury Publishing.

Lawrence, H., Furnham, A. & McClelland, A. (2021), 'Sex does not sell: Effects of sexual advertising parameters on women viewers' implicit and explicit recall of ads and brands', *Perceptual and Motor Skills*, 128(2): 692–713.

Lawson, J. (2012), 'Sociological theories of intimate partner violence', *Journal of Human Behavior in the Social Environment*, 22(5): 572–90.

Lee, C. & Wong, J. S. (2020), '99 reasons and he ain't one: A content analysis of domestic homicide news coverage', *Violence against Women*, 26(2): 213–32.

Leisring, P. A. & Grigorian, H. L. (2016), 'Self-defense, retaliation, and gender: Clarifying motivations for physical partner violence', *Journal of family violence*, 31(8): 949–53.

Leonard, H. & Ashley, C. (2012), 'Exploring the underlying dimensions of violence in print advertisements', *Journal of Advertising*, 41(1): 77–90.

Letort, D. (2020), 'The Femme Fatale of the 1990s erotic thriller: A postfeminist killer?', in C. Maury & D. Roche (eds), *Women Who Kill: Gender and Sexuality in Films and Series of the Post-feminist Era*, 33–47, London: Bloomsbury Publishing.

Liebler, C. M., Hatef, A. & Munno, G. (2016), 'Domestic violence as entertainment: Gender, role congruity and reality television', *Media Report to Women*, 44(1): 6–20.

Liem, M. & Roberts, D. W. (2009), 'Intimate partner homicide by presence or absence of a self-destructive act', *Homicide Studies*, 13(4): 339–54.

Liem, M. & Koenraadt, F. (2018), *Domestic Homicide: Patterns and Dynamics*, London: Routledge.

Ling, J. & Dipolog-Ubanan, G. (2017), 'Misogyny in the lyrics of billboard's top rap airplay artists', *International Journal of Arts Humanities and Social Science*, 2(6): 7–13.

Lippman, J.R. (2015), 'I did it because I never stopped loving you: The effects of media portrayals of persistent pursuit on beliefs about stalking', *Communication Research*, 45(3): 394–421.

Lloyd, A. (1995), *Doubly Deviant, Doubly Damned: Society's Treatment of Violent Women*, Harmondsworth: Penguin.

Lloyd, M. (2020), 'Examining domestic violence and abuse in mainstream and social media: Representations and responses', in S. Ramon, M. Lloyd and B. Penhale (eds), *Gendered Domestic Violence and Abuse in Popular Culture*, Bingley: Emerald Publishing Limited.

Lombard, N. ed (2018), *The Routledge Handbook of Gender and Violence*, 53–66, New York: Routledge.

Lombroso, C. & Ferrero, G. ([1893] 2009), *La donna delinquente, la prostituta e la donna normale*, Milan: Varesina Etal.

López Rodríguez, I. (2009), 'Of women, bitches, chickens and vixens: Animal metaphors for women in English and Spanish', *Cultura, Lenguaje y Representación/Culture, Language and Representation*, 7: 77–100.

Lorenzo-Dus, N. (2009), *Television Discourse: Analysing Language in the Media*, Basingstoke: Palgrave Macmillan.

Lotz, A. (2016), 'Really bad mothers: Manipulative matriarchs in «Sons of Anarchy» and «Justified»', in M. Buonanno (ed), *Women Behaving Badly. Anti-heroines in Crime Tv Storytelling*, 125–39, Bristol and Chicago: Intellect Books.

Lotz, A. D. (2018), *We Now Disrupt This Broadcast: How Cable Transformed Television and the Internet Revolutionized It All*, Cambridge: MIT Press.

Loughnan, S. Haslam, N. Murnane, T. Vaes, J. Reynolds, C. & Suitner, C. (2010), 'Objectification leads to depersonalization: The denial of mind and moral concern to objectified others', *European Journal of Social Psychology*, 40: 709–17.

Lynskey, D. (2013), 'Is Daniel Ek, Spotify founder, going to save the music industry … or destroy it?', *The Guardian*, 10 November. Available online: https://www.theguardian.com/technology/2013/nov/10/daniel-ek-spotify-streamingmusic (accessed 1 March 2021).

Mackay, J. Bowen, E. Walker, K. & O'Doherty, L. (2018), 'Risk factors for female perpetrators of intimate partner violence within criminal justice settings: A systematic review', *Aggression and Violent Behavior*, 41: 128–46.

Magaraggia, S. (2015), 'Il moto ondoso dei femminismi: abbiamo avvistato la quarta ondata?', in S. Magaraggia & G. Vingelli (eds), *Genere e partecipazione politica*, 23–34, Milan: FrancoAngeli.

Magaraggia, S. (2017), 'Le teorie sulla violenza maschile contro le donne', in E. Giomi & S. Magaraggia (eds), *Relazioni brutali*, 23–43, Bologna: il Mulino.

Magaraggia, S. & D. Cherubini, eds (2013), *Uomini contro le donne? Le radici della violenza maschile*, Turin: Utet.

Magaudda, P. & Santoro, M. (2013), 'Dalla popular music ai sound studies: lo studio delle culture sonore', *Studi culturali*, 10(1): 3–12.

Mallicoat, S. L. (2014), *Women and Crime: A Text/Reader*, New York: Sage.

Mallicoat, S. L. (2018), *Women, Gender, and Crime: Core Concepts*, Thousand Oaks: Sage Publications.

Mamo, C. Bianco, S. Dalmasso, M. Girotto, M. Mondo, L. & Penasso, M. (2015), 'Are emergency department admissions in the past two years predictors of femicide? Results from a case-control study in Italy', *Journal of Family Violence*, 30: 853–8.

Mandolini, N. (2020), 'Femminicidio, prima e dopo. Un'analisi qualitativa della copertura giornalistica dei casi Stefania Noce (2011) e Sara Di Pietrantonio (2016)', *Problemi dell'informazione*, 2: 247–77.

Manyiwa, S. & J. Zhongqi (2020), 'Gender effects on consumers' attitudes toward comedic violence in advertisements', *Journal of Promotion Management*, 26(5): 654–73

Mapelli, B. & Ciccone, S. (2012), *Silenzi. Non detti reticenze e assenze di (tra) donne e uomini*, Rome: Ediesse.

Marchetti, S. Mascat, J. e Perilli, V. (2012), *Femministe a parole*, Rome: Author.

Marcuello-Servós, C. Corradi, C. Weil, S. & Boira, S. (2016), 'Femicide: A social challenge', *Current Sociology*, 64(7): 967–74.

Márkus, M. (1987), 'Women, success and civil society: Submission to, or subversion of, the achievement principle', in S. Benhabib & D. Cornell (eds), *Feminism as Critique: Essays on the Politics of Gender in Late-Capitalist Society*, 96–109, London: Wiley-Blackwell.

Marotta, G. (2011), 'Devianza e criminalità femminile: un'analisi dall'antropologia criminale alla sociologia della devianza', in A. Civita, P. Massaro (eds), *Devianza e disuguaglianza di genere*, 111–37, Milan: FrancoAngeli.

Marshall, L. L. (1992), 'Development of the severity of violence against women scales', *Journal of Family Violence*, 7(2): 103–21.

Martin, P. Y. & Powell, M. (1995), 'Accounting for the second assault: Legal organization's' framing of rape victims', *Law and Social Inquiry*, 20: 853–90.

Martin, S.L. Li, Y., Casanueva, C. Harris-Britt, A. Kupper, L.L. & Cloutier, S. (2006), 'Intimate partner violence and women's depression before and during pregnancy', *Violence against Women*, 12(3):221–39.

Marway, H. & Widdows, H. eds (2015), *Women and Violence: The Agency of Victims and Perpetrators*, London: Palgrave Macmillan.

Maury, C. & D. Roche, eds (2020), *Women Who Kill: Gender and Sexuality in Films and Series of the Post-feminist Era*, London: London: Bloomsbury Publishing.

Maury, C. (2020), 'Textbook Femme Fatale, de-eroticized neo-noir heroine or postfeminist woman who kills? Genre trouble in gone girl', in D. Fincher (ed), *Women Who Kill: Gender and Sexuality in Films and Series of the Post-feminist Era*, 97–113, London: Bloomsbury Publishing.

McAllister, M. P. (1999), 'Super bowl advertising as commercial celebration', *Communication Review*, 3(4): 403–28.

McCabe, J. (2015), 'Disconnected heroines, icy intelligence: Reframing feminism(s) and feminist identities at the borders involving the isolated female TV detective in scandinavian-noir', in L. Mulvey & A. Backman Rogers (eds), *Feminisms*, 29–43, Amsterdam: Amsterdam University Press.

McCartan, A. & McMahon, F. (2020), 'Gender and advertising', in K. Ross, I. Bachmann, V. Cardo, S. Moorti & M. Scarcelli (eds), *The International Encyclopedia of Gender, Media, and Communication*, London: Wiley-Blackwell.

McClain, L.C. (1995), 'Inviolability and privacy: The castle, the sanctuary, and the body', *Yale Journal of Law and the Humanities*, 7(1): Article 9.

McClary, S. (1992), *Georges Bizet, Carmen*, Cambridge: Cambridge University Press.

McDonnell, A. (2019), 'Gender, violence, and popular culture', in L. J. Shepard (ed), *Handbook on Gender and Violence International Handbooks on Gender*, 189–201, Cheltenham: Edward Elgar Publishing.

McHugh, K. (2018), 'The female detective, neurodiversity, and felt knowledge in engrenages and Bron/Broen', *Television & New Media*, 19(6): 535–52.

Melandri, L. (2011), *Amore e violenza*, Turin: Bollati Borlinghieri.

Meltzer, H. L. Doos, P. Vostanis, T. Ford & R. Goodman (2009), 'The mental health of children who witness domestic violence', *Child and Family Social Work*, 14(4): 491–501.

Mendicino, R. (2015), 'La vittimizzazione secondaria', *Profiling. I profili dell'abuso*, 6(3).

Messerschmidt, J. W. (1993), *Masculinities and Crime: Critique and Reconceptualization of Theory*, Lanham: Rowman & Littlefield Publishers.

Meyers, M. (1994), 'News of battering', *Journal of Communications*, 44(2): 47–63.

Meyers, M. (1997), *News Coverage of Violence against Women: Engendering Blame*, Thousand Oaks: Sage.

Miller, J. (2014), 'Doing crime as doing gender? Masculinities, femininities, and crime', in R. Gartner, B. McCarthy (eds), *The Oxford Handbook of Gender, Sex, and Crime*, 19–39, Oxford: Oxford University Press.

Minowa, Y., P. Maclaran & L. Stevens (2014), 'Visual representations of violent women', *Visual Communication Quarterly*, 21(4): 210–22.

Mittell, J. (2015), *Complex Tv: The Poetics of Contemporary Television Storytelling*, New York: New York University Press.

Monckton-Smith, J. (2012), *Murder, Gender and the Media. Narratives of Dangerous Love*, New York: Palgrave Macmillan.

Moorti, S. (2002), *Color of Rape: Gender and Race in Television's Public Spheres*, Albany: State of New York Press.

Moorti, S. & Cuklanz, L. (2016), *All-American TV Crime Drama: Feminism and Identity Politics in Law and Order: Special Victims Unit*, London: Bloomsbury Publishing.

Morash, M. (2006), *Understanding Gender, Crime, and Justice*, Thousand Oaks: Sage.

Morris, K. L., Goldenberg, J. L. (2015), 'Women, objects, and animals: Differentiating between sex-and beauty-based objectification', *Revue Internationale de Psychologie Sociale*, 28(1): 15–38.

Morrissey, B. (2003), *When Women Kill: Questions of Agency and Subjectivity*, London: Routledge.

Motz, A. (2008), *The Psychology of Female Violence: Crimes against the Body*, London: Routledge.

Murphy, S. (2014), 'Transformational theory and the analysis of film music', in D. Neumeyer (ed), *The Oxford Handbook of Film Music Studies*, Oxford: Oxford University Press, 471–99.

Murray, J. P. (2008), 'Media violence: The effects are both real and strong', *American Behavioral Scientist*, 51(8): 1212–30.

Myhill, A. (2017), 'Measuring domestic violence: Context is everything', *Journal of Gender-Based Violence*, 1(1): 33–44.

Nadotti, M. (2015), *Necrologhi*, Milan: Il Saggiatore.

Naffine, N. (2017), *Female Crime: The Construction of Women in Criminology*, London: Routledge.

Nagel, I. & Hagan, J. (1983), 'Gender and crime: Offense patterns and criminal court sanctions', in N. Morris & M. Tonry (eds), *Crime and Justice*, 91–144, Chicago: University of Chicago Press.

Nail, J. (2007), 'Visibility versus surprise: Which drives the greatest discussion of super bowl advertisements', *Journal of Advertising Research*, 47(4): 412–19.

Namy, S. Carlson, C. O'Hara, K., Nakuti, J. Bukuluki, P. Lwanyaaga. J. Namakula, S. Nanyunja, B. Wainberg, M. L. Naker, D. & Michau, L. (2017), 'Towards a feminist understanding of intersecting violence against women and children in the family', *Social Science & Medicine*, 184: 40–8.

Naylor, B. (1995), 'Women's crime and media coverage: Making explanations', in R. E. Dobash, R. P. Dobash & L. Noaks (eds), *Gender and Crime, in Gender and Crime*, 77–95, Cardiff: University of Wales Press.

Neroni, H. (2005), *The Violent Woman: Femininity, Narrative, and Violence in Contemporary American Cinema*, Albany: State University of New York Press.

Ness, C. D. (2010), *Why Girls Fight: Female Youth Violence in the Inner City*, New York: New York University Press.

Nevala, S. (2017), 'Coercive control and its impact on intimate partner violence through the lens of an EU-wide survey on violence against women', *Journal of Interpersonal Violence*, 32(12): 1792–820.

Nussbaum, M. (2000), 'Women's capabilities and social justice', *Journal of Human Development*, 1(2): 219–47.

Nussbaum, M. C. (1995), 'Objectification', *Philosophy & Public Affairs*, 24(4): 249–91.

Oliver, W. (2006), 'The streets: An alternative black male socialization institution', *Journal of Black Studies*, 36:918–37.

ONS (2020), Domestic abuse in England and Wales overview: November 2020, ONS, London.

Ortner, S. (1974), 'Is female to male as nature is to culture?', in M. Z. Rosaldo & L. Lamphere (eds), *Woman, Culture, and Society*, 68–87, Stanford: Stanford University Press.

Øverlien, C. (2010), 'Children exposed to domestic violence: Conclusions from the literature and challenges ahead', *Journal of Social Work*, 10(1): 80–97.

Oware, M. (2011), 'Brotherly love: Homosociality and black masculinity in gangsta rap music', *Journal of African American Studies*, 15: 22–39.

Oware, M. A. (2009), '"Man's woman"?: Contradictory messages in the songs of female rappers, 1992–2000', *Journal of Black Studies*, 39(5):786–802.

Owen, S., Stein, S. R. & Vande Berg, L. R. (2007), *Bad Girls: Cultural Politics and Media Representations of Transgressive Women*, New York: Peter Lang Publishing.

O'Connor, T. G. Heron, J. Golding, J. Beveridge, M. & Glover, V. (2002), 'Maternal antenatal anxiety and children's behavioural/emotional problems at 4 years. Report from the avon longitudinal study of parents and children', *British Journal of Psychiatry*, 180(6):502–8.

O'Neill, M. & Seal, L. (2012), 'Violent female avengers in popular culture', in M. O'Neill, L. Seal (eds), *Transgressive Imaginations, Crime, Deviance and Culture*, 42–63, New York: Palgrave Macmillan.

Paasonen, S., K. Nikunen & L. Saarenmaa (2007), *Pornification: Sex and Sexuality in Media Culture*, 161–70, Oxford: Berg.

Paoli, M. (2013), *Femminicidio: i perché di una parola*, Florence: Accademia della Crusca.

Papadopoulos, L. (2010), *Sexualisation of Young People Review*, London: Home Office Publication.

Parikka, T. (2015), *Globalization, Gender, and Media: Formations of the Sexual and Violence in Understanding Globalization*, Lanham: Lexington Books.

Parker, S.W. & Nelson, C.A. (2005), 'The impact of early institutional rearing on the ability to discriminate facial expressions of emotion: An event-related potential study', *Child Development*, 76: 54–72.

Pascoe, C. J. (2007), *Dude You're a Fag*, Berkeley: University of California Press.

Pedace, C. F. (2019), 'Vittima/Vittimologia/Vulnerabilità', in A. Simone, I. Boiano & A. Condello (eds), *Femminismo giuridico. Teorie e problemi*, 87–99, Milan: Mondadori.

Pelvin, H. (2019), 'The "normal" woman who kills: Representations of women's intimate partner homicide', *Feminist Criminology*, 14(3): 349–70.

Pepin, J. R. (2016), 'Nobody's business? White male privilege in media coverage of intimate partner violence', *Sociological Spectrum*, 36(3): 123–41.

Peters, J. (2008), 'Measuring myths about domestic violence: Development and initial validation of the domestic violence myth acceptance scale', *Journal of Aggression, Maltreatment & Trauma*, 16(1): 1–21.

Phillips, B. J. & McQuarrie, E. F. (2010), 'Narrative and persuasion in fashion advertising', *Journal of Consumer Research*, 37(3): 368–92.

Phipps, A. (2021), 'White tears, white rage: Victimhood and (as) violence in mainstream feminism', *European Journal of Cultural Studies*, 24(1): 81–93.

Pitch, T. (1975). La devianza, Florence: Nuova Italian Editrice.

Pitch, T. (1987), 'There but for fortune. Le donne e il controllo sociale', in *Diritto e rovescio. Studi sulle donne e il controllo sociale*, Naples: Esi.

Pitch, T. (1989), *Responsabilità limitate. Attori, conflitti, giustizia penale*, Milan: Feltrinelli.

Pitch, T. (1998), *Un diritto per due. La costruzione giuridica di sesso, genere e sessualità*, Milan: Il Saggiatore.

Pitch, T. (2002), 'Le differenze di genere', in M. Barbagli & U. Gatti (eds), *La criminalità in Italia*, 171–83, Bologna: Il Mulino.

Pitch, T. (2008), 'Qualche riflessione attorno alla violenza maschile contro le donne', *Studi sulla questione criminale*, 3(2): 7–10.

Pough, G. (2004), *Check It while I Wreck It: Black Womanhood, Hip-hop Culture, and the Public Sphere*, Boston: Northeastern University Press.

Power, N. (2009), *One-Dimensional Woman*, Winchester: Zero Books.

Pravadelli, V. (2015), *Classic Hollywood. Lifestyles and Film Styles of American Cinema, 1930–1960*, Bloomington: University of Illinois Press (kindle edition).

Primack, B., Gold, M., Schwarz, E. & Dalton, M. (2008), 'Degrading and non-degrading sex in popular music: A content analysis', *Public Health Reports*, 123(5): 593–600.

Projansky, S. (2001), *Watching Rape: Film and Television in Postfeminist Culture*, New York: New York University Press.

RAI, Report sulla rappresentazione della figura femminile nella programmazione RAI del 2020 (2020) https://www.rai.it/dl/doc/1623168043362_Sintesi%20 FIGURA%20FEMMINILE_Anno%202020.pdf.

Rajiva, M. & Patrick, S. (2021), '"This is what a feminist looks like": Dead girls and murderous boys on Season 1 of Netflix's You', *Television & New Media*, 22(3): 281–98.

Ramon, S. Lloyd, M. & Penhale, B. eds (2020), *Gendered Domestic Violence and Abuse in Popular Culture*, Bingley: Emerald Group Publishing.

Rasmussen, E. E. & Densley, R. L. (2017), 'Girl in a country song: Gender roles and objectification of women in popular country music across 1990 to 2014', *Sex Roles*, 76: 188–201.

Rebollo-Gil, G. & Moras, A. (2012), 'Black women and black men in hip hop music: Misogyny, violence and the negotiation of (white-owned) space', *The Journal of Popular Culture*, 45(1): 118–32.

Redvall, E. N. (2013), *Writing and Producing Television Drama in Denmark: From «The Kingdom» to «The Killing»*, London and New York: Palgrave Macmillan.

Reichert, T. (2003), 'The prevalence of sexual imagery in ads targeted to young adults', *Journal of Consumer Affairs*, 37(2): 403–12.

Reichert, T. & Lambiase, J. eds (2003), *Sex in Advertising: Perspectives on the Erotic Appeal*, Mahwah: Erlbaum.

Reichert, T. LaTour, M. S. & Kim, J. Y. (2007), 'Assessing the influence of gender and sexual self-schema on affective responses to sexual content in advertising', *Journal of Current Issues and Research in Advertising*, 29(2): 63–77.

Reich, N. (2002), 'Towards a rearticulation of women-as-victims: A thematic analysis of the construction of women's identities surrounding gendered violence', *Communication Quarterly*, 50(3–4): 292–311.

Renzetti, C. M, Miller, S. L & Gover, A. R. eds (2013), *Routledge International Handbook of Crime and Gender Studies*, Abingdon: Routledge.

Rhym, D. (1997), 'Here's for the bitches: An analysis of gangsta rap and misogyny', *Womanist Theory and Research*, 2: 1–14.

Ribac, F. (2006), 'Dal rock alla techno. Intervista a Simon Frith', *Studi Culturali*, 3(1): 117–32.

Richards, T. N., Gillespie, L. K. & Smith, M. D. (2014), 'An examination of the media portrayal of femicide–suicides: An exploratory frame analysis', *Feminist Criminology*, 9(1): 24–44.

Richards, T. N., Gillespie, L. K., Smith, M. D. (2011), 'Exploring news coverage of femicide: Does reporting the news add insult to injury?', *Feminist Criminology*, 6(3): 178–202.

Richardson, J. & Scott, K. (2002), 'Rap music and its violent progeny: America's culture of violence in context', *The Journal of Negro Education*, 71(3): 175–92.

Richardson, L. (1991), 'Postmodern social theory: Representational practices', *Sociological Theory*, 9(2): 173–9.

Rifon, N. J., et al. (2010), 'Violence and advertising: Effects and consequences', *Journal of Advertising*, 39(4): 9–10.

Rinaldi, C. (2018), *Maschilità devianze crimine*, Milan: Meltemi.

Rivara, F. P. Anderson, M. L. Fishman, P. Bonomi, A. E. Reid, R. J., Carrell, D. & Thompson, R. S. (2007), 'Intimate partner violence and health care costs and utilization for children living in the home', *Pediatrics*, 120(6): 1270–7.

Rohlinger, D. A. (2002), 'Eroticizing men: Cultural influences on advertising and male objectification', *Sex Roles*, 46(3–4): 61–74.

Rollè, L., Santoniccolo, F., D'Amico, D. & Trombetta, T. (2020), 'News media representation of domestic violence victims and perpetrators: Focus on gender and sexual orientation in international literature', *Gendered Domestic Violence and Abuse in Popular Culture*, 149–169, Bingley: Emerald Publishing Limited.

Romain, D. M., Freiburger, T. L. (2016), 'Chivalry revisited: Gender, race/ethnicity, and offense type on domestic violence charge reduction', *Feminist Criminology*, 11(2): 191–222.

Rome, A. & Ibrahim, E. (2015), 'A cross-cultural comparison of female nudity perception in print advertising among female consumers in the UK and the Netherlands', in K. Kubacki (ed), *Ideas in Marketing: Finding the New and Polishing the Old. Proceedings of the 2013 Academy of Marketing Science (AMS) Annual Conference*, 298, Ruston: Springer.

Romito, P. & Melato, M. eds (2013), *Violenze su donne e minori: una guida per chi lavora sul campo*, Rome: Carocci Editori.

Romito, P., Turan, J.M. & De Marchi, M. (2005), 'The impact of current and past violence on women's mental health', *Social Science & Medicine*, 60: 1717–27.

Ross, S. (2004), '«Tough enough»: Female friendship and heroism in «Xena» and «Buffy»', in S. A. Inness (ed), *Action Chicks: New Images of Tough Women in Popular Culture*, 231–55, New York: Palgrave Macmillan.

Roy, W. & Dowd, T. (2010), 'What is sociological about music?', *Annual Review of Sociology*, 36: 183–203.

Royne, M. B. (2010), 'From the editor', *Journal of Advertising*, 39(4): 5–7.

Rubin, A. M. West, D. V. & Mitchell, W. S. (2001), 'Differences in aggression, attitudes toward women, and distrust as reflected in popular music preferences', *Media Psychology*, 3: 25–42.

Rudman, L.A. & Mescher, K. (2012), 'Of animals and objects: Men's implicit dehumanization of women and likelihood of sexual aggression', *Personality and Social Psychology Bulletin*, 38(6):734–46.

Ryan, J. W. & R. A. Peterson. (1982), 'The product image: The fate of creativity in country music song- writing', *Sage Annual Reviews of Communication Research*, 10:11–32.

Saavedra, L., Rebelo, A. S. & Sebastião, C. (2015), 'Gender norms in Portuguese college students' judgments in familial homicides: Bad men and mad women', *Journal of Interpersonal Violence*, 32(2):249–67.

Sabina, C. Swatt, M. (2015), *Summary Report: Latino Intimate Partner Homicide (Report No. 2013-IJ-CX-0037)*, Washington, DC: National Institute of Justice, Office of Justice Programs, U.S. Department of Justice.

Sabri, O. (2017), 'Does viral communication context increase the harmfulness of controversial taboo advertising?', *Journal of Business Ethics*, 141(2): 235–47.

Salom, C., G. M. Williams, J. M. Najman & R. Alati (2015), 'Substance use and mental health disorders are linked to different forms of intimate partner violence victimisation', *Drug and Alcohol Dependence*, 151: 121–7.

Samelius, L. Thapar-björkert, S. & Binswanger, C. (2014), 'Turning points and the "everyday": Exploring agency and violence in intimate relationships', *European Journal of Women's Studies*, 21(3): 264–77.

Sandhu, N. (2021), 'Gendering products through advertisements: A review (1973-2019) of various cues employed by advertisers', *Business Perspectives and Research*, 1–14.

Sarra, G. (2011), 'Sull'uso della violenza, in Sensibili guerriere' in F. Giardini (ed), *Sulla forza femminile*, 104–14, Rome: Iacobelli.

Sassatelli, R. (2010), 'Erving Goffman, La ritualizzazione della femminilità', *Studi culturali, Rivista quadrimestrale,* 1: 37–70.

Scannell, P. ed (1991), *Broadcast Talk,* London: Sage.

Scaptura, M. N. & Boyle, K. M. (2020), 'Masculinity threat, "Incel" traits, and violent fantasies among heterosexual men in the United States', *Feminist Criminology,* 15(3): 278–298.

Scharrer, E. (2001), 'From wise to foolish: The portrayal of the Sitcom Father, 1950s–1990s', *Journal of Broadcasting and Electronic Media,* 45(1): 23–40.

Scharrer, E. (2004), 'Virtual violence: Gender and aggression in video game advertisements', *Mass Communication and Society,* 7: 393–412.

Scharrer, E., Andrea Bergstrom, Angela Paradise & Qianqing Ren (2006), 'Laughing to keep from crying: Humor and aggression in television commercial content', *Journal of Broadcasting and Electronic Media,* 50(4): 615–34.

Scheper-Hughes, N. & Bourgois, P. eds (2004), *Violence in War and Peace: An Anthology,* Oxford: Blackwell Publishers.

Schiavon, A. (2019), 'La cyber-violenza maschile contro le donne: una nuova sfida per il diritto penale', *Studi sulla questione criminale,* 1–2: 207–22.

Schippers, M. (2012), 'Third-wave rebels in a second-wave world: Polyamory, gender, and power', in D. King & C. Smith (eds), *Men Who Hate Women and Women Who Kick Their Asses: Stieg Larsson's Millennium Trilogy in Feminist Perspective,* 1152–342, Nashville: Vanderbilt University Press (kindle edition).

Schneider, E. (2000), *Battered Women and Feminist Lawmaking.* New Haven; London: Yale University Press.

Scholz, C. (2014), *Generation Z: wie sie tickt, was sie verändert und warum sie uns alle ansteckt,* Weinheim: Wiley-VCH.

Schroeder, J. E. & J. L. Borgerson. (1998), 'Marketing images of gender: A visual analysis', *Consumption Markets & Culture,* 2: 161–201.

Schroeder, J. E. & J. L. Borgerson (2003), 'Dark desires: Fetishism, ontology and representation in contemporary advertising', in T. Reichert & J. Lambiase (eds), *Sex in Advertising: Perspectives on the Erotic Appeal,* 65–87, Mahwah: Lawrence Erlbaum Associates.

Schroeder, J. E. & Zwick, D. (2004), 'Mirrors of masculinity: Representation and identity in marketing communication', *Consumption, Markets and Culture,* 7(1): 21–52.

Schubart, R. (2007), *Super Bitches and Action Babes: The Female Hero in Popular Cinema, 1970–2006,* Jefferson: McFarland (kindle edition).

Scott, H. (2005), *The Female Serial Murderer: A Sociological Study of Homicide and the«Gentler Sex»*, Lewiston: Edwin Mellen.

Scott, K. (2014), 'Violence against children in families', in R. Gartner, B. McCarthy (eds), *The Oxford Handbook of Gender, Sex and Crime*, 379–402, Oxford: Oxford University Press.

Seabrook, R. C., Ward, L. M. & Giaccardi, S. (2019), 'Less than human? Media use, objectification of women, and men's acceptance of sexual aggression', *Psychology of Violence*, 9(5): 536–45.

Seal, L. (2010), *Women, Murder and Femininity: Gender Representations of Women Who Kill*, New York: Palgrave Macmillan.

Sellers, B. G., Desmarais, S. L. & Tirotti, M. (2014), 'Content and framing of male- and female-perpetrated intimate partner violence in print news', *Partner Abuse*, 5(3): 259–78.

Shanahan, K. J., C. M. Hermans & M. R. Hyman (2003), 'Violent commercials in television programs for children', *Journal of Current Issues and Research in Advertising*, 25(1): 61–69.

Sharpe, G. (2013), *Offending Girls: Young Women and Youth Justice*, New York: Routledge.

Shepherd, L. J. (2012), *Gender, Agency and Political Violence*, ed. L. Åhäll, Basingstoke: Palgrave Macmillan.

Shepherd, L. J. (2013), *Gender, Violence and Popular Culture: Telling Stories*, New York: Routledge (kindle edition).

Shepherd, L. J. (2019), 'Gender and violence: Tools to think with', *Handbook on Gender and Violence*, Cheltenham: Edward Elgar Publishing.

Shoos, D. (2010), 'Representing domestic violence: Ambivalence and difference', in M. Mesropova, S. Weber-Fève (eds), *«What's Love Got to do with it», Being and Becoming Visible*, 115–33, Baltimore: Johns Hopkins University Press.

Shoos, D. L. (2017), *Domestic Violence in Hollywood Film: Gaslighting*, Cham: Palgrave Macmillan.

Shoos, D. L. (2021), 'Hollywood and beyond: Rescreening domestic violence', in S. Ramon, M. Lloyd & B. Penhale (ed), *Gendered Domestic Violence and Abuse in Popular Culture*, 104–31, Bingley: Emerald Publishing Limited.

Sibielski, R. (2010), '«Nothing hurts the cause more than that»: Veronica Mars and the business of the backlash', *Feminist Media Studies*, 10(3): 322–34.

Silvaggi, M. A. Fabrizi, R. Rossi, F. Tripodi & C. Simonelli (2016), 'Oggettivazione del femminile e sessualizzazione precoce delle bambine: implicazioni sullo sviluppo psicosessuale', *Rivista di Sessuologia Clinica*, 2: 5–19.

Silvestri, M., Crowther-Dowey, C. (2016), *Gender and Crime: A Human Rights Approach*, London: Sage.

Simkin, S. (2014), *Cultural Constructions of the Femme Fatale: From Pandora's Box to Amanda Knox*, London: Palgrave Macmillan.

Simon, R. J. (1975), *Women and Crime*, Toronto: Lexington Books.

Simone, A. Boiano, I. & Condello, A. eds (2019), *Femminismo giuridico. Teorie e problemi*, Milan: Mondadori.

Sims, C. D. L. (2008), 'Invisible wounds, invisible abuse: The exclusion of emotional abuse in newspaper articles', *Journal of Emotional Abuse*, 8(4): 375–402.

Sjoberg, L. & Gentry, C. (2007), *Mothers, Monsters, Whores: Women's Violence in Global Politics*, London: Zed Books.

Skeggs, B. (1993), 'Two Minute brother: Contestation through gender, "race" and sexuality', *Innovation: The European Journal of Social Science Research*, 6(3): 299–322.

Smith, A. L., Bond, C. E. & Jeffries, S. (2019), 'Media discourses of intimate partner violence in Queensland newspapers', *Journal of sociology*, 55(3): 571–86.

Soley, L. C. & Kurzbard, G. (1986), 'Sex in advertising: A comparison of 1964 and 1984 magazine advertisements', *Journal of Advertising*, 15(3): 46–54.

Sontag, S. (2004), *Regarding the Pain of Others*, London: Penguin Books.

Soothill, K. & Walby, S. (1991), *Sex Crimes in the News*, London: Routledge.

Sotirovic, M. (2003), 'How individuals explain social problems: The influences of media use', *Journal of Communication*, 53: 122–37.

Spangaro, J. (2019), 'Intimate partner violence' in L. J. Shepherd (ed), *Handbook on Gender and Violence*, 265–78, Northampton: Edward Elgar Publishing.

Stabile, C. A. (2006), *White Victims, Black Villains: Gender, Race, and Crime News in US Culture*, New York: Routledge.

Statista (2020), *Number of Femicide Victims in Europe in 2018*, Author.

Statista (2019), *Murder in the U.S.: Number of Offenders by Gender 2018*, Author.

Steemers, J. (2016), 'International sales of UK television content: Change and continuity in "the space in between" production and consumption', *Television & New Media*, 17(8): 734–53.

Steenberg, L. (2017), 'The fall and television noir', *Television & New Media*, 18(1): 58–75.

Stern, B. (2003), 'Masculism(s) and the male image: What does it mean to be a man?', in T. Reichert, J. Lambiase (eds), *Sex in Advertising: Perspectives on the Erotic appeal*, 215–28, Mahwah: Lawrence Erlbaum.

Sternadori, M. (2014), 'The witch and the warrior', *Feminist Media Studies*, 14(2): 301–17.

Stöckl, H., Devries, K., Rotstein, A., Abrahams, N., Campbell, J., Watts, C. & Moreno, C. G. (2013), 'The global prevalence of intimate partner homicide: A systematic review', *The Lancet*, 382(9895): 859–65.

Straus, M. A. (1979), 'Measuring intrafamily conflict and violence: The conflict tactics (CT) scales', *Journal of Marriage and the Family*, 41: 75–88.

Straus, M. A. (2015), 'Dyadic concordance and discordance in family violence: A powerful and practical approach to research and practice', *Aggression and Violent Behavior*, 24: 83–94.

Straus, M. A. Hamby, S. L. Boney-mccoy, S. & Sugarman, D. B. (1996), 'The revised conflict tactics scales (CTS2): Development and preliminary psychometrics data', *Journal of Family Issues*, 17(3): 283–316.

Sturken, M. & Cartwright, L. (2002), *Practices of Looking: An Introduction to Visual Culture*, Oxford: Oxford University Press.

Suarez, M. (2020), 'Motherhood, domesticity, and nurture in the postapocalyptic world: Negotiating femininity in the walking dead', in C. Maury, D. Roche (eds), *Women Who Kill: Gender and Sexuality in Films and Series of the Post-feminist Era*, 154–71, London: Bloomsbury Publishing.

Surette, R. (1998), *Media, Crime, and Criminal Justice. Images and Realities*, Belmont: Wadsworth.

Sutherland, G., McCormack, A., Pirkis, J., Holland, K. & Vaughan, C. (2015), *Media Representations of Violence against Women and Their Children: State of Knowledge Paper*, Sydney: ANROWS.

Tait, S. (2006), 'Autoptic vision and the necrophilic imaginary in «CSI»', *International Journal of Cultural Studies*, 9(1): 45–62.

Tamburro, R. R. Gordon, P. L. D'Apolito, J. P. & Howard, S. C. (2004), 'Unsafe and violent behavior in commercials aired during televised major sporting events', *Pediatrics*, 114(6): 694–98.

Tarzia, L. (2021), '"It went to the very heart of who I was as a woman": The invisible impacts of intimate partner sexual violence', *Qualitative Health Research*, 31(2):287–97.

Tasker, Y. (1993), *Spectacular Bodies: Gender, Genre and the Action Cinema*, New York: Routledge.

Tasker, Y. (1998), *Working Girls: Gender and Sexuality in Popular Cinema*, London: Routledge.

Tasker, Y. & Steenberg, L. (2016), 'Women warriors from chivalry to vengeance', *Women of Ice and Fire, Gender, Game of Thrones and Multiple Media Engagements*, 171–192, London: Bloomsbury Publishing.

Taylor, J. (2014), 'Romance and the female gaze obscuring gendered violence in the Twilight saga', *Feminist Media Studies*, 14(3): 388–402.

Taylor, R. (2009), 'Slain and slandered: A content analysis of the portrayal of femicide in the news', *Homicide Studies*, 13: 21–49.

Thaller, J. & Messing, J. (2014), '(Mis)perceptions around intimate partner violence in the music video and lyrics for «Love the Way You Lie»', *Feminist Media Studies*, 14(4): 623–39.

The Codes of Gender: Identity and Performance in Pop Culture (2009), [videorecording], S. Jhally, Northampton, MA: Media Education Foundation.

Thornham, S. & Purvis, T. (2005), *Television Drama: Theories and Identities*, London: Palgrave Macmillan.

Tipler, C. N. & Ruscher, J. B. (2019), 'Dehumanizing representations of women: The shaping of hostile sexist attitudes through animalistic metaphors', *Journal of Gender Studies*, 28(1): 109–18.

Tolman, D. L. & McClelland, S. I. (2011), 'Normative sexuality development in adolescence: A decade in review, 2000–2009', *Journal of Research on Adolescence*, 21: 242–55.

Torres, M. G. & Yllö, K. eds (2021), *Sexual Violence in Intimacy: Implications for Research and Policy in Global Health*, New York: Routledge.

Tuchman, G. (1978), 'The symbolic annihilation of women by the mass media', in G. Tuchman, A. K. Daniels & J. Benet (eds), *Hearth and Home: Images of Women in the Mass Media*, 3–38, New York: Oxford University Press.

Turner, J. (2011), 'Sex and the spectacle of music videos: An examination of the portrayal of race and sexuality in music videos', *Sex Roles*, 64: 173–91.

Un Broadband Commission For Digital Development (2015), *Cyber Violence against Women and Girls: A WorldWide Wake-Up Call*, New York: United Nations.

United Nations (1980), *Report of the World Conference on Human Rights: Vienna Declaration and Programme of Action*, New York: Author.

United Nations (2020), *The World's Women 2020: Trends and Statistics*, New York: Author.

United Nations Population Fund (2016), *Gender-based Violence*. www.unfpa.org.

UNODC, *Global Study on Homicide* (2018), Vienna.

Vaes, J. Paladino, P. & Puvia, E. (2011), 'Are sexualized female complete human beings? Why males and female dehumanize sexually objectified women', *European Journal of Social Psychology*, 41: 774–85.

Vance, K. Sutter, M. Perrin, P. & Heesacker, M. (2015), 'The media's sexual objectification of women, rape myth acceptance, and interpersonal violence', *Journal of Aggression, Maltreatment & Trauma*, 24(5): 569–87.

Van Oosten, J., Peter, J. & Valkenburg, P. (2015), 'The influence of sexual music videos on adolescents' misogynistic beliefs: The role of video content, gender, and affective engagement', *Communication Research*, 42(7): 986–1008.

Vatnar, S. K. B. Friestad, C. & Bjørkly, S. (2018), 'Differences in intimate partner homicides perpetrated by men and women: Evidence from a Norwegian National 22-year cohort', *Psychology, Crime & Law*, 24(8): 790–805.

Venäläinen, S. (2016), 'What are true women not made of? Agency and identities of «violent» women in tabloids in Finland', *Feminist Media Studies*, 16(2): 261–75.

Verdolini, A. (2019), 'Devianza/Questione criminale/Sicurezza', in A. Simone, I. Boiano, A. Condello, *Femminismo giuridico. Teorie e problemi*, 69–86, Milan: Mondadori.

Vincent, R., Davis, D. & Boruszkowski, L. (1987), 'Sexism on MTV: The portrayal of women in rock videos', *Journalism Quarterly*, 64: 750–5.

Violence Policy Center (2015), *When Men Murder Women*. An Analysis of 2013 Homicide Data.

Vitis, L. & Gilmour, F. (2016), 'Dick pics on blast: A woman's resistance to online sexual harassment using humour, art and Instagram', *Crime Media Culture*, 1–21.

Volpato, C. (2011), *Deumanizzazione. Come si legittima la violenza*, Bari-Rome: Laterza.

Wakeman, S. (2018), 'The "one who knocks" and the "one who waits": Gendered violence in Breaking Bad', *Crime, Media, Culture*, 14(2): 213–28.

Walby, S. (2005), 'Improving the statistics on violence against women', *Statistical Journal of the United Nations Economic Commission for Europe*, 22: 193–216.

Walby, S., Towers, J. (2017), 'Measuring violence to end violence: Mainstreaming gender', *Journal of Gender-Based Violence*, 1(1): 11–31.

Waling, A. (2019), 'Rethinking masculinity studies: Feminism, masculinity, and poststructural accounts of agency and emotional reflexivity', *The Journal of Men's Studies*, 27(1): 89–107.

Walklate, S. (2004), *Gender, Crime and Criminal Justice*, Cullompton, Devon: Willan Publishing.

Walklate, S. ed (2012), *Gender and Crime*, London: Routledge.

Wallis, C. (2011), 'Performing gender: A content analysis of gender display in music videos', *Sex Roles*, 64: 160–72.

Walser, R. (1999), *Keeping Time: Readings in Jazz History*, New York: Oxford University Press.

Walter, N. (2010), *Living Dolls: The Return of Sexism*, London: Virago Press.

Walters, S. & Harrison, L. (2014), 'Not ready to make nice: Aberrant mothers in contemporary culture', *Feminist Media Studies*, 14(1): 38–55.

Weitzer, R. & Kubrin, C. (2009), 'Misogyny in rap music. A content analysis of prevalence and meanings', *Men and Masculinities*, 12: 3–29.

West, C. (1996), 'Goffman in feminist perspective', *Sociological Perspectives*, 39(3),353–69.

West, C. & Zimmerman, D. H. (1987), 'Doing gender', *Gender & Society*, 1(2): 125–51.

West, C. M. (2008), '"A thin line between love and hate"? Black men as victims and perpetrators of dating violence', *Journal of Aggression, Maltreatment & Trauma*, 16(3): 238–57.

WHO (2011), *Intimate Partner Violence During Pregnancy*.

WHO (2013), *Global and Regional Estimates of Violence against Women*.

Wilczynski, A. (1997), 'Mad or bad?: Child killers, gender and the courts', *British Journal of Criminology*, 37(3): 419–36.

Willem, C., Araüna, N. & Tortajada, I. (2019), 'Chonis and pijas: Slut-shaming and double standards in online performances among Spanish teens', *Sexualities*, 22(4): 532–48.

Williams, J. R., Ghandour, R. M. & Kub, J. E. (2008), 'Female perpetration of violence in heterosexual intimate relationships: Adolescence through adulthood', *Trauma, Violence & Abuse*, 9(4): 227–49.

Williamson, E., Morgan, K. & Hester, M. (2018), 'Male victims: Control, coercion and fear?', in Lombard, N. (ed), *The Routledge Handbook of Gender and Violence*, 53–66, Routledge: New York.

Willie, T. C. & Kershaw, T. S. (2019), 'An ecological analysis of gender inequality and intimate partner violence in the United States', *Preventive Medicine*, 118: 257–63.

Wilson, B. J. Smith, S. L. Potter, W. J. Kunkel, D. Linz, D. Colvin, C. M. & Donnerstein, E. (2002), 'Violence in children's television programming: Assessing the risks', *Journal of Communication*, 52(1): 5–35.

Wilson, M. & Daly, M. (1992), 'Who kills whom in spouse killings? On the exceptional sex ratio of spousal homicides in the United States', *Criminology*, 30: 189–215.

Wolbers, H. & J. Ackerman (2020), 'The degree of specialization among female partner violence offenders and the role of self-defense', *Its Explanation, Victims & Offenders*, 15(2): 197–217.

Wolin, L. D. (2003), 'Gender issues in advertising: An oversight synthesis of research: 1970–2002', *Journal of Advertising Research*, 43(1): 111–30.

Worden, A. & Carlson, B. (2005), 'Attitudes and beliefs about domestic violence: Results of a public opinion survey: II', *Journal of Interpersonal Violence*, 20(10): 1219–43.

Worrall, A. (1990), *Offending Women. Female Lawbreakers and the Criminal Justice System*, New York: Routledge.

Wozniak, J. A. & Mccloskey, K. A. (2010), 'Fact or fiction? Gender issues related to newspaper reports of intimate partner homicide', *Violence against Women*, 16(8): 934–52.

Wright, L. (2017), 'Black, white, and read all over: Exploring racial bias in print media coverage of serial rape cases', Doc. diss., College of Sciences, University of Central Florida.

Wright, C. L. & Centeno, B. (2018), 'Sexual content in music and its relation to sexual attitudes and behaviors among consumers: A meta-analytic review', *Communication Quarterly*, 66(4): 423–43.

Wykes, M. (2001), *News, Crime, and Culture*, London: Pluto Press.

Wykes, M. & Welsh, K. (2009), *Violence, Gender, Justice*, London: Sage.

Yllo, K. A. (1993), 'Through a feminist lens: Gender, power and violence', in R. J. Gelles & D. R. Loseke (eds), *Current Controversies on Family Violence*, 47–62, Newbury Park: Sage.

Zeitlin, D. Dhanjal, T. & Colmsee, M. (1999), 'Maternal-foetal bonding: The impact of domestic violence on the bonding process between a mother and child', *Archives of Women's Mental Health*, 2(4):183–9.

Index

gender ratio 35, 52, 79
  in England and Wales 35–6
  in Italy 37–8
  problem 16
  in United States 32–5
gender symmetry 20–1, 32, 51, 146
GenZ 96, 101
Gilbert, P. R. 41, 45, 139
Girl with the Dragon Tattoo, The
  (Fincher) 75
Glueck, E. L. 41
Glueck, S. 41
Goffman, E., courtship system 27–8
Gone Girl (Fincher) 87
Good Wife, The (CBS) 84
Graham, L. M. 53. *See also* self-help/
  self-defence theory
guardians of resilience 18

Hagan, J. 46–7
Hanna (Amazon Video) 1–2, 77, 84
Happy Valley (BBC) 83
Hearn, J. 11–12, 19, 21, 23, 105
Hearts Afire (3×3) 141
hegemonic masculinity 93, 97, 100,
  103, 124, 174, 176
  emotional detachment 103–4
  heterosexuality 98
  self-celebration 101–2
  status degradation ceremonies
   98–101
  violent actions 104–7
heterosexuality 30, 48, 77–8, 97–8,
  100, 109
HIV 18
Hollywood 71, 74, 76, 102, 137
  domestic violence films 58
Homeland (Showtime) 84
homicide 12, 16–17, 44, 57, 79
  global studies 16–17
Homolka, K. 80–1, 86
homosexuality 40, 100, 109, 176
Horek, K. 127
Hotel Beau Séjour (Netflix) 65

human rights, violation 9, 11, 31
Hunger Games, The (Ross) 1, 74, 77, 84

Illouz, E. 26
I May Destroy You (HBO/BBC One)
  76
infanticide 38–9, 44, 50
Infanticide Act 44
Institute for Self-regulation of
  Advertising (IAP) 124
interactive technologies 5
interdisciplinary approach 31
interpersonal violence 3–4, 38, 50,
  127
  female 31–2
  gender and 31
intimate partner homicide (IPH) 13,
  52–4
  common offences 129
  in crime series 140–1, 156
  female-perpetrators 54, 73, 79,
   117, 129, 139
  gender ration in Europe 52–3
  individual and situational
   characteristics 76, 132
  media representation 57
  nuanced conceptualization 13
  U.S. statistics 146
intimate partner violence (IPV) 4, 9,
  12, 16–22, 25, 50
  American press coverage 57
  Canadian press 57
  in commercial advertisement 112
  conflict and romance 59–63, 174
  heterosexual relationships 4
  lethal female-perpetrators 52–4
  male-perpetrated 25, 51
  male perpetration and female
   experience 25, 87
  male psychological traits 41
  media coverage 56
  myth-based belief 69, 76
  news reports 121
  nonlethal 17, 50